Engaging Place, Engaging Practices

In the series *History and the Public*,
edited by Steven Conn

EDITED BY ROBIN F. BACHIN
AND AMY L. HOWARD

Engaging Place, Engaging Practices

Urban History and Campus-Community Partnerships

TEMPLE UNIVERSITY PRESS
Philadelphia • *Rome* • *Tokyo*

TEMPLE UNIVERSITY PRESS
Philadelphia, Pennsylvania 19122
tupress.temple.edu

Library of Congress Cataloging-in-Publication Data

Names: Bachin, Robin Faith, editor. | Howard, Amy Lynne, 1971– editor.
Title: Engaging place, engaging practices : urban history and
 campus-community partnerships / edited by Robin F. Bachin and Amy L.
 Howard.
Other titles: History and the public (Philadelphia, Pa.)
Description: Philadelphia : Temple University Press, 2023. | Series:
 History and the public | Includes bibliographical references and index.
 | Summary: "Engaging Place, Engaging Practices is an edited volume that
 explores the challenges and successes of campus-community collaborations
 grounded in urban history as catalysts for community development"—
 Provided by publisher.
Identifiers: LCCN 2022017985 (print) | LCCN 2022017986 (ebook) | ISBN
 9781439920961 (cloth) | ISBN 9781439920978 (paperback) | ISBN
 9781439920985 (pdf)
Subjects: LCSH: Urban universities and colleges—United States $$x Public
 services. | Community and college—United States. | Education,
 Urban—Social aspects—United States. | Education, Higher—Social
 aspects—United States.
Classification: LCC LB2331.44 .E56 2023 (print) | LCC LB2331.44 (ebook) |
 DDC 378.1/03—dc23/eng/20220706
LC record available at https://lccn.loc.gov/2022017985
LC ebook record available at https://lccn.loc.gov/2022017986

Printed in the United States of America

9 8 7 6 5 4 3 2 1

For Marissa, Daniel, and Meseret
Our bright lights in a changing world.

Contents

Acknowledgments

This collection emerged out of a dynamic roundtable discussion on "Civic Engagement and Community Development: Public Humanities, Place-Making, and the Uses of Urban History" at the ninth biennial Urban History Association conference in 2014 in Philadelphia. Eugenie Birch facilitated a lively conversation we both participated in with Joseph Heathcott, Ira Harkavy, and Catherine Gudis. These wonderful colleagues began what has become a sustained dialogue with many other community-engaged scholars, teachers, administrators, and community partners across the country. We are grateful for the wonderful contributors to this volume as well as the larger network of community-engagement advocates who support, sustain, critically reflect on, and work to improve higher education's responsibility to enhance democracy and make a positive difference in the communities they share. Our individual and collective work is better because of thoughtful, talented colleagues and friends who have informed our community-engaged work and this volume: Kal Alston, Davarian Baldwin, Anna Bartel, Gretchen Beesing, Eugenie Birch, Trenise Bryant, Mileyka Burgos-Flores, Adam Bush, Alexandra Byrum, N.D.B. Connolly, Anthony Crenshaw, Nicole Crooks, Kim Dean-Anderson, Jorge Damian de la Paz, Terry Dolson, Lena Dostilio, Timothy Eatman, Emily Eisenhauer, Julie Ellison, Scotney Evans, Tiffany Fajardo, Ashley Finley, Kamalah Fletcher, Sylvia Gale, William S. Green, Catherine Gudis, Ira Harkavy, Joseph Heathcott, Ashley Hemm, Marisa Hightower, Rita A. Hodges, Andrew Hurley, Matthew Johnson, Erica Kohl-Arenas, Laura Kohn-Wood, Lisa Lee, Annie Lord, Derek Miller, Marisol Morales, Daniel Neal, Robert K. Nelson, Scott Peters, Adrienne Piazza, John L. Puckett, Jyotika Ramaprasad, Darby Ray, John Saltmarsh, George Sanchez, Paul Schadewald, David Scobey, Andrew Seligsohn, J. Mark Souther, Blake Stack, Joann Weeks, LaDale Winling, and Jocelyn Zanzot. We also thank our fabulous colleagues on the National Advisory Board of Imagining America, some of whom are listed individually above, for providing an engaging, supportive, and vibrant home in which to advance the work of public scholarship, cultural organizing, and campus and community change.

We are grateful to Aaron M. Javsicas and Steven Conn and the staff at Temple University Press for their patience and support in seeing this volume to fruition. We also appreciate the time and helpful feedback provided by our reviewers.

Engaging Place, Engaging Practices

Introduction

The Past as Prologue

Engaging Urban Places and Public Purpose in the Twenty-First Century

Robin F. Bachin and
Amy L. Howard

During the first two decades of the twenty-first century, cities have been touted as epicenters for creativity and innovation, magnets for the coveted millennial workforce, and optimal retirement locations for privileged retirees who desire easy access to arts and culture as well as walkability. Richard Florida's recipe for postindustrial urban success—technology, tolerance, and talent to attract the "creative class"—inspired ideas about the future growth and potential of urban America.[1] Large and midsize cities have competed for "most livable," "best arts scene," and "healthiest" rankings. They have also dealt with long-standing localized challenges, including poverty, affordable housing, segregated schools, and gentrification. At the same time, colleges and universities located in urban areas have leveraged their locales to appeal to students while also taking a more active role in addressing local challenges. Institutions of higher education across the country have embraced civic engagement, supporting academically grounded community service, community-based learning courses tying course content to community-identified needs, and even large-scale university-community collaborations such as lab schools, downtown centers, and innovation hubs. As colleges and universities strive to matter in the places where they are located, a grounding in urban history has emerged as an important framework for helping situate a wide-range of campus-community collaborations.

This volume highlights how the academy, in general, and urban history, in particular, can play a significant role in fostering these connections. Urban historians have highlighted the important role of urban universities as place-based anchor institutions with extraordinary resources that can and should help contribute to collaboratively addressing the most pressing issues facing cities and their communities through the lens of the past. Cities serve as a crucible for analyzing macrolevel processes, such as changes in the nature of work, concentrations of capital, and government disinvestment in the public realm. Studying people's interactions in, engagement with, and conflict over urban spaces provides scholars of the city with tools for examining the relationship both between the built environment and culture and between large-scale social processes and daily lived experience. At the same time, delving into the past provides opportunities for urban historians to connect the history of urban policy to present-day practices, fostering publicly engaged scholarship that brings campus and community together to promote vibrant urban futures. By developing teaching, research, and institutional strategies that directly link academic scholarship to public practice and civic engagement, universities can help fulfill their mandate to produce the next generation of citizens who have the knowledge, skills, and values to be effective civic leaders.

The stated purpose of higher education to advance democracy and citizenship and the additional responsibility of urban universities to contribute locally has deep roots. A century ago, philosopher and educator John Dewey laid the foundation for understanding the valuable role all citizens could play in urban community problem-solving. Dewey believed in the intimate connections between the search for knowledge, the process of social engagement in urban communities, and deliberative democracy. For Dewey, knowledge and truth were not contained within the walls of the university. The processes of shaping knowledge and building community would be dynamic and dialogic; they would inform one another and unravel in new and spontaneous ways.[2] He wrote, "Democracy is freedom. If truth is at the bottom of things, freedom means giving truth a chance to show itself, a chance to well up from the depths."[3] All citizens, according to Dewey, had both a right and a responsibility to be part of this process. So-called experts, according to Dewey, needed to recognize their role as members of the public, applying their specialized knowledge in the service of the public good. That way, a variety of models of expertise, from localized knowledge to large-scale solutions for urban problem-solving, could be brought to bear equally in confronting urban challenges.[4]

The gap between Dewey's ideal and the complex role higher education institutions have played within their host cities has at times widened and narrowed. The contradictions are many: higher education has both contributed to knowledge creation, reciprocal partnerships, community development, and access programs for addressing the pressing needs of cities and residents and leveraged power to exploit the human, intellectual, and real estate assets of the communities in which they are located. During the twentieth century, universities benefited from government-sanctioned policies ranging from urban renewal to large tax breaks to fuel their growth and expansion, often at the expense of low-income and Black and Brown neighbors and neighborhoods. Even before federal policies began influencing university land use practices in urban areas, institutions of higher education often relied on more informal and market-based practices to shape their neighborhoods. At the time of its founding in the late nineteenth century, the University of Chicago sought to create a buffer between the campus and the surrounding community by buying up adjacent real estate. The university razed tenements and in their place built modern apartment buildings that could be rented to faculty, students, and professionals in the area. During and after World War I, as the Great Migration brought more Black Southerners to Chicago and other Northern cities, universities affected by these demographic shifts often were party to restrictive covenants that forbade renting or selling properties to Black people. The *Chicago Defender*, the leading Black newspaper in the city, referred to restrictive covenants as "the University of Chicago Agreement to get rid of Negroes."[5]

From the beginning of the federal government's urban renewal program in 1949, and its expansion and university-focused Section 112 introduced in 1959 and ending in 1964, 120 colleges and universities received funds to acquire land, demolish or rehabilitate buildings, and/or relocate occupants of buildings located in the vicinity of the project site.[6] Columbia University united with other institutions in Morningside Heights to stop "the encroachment of Harlem" by razing tenements occupied mostly by African Americans and Puerto Ricans and replacing them with middle-income cooperative apartments through a slum-clearance project.[7] In response to protests from local community organizations about Columbia's continued expansion, Jacques Barzun, the university's provost, argued that if its urban renewal plans were blocked, Columbia would not be able to continue to produce the leaders who would serve the city and the nation in the future.[8] Leveraging federal funds received through an amendment in the 1959 Housing Act, Fordham University purchased three hundred twenty thousand square feet in a low-income neighborhood near Central Park in which to expand. Despite protests and court challenges by homeowners, tenants, and small business owners slated to be displaced by the project, the Lincoln Center, new Fordham law school, and other university buildings opened in 1961.[9]

In the later decades of the twentieth century, criticism intensified over expanding campuses, public universities' exemption from paying real estate taxes, and local research projects based on "surveying local residents constantly"—often Black and Brown people living in lower-income communities—without producing results that benefited those who were surveyed.[10] The power, privilege, and resources of higher education cut both ways for cities, producing new knowledge, generating economic and community development, and serving as major employers while also extracting data, land, and taxes from surrounding communities. These examples show the often antagonistic relationship between urban universities and their cities, and the various ways in which university administrators have justified their antidemocratic practices by pointing to their supposed role in promoting the public good.[11]

Engaging with the complex history of cities alongside college and universities' roles as potent players in shaping and being shaped by their locales requires an honest reckoning with higher education's misuse of power and missteps. More recently, educators across the country have called for stronger connections between universities and their communities in addressing pressing societal concerns. Nancy Cantor, chancellor at Rutgers University–Newark, has championed the role of universities as a public good. "We educate the next generation of leaders," she explains. "We address important societal issues with discoveries that change our world. We preserve our cultural past while laying the groundwork for the future. And we experiment with ways of building community."[12] This last idea reflects the vision of numerous university leaders who have called for stronger ties between universities and their communities, whereby scholars, students, activists, and residents can join together in the act of collaborative knowledge building, problem-solving, and creativity. This process recognizes that different groups bring different kinds of expertise, and all have a vital role to play in fostering connections between people and across cultures. By engaging more directly and intentionally with communities, universities not only bring skills and resources to the public but also transform the process of knowledge production itself by fostering a symbiotic relationship with people and groups outside of the confines of the campus. This act of "collaborative co-creation," as historian David Scobey calls it, places knowledge building and culture making at the heart of democratic public life, thereby reconnecting the university with its publics.[13]

From Los Angeles to St. Louis, Richmond to Miami, colleges and universities are working to intentionally connect to and build capacity in the cities where they are located. Each chapter in *Engaging Place, Engaging Practices* highlights how these projects provide opportunities to present multiple components of a city's history to give context and promote a sense of cultural belonging. These projects help forge civic identity, shared meaning, and respect for groups that have come before while allowing new groups to feel part of a city's history by reconnecting fragments of its past to its present and future. These links to the past, and the process of including multiple voices and community knowledge within the narrative of place, can help forge a stronger sense of place attachment and civic identity at a time when transience and disengagement define much of our urban culture.

In the first chapter, Alexandra Byrum and Amy L. Howard of the University of Richmond (UR) take up the theme of historical injustice and its role in shaping present-day community development concerns in "Historicizing Richmond's Future: UR Downtown and the Geography of Community Engagement." This chapter explores the possibilities and challenges of campus-community connectivity rooted in the urban history of an emerging Southern city. The authors reflect on UR Downtown as part of both the burgeoning downtown renaissance and the university's commitment to civic engagement. What does it mean for a liberal arts college to open a downtown hub? What possibilities for learning and community impact emerge? What obstacles exist and how can they be overcome? And, what role does the history of the city and its current challenges play in shaping UR Downtown and its programs? After reflecting on a decade of work to start and sustain the space and programming, the authors provide a practical guide to the challenges and possibilities of the work.

In Chapter 2, "Toward Creating the Democratic, Engaged Urban University: Penn's Partnership with West Philadelphia as an Experiment in Progress," University of Pennsylvania colleagues Ira Harkavy, Rita A. Hodges, John L. Puckett, and Joann Weeks examine what role, if any, an urban university should play in addressing historic and systemic injustices in place? What challenges must universities overcome to engage meaningfully in this work? This chapter argues for the development of "truly engaged universities" that embrace the comprehensive and sustained involvement of all aspects of the university with the community. By focusing on democratic practices that value the expertise "on the ground" and working with communities in respectful and collaborative ways, urban universities, like Penn, can address both the historic institutional harm inflicted on neighboring areas and the inequities of extreme poverty, persistent deprivation, and pernicious racism afflicting communities in the shadows of powerful and relatively wealthy urban universities.

J. Mark Souther, from Cleveland State University, examines how digital humanities has emerged as an important methodology for connecting history to its publics. In Chapter 3, "Digital Storytelling and University-Based Community Engagement in Cleveland," he reflects on his experience in modeling university-based community engagement through digital public history. The chapter highlights the work of the Center for Public History + Digital Humanities at Cleveland State University by focusing on how the *Cleveland Historical* web and app project, along with the *Cleveland Voices* oral history initiative, created opportunities for location-based digital storytelling that have made the city a humanities-based, public-facing learning laboratory. The author shares examples of student-centered and public-facing outcomes associated with these projects and presents case studies of how these projects have contributed to placemaking and community-development initiatives in a Cleveland neighborhood. The chapter also addresses the implications of deploying digital history to construct bridges between traditional scholarly practice and the imperative of public engagement.

Robin F. Bachin of the University of Miami continues the theme of digital history and public practice in Chapter 4, "Mapping Miami: Affordable Housing, Equitable Community Development, and Grassroots Engagement in South Florida." This chapter addresses the variety of initiatives in affordable housing, land use, and placemaking that have brought together University of Miami faculty and students with local planners, architects, policy makers, advocacy groups, and community organizers in Miami. It examines the roles that digital mapping tools, planning history, and grassroots activism are playing in efforts to promote urban equity and resilience. It also focuses on the impact that cross-sector collaboration between campuses and community organizations can have in using both innovative technological tools and grassroots organizing to shape community development. A central theme of the chapter is the significant role racial displacement has played in shaping housing access and land use patterns in Miami over the past century. The chapter explores how local residents and activists have used oral history, historic preservation, and archival documentation to tell their stories. It highlights how campus-community partnerships have carved out new opportunities for resident engagement in the planning process, and how communities are using data-driven solutions along with historical narratives to shape the future of urban growth and resilience in their neighborhoods.

University of Missouri–St. Louis history professor Andrew Hurley links urban and environmental history in Chapter 5, "Engaging Neighborhoods in Climate Change Planning with Public History." This chapter highlights the powerful role that historical understanding plays in building community resilience in the face of climate change and extreme weather events. If current projections of planetary-scale climate change come to pass, urban areas in the United States and throughout the world will face unprecedented threats to their viability. Typically, planning related to climate change revolves around emergency preparedness at the scale of counties and municipalities. Yet, this chapter shows there is much that grassroots organizations can do to build resilience capacity at the scale of neighborhoods. Low-income urban districts present a special challenge due to the vulnerability of populations and the numerous issues that compete with climate change for the attention of residents. The author showcases how the students and faculty at the University of Missouri–St. Louis partnered with inner-city civic, environmental, and religious organizations to identify climate-related liabilities and assets through the production of local landscape histories and citizen-generated photo narrations about meaningful places. The chapter concludes with a call for public historians to intercede more adventurously in arenas of policy and planning not normally associated with historical or humanities inquiries.

In Chapter 6, Catherine Gudis from the University of California, Riverside, explores the ways in which critical tourism and embodied geographies can provide frameworks for examining and interpreting cultural landscapes, in particular, the historical, socioeconomic, and environmental issues related to urban infrastructure in Southern California. "Critical Tourism and Embodied Geographies: Touring Southern California with the Bureau of Goods Transport" takes as a primary case study the logistics industry in the Inland Empire and a tour and guidebook produced by the Bureau of Goods Transport focused on heritage and historic sites related to the goods movement industry. The bureau was developed out of a series of projects by the University of California, Riverside, faculty and students that aimed to bridge social science research and artistic practice, community engagement and broad-based outreach. The bureau's Goods Movement Industry Tour derived from exploring models for alternative pedagogy, social engagement, and modes of research and knowledge production that exceed the traditional boundaries of the university. It is rooted in research developed through work with local union organizers, activists, and business leaders exploring the economic, sociopolitical, and environmental effects of moving goods through a congested, demographically diverse, and environmentally rich region. Yet, by reframing and representing this research through practices of critical tourism and embodied geography, the bureau's tour poses additional questions regarding the university and civic engagement. Here are some central questions: How can we create spaces for nontraditional learning and for participatory site-based engagement? How might we employ urban interventions and touristic modes of exploration as entertaining and engaging means of building constituencies for social change? And, might such critical pedagogical practices also help bridge divides between scholars, the general public, and industry as well as effect policy change?

Individually these case studies highlight a range of methods and modes for advancing collaborative campus-community partnerships rooted in a clear-eyed understanding of urban history and the power differential between urban campuses and their communities. Collectively, the successes and challenges of each study demonstrate the possibilities for colleges and universities to make good on their stated democratic purpose as well as the need for continued work to center and value community-engaged work within the academy and to fully embrace community-based knowledge as a critical factor in promoting the health and thriving of cities. The embrace of collaboration, knowledge sharing, and co-creation between communities and colleges and universities is even more urgent as the nation and world grapple with the death, disruption, and economic decline wrought by COVID-19. The impact of the COVID-19 pandemic on both cities and their universities has called into question the future of both. Will city dwellers move back to urban centers after virtual meetings and remote work from small suburbs, beach towns, and mountain lodges became so widespread? Will people return to crowded theaters, museums, restaurants, and bars that have given cities their historic vitality? And can universities continue to thrive as anchor institutions in cities when Zoom classes and asynchronous learning can deliver content more efficiently and inexpensively? Partly what the pandemic has shown is that we need to rethink what cities are, whom they serve, and how they can be made more inclusive and just. As Farhad Manjoo argues, "What's important here aren't the specific ideas, but the larger push for civic revitalization. The coronavirus does not have to kill cities—just our old idea of what cities were, how they worked, and who they were for."[14] As higher education and cities nationwide and globally grapple with the serious social, economic, cultural, environmental, and political consequences of the COVID-19 pandemic, *engaging place* through *engaging practices* in campus-community collaborations has become even more important. Joining the educational and public purpose of higher education with community-based knowledge and an understanding of historical context can contribute to a more equitable, just, and sustainable future.

NOTES

1. Richard Florida, *The Rise of the Creative Class* (New York: Basic Books, 2002). In subsequent books, including *Cities and the Creative Class* (New York: Routledge, 2005) and *The New Urban Crisis: How Our Cities Are Increasing Inequality, Deepening Segregation, and Failing the Middle Class—And What We Can Do about It* (New York: Basic Books, 2017), Florida addressed the debate and criticism that arose after publication of *The Rise of the Creative Class*, especially his failure in the original book to address the impact that appealing to "creatives" to remake cities would have in exacerbating urban inequality, promoting gentrification, and making cities more unaffordable.

2. John Dewey, *Democracy and Education* (New York: Macmillan, 1916), 99.

3. John Dewey, "Christianity and Democracy: An Address to the University of Michigan Christian Association" (March 27, 1892), in *John Dewey, The Early Works, 1882–1898*, volume 5, ed. Jo Ann Boydston (Carbondale: Southern Illinois University Press, 1972), 4.

4. John Dewey, *Experience and Education* (New York: Collier Books, 1938), 82–86. For more on John Dewey's philosophy of education, see Robin F. Bachin, *Building the South Side: Urban Space and Civic Culture in Chicago, 1890–1919* (Chicago: University of Chicago Press, 2004), 67–72; Andrew Feffer, *The Chicago Pragmatists and American Progressivism* (Ithaca, NY: Cornell University Press, 1993), 117–123; Alan Ryan, *John Dewey and the High Tide of American Liberalism* (New York: W. W. Norton, 1995); Robert Westbrook, *John Dewey and American Democracy* (Ithaca, NY: Cornell University Press, 1991).

5. *Chicago Defender*, September 25, 1937, quoted in Bachin, *Building the South Side*, 60.

6. Steven J. Diner, *Universities and Their Cities* (Baltimore, MD: Johns Hopkins University Press, 2017), 53. Section 112 of the U.S. Housing Act of 1959 granted a city two to three dollars of federal urban renewal money for each dollar an educational institution spent on land, demolition, building, and relocation. Diner, *Universities and Their Cities*, 52.

7. Andrew S. Dolkart, *Morningside Heights: A History of Its Architecture and Development* (New York: Columbia University Press, 1998), 330–332.

8. Brian D. Goldstein, *The Roots of Urban Renaissance: Gentrification and the Struggle over Harlem* (Cambridge, MA: Harvard University Press, 2017), 32.

9. Diner, *Universities and Their Cities*, 58. As Diner notes, Fordham's president at the time had ties to New York City's powerful planner, Robert Moses. The federal government provided two-thirds of the funding for the project, which included Lincoln Center.

10. Comment from a community partner and leader of a nonprofit in Richmond, Virginia, who has regularly worked with Virginia Commonwealth and University of Richmond undergraduate and graduate students over the past twenty years.

11. See Davarian L. Baldwin, *In the Shadow of the Ivory Tower: How Universities Are Plundering Our Cities* (NewYork: Bold Type Books, 2021) for a discus-

sion of the inequitable relationships that continue to exist between cities and urban universities and the ways in which scholars, students, and community organizers are forging alliances that have the potential to transform both campus and community.

12. Nancy Cantor, "Transforming America: The University as Public Good," *Foreseeable Futures #3* (Ann Arbor, MI: Imagining America, 2003), 4.

13. David Scobey, "Putting the Academy in Its Place: A Story about Park Design, Civic Engagement, and the Research University," lecture delivered February 10, 2000, University of Miami.

14. Farhad Manjoo, "Should We Ever Return to Living and Working So Close Together?" *New York Times*, December 22, 2020, available at https://www.nytimes.com/2020/12/22/opinion/cities-coronavirus.html. Accessed on December 23, 2020.

1

Historicizing Richmond's Future

*UR Downtown and the Geography
of Community Engagement*

Amy L. Howard and
Alexandra Byrum

Introduction

"Each cobblestone and street corner has a powerful history of its own," wrote Chelsey Davidson, '17, as she reflected on Dr. Edward L. Ayers's First-Year Seminar, "Touching the Past: The Purposes and Strategies of American History." For a class project, the students were invited to photograph one building in Shockoe Bottom in Richmond, Virginia, and tell its antebellum history. The photographs and accompanying labels became a part of *Missing Richmond*, a 2014 exhibition for the Wilton Companies Gallery at the University of Richmond (UR) Downtown. Shockoe Bottom was the center of Richmond's slave trade, the second-largest market of enslaved people in the South.[1] Apart from Richmond Slave Trail markers, little of this history is evident today to people walking the streets teeming with apartments, restaurants, bars, and other businesses. The students' discoveries were eye opening for the many visitors who came to see the exhibition. A line in the introductory panel read, "How would your perception of Richmond change if you knew that your apartment building was once a slave auction floor, that your favorite restaurant stood in the footprint of a slave jail, or that your morning commute casually traversed the unmarked graves of thousands of African American men, women, and children?" These questions, fostered through a community-based learning course at a liberal arts university and posed in an exhibition in the heart of downtown, sparked new ways of reading and understanding the city. Students left the University of Richmond's "bubble" in the city's suburban west end to explore the past, engage with urban history on-site, and invite community members into a nearby space to share their discoveries. Taken together, these elements created a deep learning experience for students and a nuanced look into the complexities of Richmond's history for visitors to the exhibition. UR Downtown, seven miles away from University of Richmond's suburban campus, provided the foundation for this engaged learning and connection between regional residents and first-year students who became invested in Richmond's past, present, and future and who began to see Richmond as home.

In 2009, the University of Richmond, a small private liberal arts university in Richmond, Virginia, opened UR Downtown, occupying five thousand square feet on the first floor of a forty-five thousand square foot former bank building in the heart of downtown. The Edward Sinnott-designed International Style building housed Franklin Federal Savings and Loan Association of Richmond from 1954 until the 1990s. The university was the first tenant back in the building, located blocks from Richmond City Hall, Capitol Square, the federal courthouse, and the Dominion Energy Center for the Performing Arts. (See Figure 1.1.) The decision for the university to invest in Richmond's downtown built on a long history of community engagement and served as an important symbol of the institution's deepened commitment to be the "University of, for, and with Richmond."[2] Aligned with "The Richmond Promise: A Strategic Plan for the University of Richmond, 2009–14" under president and prominent historian Dr. Edward L. Ayers, UR Downtown created an opportunity for the five schools of the university to connect to and collaborate with organizations in the business, government, arts and culture, and legal hubs situated in the slowly reemerging downtown core. Both a space and a place, UR Downtown centered Richmond's history and community knowledge and needs in the programs that developed there.

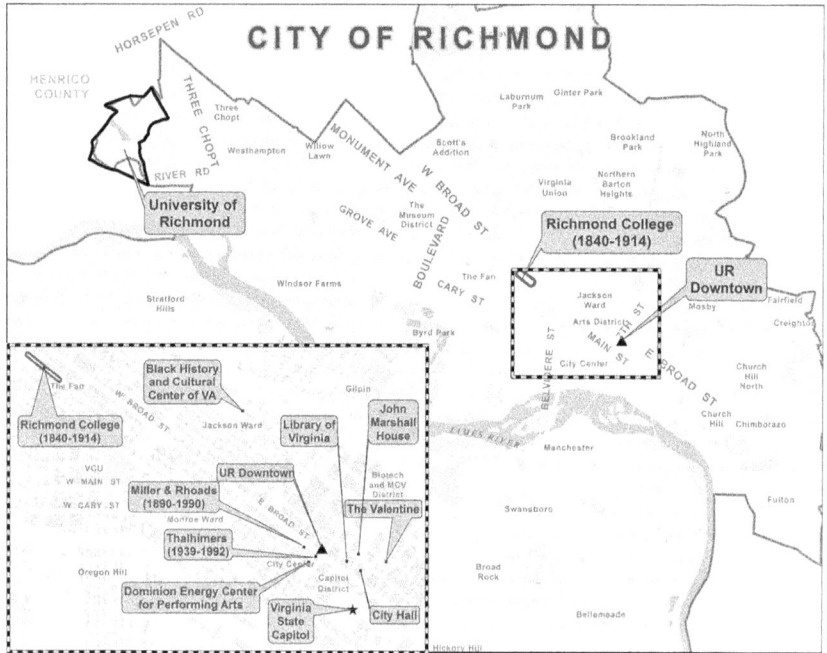

Figure 1.1 *City of Richmond*, 2018. (Courtesy of Taylor Holden)

Rooted in Richmond's past and aiming to collaborate for a better future, UR Downtown provides a unique vehicle for examining the role of a liberal arts university in community and economic development in a growing Southern city. In this chapter, we examine the creation and evolution of UR Downtown both as a marker of the university's growing commitment to community engagement and as a catalyst for strengthening campus-community collaborations that contribute to a more just city. What does it mean for a predominantly white private liberal arts college to have a downtown hub rooted in community engagement? What possibilities for learning and community impact emerge? What obstacles exist and how can they be overcome? And what role does the legacy of the college and the history of the city play in shaping UR Downtown and its programs? The history and geography of the University of Richmond in relationship to the development of the city are critical to the exploration of these questions.

A (Liberal Arts) University and Its City

The creation of UR Downtown was a return to the city where the university opened nearly two hundred years ago.[3] Established by Virginia Baptists as a seminary from 1830 to 1832, the school that later became the University of Richmond founded Richmond College for white men in 1840, providing training in the liberal arts and the ministry. Located in the former Haxall Mansion, Richmond College expanded to more buildings and the campus became a new landmark in the city while providing "easy access to Richmond and its many opportunities for the intellectual and social developments of students."[4] As the school gradually increased its enrollment over the next two decades, the city's slave trade grew significantly with an estimated value of between $3.5 million and $4 million in 1857.[5] During the Civil War, the college erroneously invested its endowment in Confederate bonds and faced near financial collapse as it reopened after serving as a hospital and quarters for Union troops when the war ended with the burning of Richmond in 1865. Leadership by President Fredric Boatwright and a generous gift, combined with a growing commitment to educate women as well as men, propelled the college forward. The college added the study of law, in 1870, and an endowment, in 1890, secured the future of the School of Law.[6] That same year, the resurgence of Confederate sentiment, rooted in continued efforts to oppress African Americans, resulted in the unveiling of the twelve-ton, twenty-one-foot-high statue of Robert E. Lee, the first Confederate on what became Monument Avenue. The monument was the centerpiece of a new real estate development that edged the city westward and further hastened residential segregation by race and class.[7] Lee's statue paved the way for the placement of other towering markers of Confederate memory and white supremacy on Monument Avenue over the next few decades.[8]

Improved and expanded transportation services fueled outward expansion of the region, and Richmond College, at first looking to grow in the city, joined the move west.[9] In 1914, as streetcar lines spurred urban development and the growth of suburbs, the college moved to a new three-hundred-fifty-acre campus, where Westhampton College for women was established along with Richmond College on the former site of a plantation, an African American mutual benefit association, and the Westham Amusement Park located at the end of the streetcar line.[10] These coordinate colleges formed the University of Richmond, in a quiet, leafy developing suburb. In the following years, developers extended Monument Avenue and Horsepen and Three Chopt Roads, creating a "thoroughfare" to connect the college with the city.[11]

The first half of the twentieth century spurred more expansion for the university and the city of Richmond. As the university's enrollment increased, between 1900 and 1920, the city grew rapidly in size and population through annexation.[12] This growth exacerbated pressing issues, including a deteriorating physical environment, substandard housing, and land use conflicts. The persistence of race-based segregation in education, housing, and transportation pervaded planning, policies, and politics and shaped the city's development.[13] In 1937, the federal Home Owners' Loan Corporation gave African American neighborhoods in Richmond (and elsewhere) the lowest grade, "D," colored red on maps, resulting in reduced opportunities for mortgages and home insurance for residents living in the "redlined" areas.[14] That same year, tobacco workers, mostly disenfranchised African American women, led a strike in the heart of downtown to protest low wages. By claiming the downtown city streets for twenty-four hours, they won minor improvements in hours and working conditions.[15] Richmond economically weathered the Great Depression better than most cities because of the depression-proof tobacco industry that most benefited its wealthiest citizens.

Through World War II and into 1950, when Richmond was named an "All American City" by the National Civic League, the city's economic and population growth remained steady. During this time, the University of Richmond continued its "close connection" to the city, with the majority of enrolling students coming from Richmond and Virginia.[16] The university expanded its offerings by opening a business school in 1949, later named the E. Claiborne Robins School, in 1979, after a 1931 alumnus who grew up in the city and sold newspapers downtown to support his family before attending the university on a scholarship. Robins went on to grow his family's pharmacy business and invest in both the university and the city of Richmond.[17]

In Richmond and across the South, systemic segregation ensured that the opportunities and resources offered to white people were paramount to those offered to Black people. Against this backdrop, the civil rights movement in Richmond unfolded with the epicenter in Jackson Ward and nearby on Broad Street. Located north of downtown and claimed by free Black people during Reconstruction, Jackson Ward, known as the "Harlem of the South," was a vibrant African American neighborhood by 1920. The headquarters of the firm Hill, Martin, and Robinson, with landmark cases filed on behalf of the NAACP and others, was located there.[18] *Morgan v. Commonwealth of Virginia* led the U.S. Supreme Court in 1946 to outlaw segregated interstate transportation. In 1950, *Davis et al. v. County School Board of Prince Edward County* led to the U.S. Supreme Court decision in *Brown v. Board of Education of Topeka* to desegregate public schools, launching a period of "massive resistance" in Virginia through the end of the decade.

As African Americans and allies continued to challenge inequality, the city and state chipped away at Jackson Ward. The newly formed Richmond Redevelopment and Housing Authority "took the first bite out" of the neighborhood with the destruction of Apostle Town to build Richmond's first public housing complex, Gilpin Court, in 1941.[19] Over the next twenty years, public housing for Black people was heavily concentrated in a formerly redlined area in the East End, where five complexes went up within one square mile.[20] The construction of I-95 by state approval, in 1957, destroyed the fabric of Richmond's most prestigious Black community, egregiously splitting the neighborhood in two and displacing seven thousand African Americans, a pattern repeated in Miami and elsewhere.[21] Divided by the highway are Sixth Mount Zion Baptist Church, founded by the Reverend John Jasper, and the Order of St. Luke building where Maggie L. Walker opened St. Luke Penny Savings Bank, in 1903, to serve the African American community that was denied equal rights across the city.[22] To stand in either location and look across the lanes is to see racial injustice through the scars in the landscape.

Five blocks away from Jackson Ward, in 1954, Franklin Federal Savings and Loan Association of Richmond opened a new headquarters at the corner of Seventh and Broad Streets—the future home of UR Downtown—across the street from Thalhimers and Miller & Rhodes department stores. (See Figure 1.2.) The bank was the only building constructed on the north side of Broad Street in the 1950s and one of the first new buildings on that side of the street in over thirty years.

Figure 1.2 Franklin Federal Savings and Loan Association from *Richmond: Her Triumphs, Tragedies, and Growth*, compiled and edited by James K. Sanford (1975), 240. (Courtesy of the Richmond Chamber of Commerce)

As the unofficial dividing line between the Black and white communities, Broad Street was the main commercial artery downtown and a flashpoint for civil rights activism. The department stores drew visitors from across Central Virginia and beyond. The Tea Room at Miller & Rhodes and the Richmond Room at Thalhimers were swanky and popular eateries for white locals and visitors alike.[23] They were segregated. In 1960, two hundred African American students from Virginia Union University marched from campus to Broad Street to sit in at segregated lunch counters. Two days later, the Richmond thirty-four from Virginia Union University endured verbal abuse, scalding coffee, and arrest as they led a sit-in at the Thalhimers's Richmond Room, part of a nationwide effort to end segregation and racial inequality.[24] Their effort spurred a shopping boycott that stung local retailers.

Amid civil rights protests and shifting residential patterns, Franklin Federal Savings and Loan Association and other downtown businesses expected the new interstate to serve as a catalyst for increased traffic from the surrounding region. The opposite happened: I-95 led more Richmonders to the suburbs. In the years that followed, many efforts were made by Richmond civil servants to counter the decline of the downtown area. One such example was the Sixth Street Marketplace, built in 1984. The enclosed mall and bridge across Broad Street were anchored by the then flagging Thalhimers and Miller & Rhodes department stores. For many Richmonders, connecting the two sides of Broad Street was seen as a symbol of racial unity, connecting the Black and the white communities.[25] Over time, as suburban commercial options expanded and marketplace tenants complained about building and marketing challenges, business ground to a halt. The Sixth Street Marketplace bridge was torn down, in 2003, and the building on East Marshall Street adjacent to the Richmond Coliseum remains vacant.[26]

Despite growth in businesses and the creation of the civic center, and, later, the Richmond Coliseum in 1971, Richmond's population began to decline in the wake of school desegregation. In response to the *Brown v. Board of Education* ruling, white local officials enacted "passive resistance" policies from 1954 to 1970, including freedom of choice plans and pupil assignments "aimed at keeping black and white children in separate schools." Other heavily used segregationist practices included families moving to white suburban enclaves or enrolling their children in the growing number of private schools.[27] The University of Richmond mirrored Richmond's entrenched segregationist stance, enrolling white students until 1968, when Barry Greene became the first African American undergraduate student to matriculate.

As the city struggled with a declining tax base, continued white flight, and the growth and prosperity of the surrounding counties, the University of Richmond expanded its curricular offerings. The university established University College, in 1962, to meet the lifelong learning needs of Richmond's working professionals. Located on the original campus at Grace and Lombardy Streets, University College began enrolling African American students four years before the main campus did, when Walter Carpenter was transferred, in 1964, to the college from Fort Lee.[28] Ten years later, University College moved to the west end campus.[29] At the time, the university was slowly integrating and expanding its reach to prospective students beyond Virginia. The geography and expanded profile of the university shaped a growing perception in the region of the institution as increasingly exclusive and isolated.

Over the next three decades, the university challenged local stereotypes by increasing efforts to contribute to the region, building on University College's (later named the School of Professional and Continuing Studies) and the School of Law's community outreach and undergraduate students' continued commitment to community service. The Jepson School of Leadership Studies was founded in 1992 with a curricular emphasis on service learning. One year later, through a generous endowment from the Bonner Foundation, the University of Richmond launched the Bonner Scholars Program—an access and service program for one hundred students.

On the foundation of decades of volunteerism by students, strong clinical education in the School of Law, and the strengths of its five schools, the University of Richmond established the Bonner Center for Civic Engagement (BCCE) in 2004. Located in Academic Affairs and reporting to the provost, with close ties to Student Development, the BCCE prioritized the building of sustained and reciprocal campus-community partnerships, supporting faculty in community-engaged teaching and scholarship, educating and connecting students with nonprofit and governmental organizations in the Richmond region, and catalyzing stakeholders for social change. Aimed at piercing the campus "bubble," experienced by students living on the well-maintained suburban residential campus and perceived by the community as a geographic and relational barrier, the BCCE began forming and strengthening relationships, collaborating on and off campus, and creating new programs.[30] Through presidential and institutional support, which spurred rapid growth, the BCCE worked to embed civic engagement into a Richmond education and to do so through the values of collaboration, intentionality, full participation, and lifelong learning.[31] The BCCE's mission is to prepare students for lives of purpose and connect student, faculty, staff, and community stakeholders in social change efforts that value the knowledge and potential in our communities.[32]

A university-wide center, with expanding and reciprocal partnerships with community organizations, the BCCE became a keystone for the University of Richmond's bold return downtown.

UR Goes (Back) Downtown

In 2008, the BCCE and the School of Law began discussions on ways to more intentionally collaborate and partner with nonprofits for social change in the region. With the creation of two new community-engaged programs in the School of Law and one in the BCCE with shared commitments, the opportunity to colocate outreach efforts off campus emerged.[33] The ideal became to develop educational programming for law and undergraduate students to strengthen their civic agency while meeting community-identified needs in the city center, nearer to nonprofits, courts, and clients seeking legal services. While looking for space to rent downtown, a serendipitous conversation at a board of trustees dinners between the Wilton Companies president and CEO Rich Johnson, a 1973 alumnus, and the founding director of the BCCE Dr. Douglas A. Hicks resulted in the creation of UR Downtown in part of the former Franklin Federal Savings and Loan Association of Richmond building.

Vacant since the mid-1990s, in 2008, the former bank's worn-out interior served as a reminder of the larger struggles Richmond's downtown faced in the second half of the twentieth century. With a generous donation of the rental value of the five thousand square feet annually for five years, the renovation and retrofitting of the bank building into UR Downtown began.[34] During this nine-month process, amid the ripped up carpet and hidden behind boards, a mural that once served as the backdrop of bank activity was uncovered. The 1956 sgraffito mural, *The Circulation of Money*, carved by German artist Hans Gassman, depicts the story of money over time, combining biblical and classical figures with symbols of Virginia and industries, such as tobacco, critical for the growth of our region. (See Figure 1.3.) In 2009, The Wilton Companies also discovered and purchased Hans Gassman's collection and an opportunity was born. Supported by University Museums with faculty guidance on the mural by associate professor of art history Dr. Margaret Denton, Layla Hedges, '12, Mary Ellen Stanley, '11, and Elizabeth Moore, '11, took on the study of this

Figure 1.3 Hans Gassman, *The Circulation of Money*, 1956.
(From the author's collection)

relatively unknown artist who immigrated to the United States in 1947. The students organized, photographed, and accessioned over five hundred objects, traced the artist's steps across Virginia to see other murals in person, and curated an exhibition for the newly named Wilton Companies Gallery. The mural contributed to the building's designation as a historic building within the Grace Street Commercial District by the Virginia Department of Historic Resources, but, for the enrichment of our students' learning, it presented much more. This early project, and others that followed, showed the value in pursuing ventures not only of a student or faculty's own making but also of those cultivated by community connections and shared discovery. It also cemented the BCCE's decision to fully embed community-based arts and public humanities programming as a core feature of UR Downtown.

UR Downtown officially opened in the spring of 2009 as a "visible marker of the University of Richmond's commitment to engaging with our community" and a catalyst for collaborative cross-school and community-based partnerships.[35] University Transportation began operating a free shuttle to transport the campus community back and forth from the new downtown hub. The BCCE and the School of Law collaborated in anchoring and opening the space that the BCCE went on to manage. A community room, conference room, classroom, and gallery off of a long hallway at the entrance of the space provide opportunities for multiple classes and community meetings to happen simultaneously. At the end of the hallway, a small waiting area anchors the office spaces, which include a larger coworking space for law clinic students. The former bank vault adjacent to the conference room serves as a reminder of the building's history. From the beginning, all of the spaces have been free for nonprofits, government, and university groups to use for meetings and public events.

During the first year, UR Downtown became home to four community-engaged programs of the School of Law, BCCE, and School of Professional and Continuing Studies. Together these programs created a set of community resources conveniently colocated in "one stop" downtown:

- The Harry L. Carrico Center for Pro Bono & Public Service "connects the skills and talents of its student body with the greater Richmond community and a network of regional, national, and international programs." The center offers a wide range of pro bono opportunities from helping victims of domestic violence to assisting nonprofit organizations in incorporation.[36]
- The Jeanette S. Lipman Family Law Clinic, in the first four years and in partnership with Virginia Commonwealth University, provided local low-income families in Richmond with legal and social work services under the supervision of a faculty member as part of a yearlong course taught at UR Downtown.[37]
- Partners in the Arts, a program of the School of Professional and Continuing Studies, trains educators to integrate the arts into their pre-K-12 curriculum and to support the implementation of school-based projects created in workshops, courses, and professional development sessions.[38]
- The Richmond Families Initiative was a BCCE program aimed at leveraging university student and faculty resources and community knowledge through partnerships with nonprofits to support children and families in the city of Richmond.[39]

Over the next five years, the UR Downtown experiment changed and grew. UR Downtown's four programs activated the rooms and capitalized on the location, as did the many community organizations that used the space for free. The Carrico Center for Pro Bono & Public Service began offering lunchtime Continuing Legal Education programs for local attorneys who could walk from their downtown offices and providing a range of programs for law students in partnership with area firms, including the Wills Pro Bono Program and the Immigration Assistance Project. The Family Law Clinic held weekly class sessions in the space where public defenders and social workers were regular guest lecturers. Clinic students met with clients and worked on cases before walking to court. Located blocks from the Virginia State Capitol, advocacy groups held breakfasts at UR Downtown when the Virginia General Assembly was in session. Fan Free Clinic, now Health Brigade, hosted regular HIV testing days at UR Downtown. BCCE staff hired UR Downtown student coordinators to support community-sponsored events, ongoing programming, and gallery exhibitions.

In 2012, UR Downtown became a Volunteer Income Tax Assistance (VITA) site in the MetroCASH coalition of the United Way of Greater Richmond and Petersburg to provide free tax assistance for low- to moderate-income families and individuals. The partnership emerged after three years of discussions, planning, and needs assessment with MetroCASH to ensure UR Downtown would add value to the program and clients through a new location. The VITA site presented Robins School of Business faculty with direct avenues for students to gain real-world tax experience through classes and eligible Richmonders a convenient location for tax assistance as UR Downtown is among the few sites with easy access to multiple bus routes. As university students' applied learning met a community-identified need, the partnership between MetroCASH and UR Downtown gained quick traction. By 2018, out of 197 community volunteers in the region, 70 were University of Richmond students who volunteered more than 930 hours of service through community-based learning courses.[40] As a coalition, MetroCASH was able to file more than thirty-four hundred returns and refunded over $2.5 million to area customers.

The same year the VITA site was launched, the university increased the size of UR Downtown with an additional 7,741 square feet. The

Figure 1.4 The UR Downtown blade sign, February 11, 2013.
(Courtesy of Kim Lee Schmidt)

space included the entire lower level of the building for programming and offices and the first floor corner space to open the university-operated Richmond on Broad Café, a fast-casual restaurant sourcing some local ingredients, created in response to surveys from workers in the area about limited downtown dining options for breakfast and lunch. With increased space for campus-community engagement and programming, the University of Richmond sought to increase both its visibility downtown and its presence as a partner. Previous attempts to signal the university's location in the building through a UR Downtown flag out front and some signage on the windows were not successful. With a generous donation, UR brought back the style of historic signage with the UR Downtown blade sign, referencing the original architecture and signage of the building and Broad Street's rich history as a commercial thoroughfare for the city. (See Figure 1.4.)

Through these efforts, the University of Richmond supported the city of Richmond's goals for community and economic development. Based on a high level of citizen participation, the city's dynamic 2009 "Downtown Plan" called for creating a more connected, green urbanist environment, with increased public space, small blocks, a tight grid, and the creation of a continuous riverfront park with public access along the James River.[41] For the "City Center" area of the plan, where UR Downtown is located, the University of Richmond contributed to the recommendations in the plan by retrofitting and reoccupying the Franklin Federal Saving and Loan Association of Richmond building, adding commercial uses on the ground floor through the Richmond on Broad Café, and erecting historically aligned signage through the blade sign. At the end of its first five years downtown, the university began paying rent on the leased space, contributing to the tax base for the city.

The expansion of UR Downtown presented increased opportunities for catalyzing connections in a revitalizing downtown. In the spring of 2012, the city established the Richmond Arts District downtown in "recognition of the importance of arts, culture, and entertainment as catalysts for the economic vitality of the city" and offered financial and marketing incentives within the designated area.[42] UR Downtown is located at the eastern edge of the walkable neighborhood featuring galleries, restaurants, and businesses and home to the RVA First Fridays monthly art walk.[43] The university became a fiscal sponsor of RVA First Fridays and incorporated UR Downtown's Wilton Companies Gallery into an RVA First Fridays stop, where hundreds of participants could view collaborative student/faculty/community curated exhibitions. (See Figure 1.5.) An early option in a now more robust food scene in the area, Richmond on Broad Café became a magnet for downtown workers from the federal courthouse and city hall to the Virginia General Assembly and the Richmond Symphony to get a quick lunch in a footprint with few other choices and for students to use their university meal plan while feeling connected to the city.

Additional office space enabled UR Downtown's Faculty-in-Residence Program to support faculty in their community-engaged scholarship and teaching. The first faculty member to step into this role in 2012 was Dr. Thad Williamson, associate professor of leadership studies and in the philosophy, politics, economics, and law program. Dr. Williamson served on the Mayor's Anti-Poverty Commission[44] and was the principal author of the commission's final report, completed during his residency and the foundation for the city's poverty reduction strategy. He went on to cochair the Maggie L. Walker Initiative for

Figure 1.5 Wilton Companies Gallery, March 9, 2013.
(Courtesy of Kim Lee Schmidt)

Expanding Opportunity and Fighting Poverty and became the first director of the city's Office of Community Wealth Building. The Office is charged with implementing a comprehensive poverty reduction initiative encompassing education, employment, housing, and transportation, aligned with the recommendations of the Mayor's Anti-Poverty Commission. The Office of Community Wealth Building has been recognized nationally (including grant support from the W. K. Kellogg Foundation) as a promising municipal model for tackling systemic poverty in urban communities. In 2014, Dr. Williamson hosted many class sessions for the "Research Workshop on Richmond Politics" at UR Downtown, where guest lecturers often came from city hall just a couple of blocks away. It is the proximity of UR Downtown to local and state government that catalyzed more and more programming for University of Richmond students as the initiative matured.

In the summer of 2014, the BCCE supported two students, Peter CampoBasso, '14, and Andrew Talbot, '15, in the launch of RVAGOV. org, a new website dedicated to educating Richmonders about local government. CampoBasso had participated in Dr. Williamson's class the semester before. Finding few online resources for community members on our local government, CampoBasso envisioned RVAGOV to be a resource for students and city of Richmond residents to learn more about the mayor, Richmond City Council, Richmond School Board, and the city budget and to update citizens on monthly meetings. A newsfeed provides recaps of nearly every Richmond City Council and Richmond School Board meeting written by University of Richmond students during the academic year. Dedicated students working at UR Downtown have helped the site remain effective. Bonner Scholar Alicia Jiggets, '19, combined her work on RVAGOV with internships in local and state government. This model of hiring Bonner Scholars and Federal Work-Study students who support UR Downtown programming and volunteer at nearby partner organizations has both enriched the students' experience, providing them with opportunities for learning and leadership, and deepened the university's connections to downtown. Every semester, UR Downtown and RVAGOV team members also host dinners at UR Downtown before Richmond City Council and Richmond School Board meetings for undergraduate, graduate, and law students to review the agenda and current political landscape together.

The immense value in bringing diverse perspectives to the table has consistently been an important driving principle of UR Downtown. Frequently, UR Downtown is a convener. At RVA Connections dinners, for example, BCCE staff at UR Downtown intentionally bring together faculty, staff, and community leaders around issues of shared interest in the hope of uncovering new opportunities for collaboration. In conjunction with *The Community Voice*, a photovoice exhibition illuminating challenges related to health and health care,[45] UR Downtown hosted a dinner on health care access with University of Richmond and Virginia Commonwealth University faculty from multiple disciplines and representatives from Richmond City Health District, CrossOver Healthcare Ministry, the Daily Planet, YMCA of Greater Richmond, Capital Area Health Network, Hands Up Ministries, and Bon Secours Richmond Health System—community partners who rarely have the opportunity to connect one-on-one but whose work is critically aligned. Each RVA Connections dinner brings unexpected results, and we do not always hear about every outcome. We do know from speaking with attendees of this dinner that the Daily Planet and

Richmond City Health District deepened their partnership in connecting homeless and low-income individuals with health care services. Hands Up Ministries learned new information about health care services that affects their residents in Highland Park. Dr. John Vaughan, director of prehealth education, heard about new potential internship opportunities, and Dr. Jennifer Nourse, associate professor of anthropology, began exploring community-based learning opportunities with Richmond City Health District.

The Community Voice was a catalyst for the RVA Connections dinner, and the public exhibition space at UR Downtown has offered many possibilities for engagement with our community. Curatorial decisions impart clear messages to public audiences, and exhibitions invite new visitors, conversations, and learning. At UR Downtown, each exhibition has engaged students in curatorial practice, research, installation, and programming and has revealed what might happen when a university becomes a part of a larger conversation reverberating in the city. When diverse audiences connect on housing or transportation or archaeology or protest,[46] to name just a few of the different subjects explored through UR Downtown exhibitions, new perspectives and connections emerge. Students grow from the experience and the learning. Faculty discover avenues for high-impact teaching. But, even more importantly, the campus community learns what it means to be *a part* of a community, to know its complex history, and to seek reconciliation and change together with community residents. UR Downtown's potential to catalyze interdisciplinary campus-community collaboration rooted in the liberal arts and aimed at contributing to the vitality of the city coalesced around an unexpected and forgotten place, East End Cemetery.

East End Cemetery Collaboratory: A Case Study

On February 10, 2015, community historians and museum professionals gathered at UR Downtown for a "Curating Civil Rights" breakfast featuring Dan Neil, curator of the Rosa Parks Museum in Montgomery, Alabama, and codirector of the Mobile Studio. Neil was visiting the University of Richmond to teach, with Mobile Studio codirector Jocelyn Zanzot, a class of intrepid students in "Public Art and Social Change in the River City" about participatory design and to build with them a mobile studio for our own community. The convening gave community leaders an opportunity to hear from a fellow expert and connect with each other. Among those who joined the conversation was Brian Palmer, veteran photojournalist and new Richmond resident who was working on a documentary, "Make the Ground Talk," focused on African American history with his partner Erin Holloway Palmer. It was in conversations after the breakfast that the seeds were planted for a new UR Downtown exhibition focused on Palmer's photographs of nearby East End Cemetery, a historic burial ground in Richmond City and Henrico County, Virginia, where ivy and Virginia creeper have slowly covered the graves of thousands of African Americans who were buried from 1897 to the 1980s.

East End Cemetery is the resting place of an estimated thirteen thousand prominent citizens of Richmond, many of whom called Jackson Ward or Church Hill home after Reconstruction. William Custalo owned and operated a restaurant at Seventh and Broad, across the street from UR Downtown today. Dr. Richard Tancil met patients at an office in Church Hill further down Broad Street, where he also opened a bank. Hezekiah F. Jonathan was the vice president of the Mechanics' Savings Bank, founded by John Mitchell Jr., longtime editor of the *Richmond Planet* who is buried at Evergreen Cemetery adjacent to East End Cemetery. Evergreen Cemetery is also the resting place of Maggie L. Walker, the first woman to charter a bank in the United States and a beacon for Richmond's African American community in Jackson Ward. The story of East End Cemetery is one that needs to be told, and on September 4, 2015, *All Our Sorrows Heal: Restoring Richmond's East End Cemetery* opened at UR Downtown in conjunction with the RVA First Fridays downtown art walk.[47] The exhibition featured the photographs and words of Brian Palmer and Erin Holloway Palmer as well as a wall dedicated to the families buried at East End Cemetery.[48]

All Our Sorrows Heal: Restoring Richmond's East End Cemetery launched a year of engagement around the historic African American cemetery and invited students and faculty across disciplines into a collaborative effort to reclaim the grounds and our history. UR Downtown student coordinator Aadil Adatia, '17, and American Studies major Victoria Charles, '16, supported the installation efforts. Charles and UR Downtown student coordinator Nia Carter, '19, helped plan and execute educational programming for the exhibition, including community dinners on public memory and Black leadership. "Finding Tomorrow: Experiences in Black Leadership" was a facilitated dinner conversation with Marc Cheatham, creator of The Cheats Movement; Hamilton Glass, artist; and Dr. Tawnya Pettiford-Wates, associate professor of theater at Virginia Commonwealth University and founder and artistic director of The Conciliation Project. "What Is Public Memory and Why Does It Matter?" was facilitated by Benjamin Campbell, author of *Richmond's Unhealed History*, and Dr. Nicole Maurantonio, assistant professor of Rhetoric and Communications Studies. Biology classes also visited the exhibition to learn about East End Cemetery before volunteering on the grounds as part of their study of human demography.

Convening additional curated conversations at UR Downtown with engaged faculty and community members resulted in a web of new possibilities. BCCE staff hosted two RVA Connections dinners to bring together faculty and community members with shared interests in African American history and cemeteries. Members of the Friends of East End, descendants of those buried in the cemetery, faculty, and staff gathered for dinner from Richmond on Broad Café and discussed what could be done together. Elizabeth Baughan, associate professor of Classics, learned about the site at one of the dinners, and, the next semester, included a single workday at East End Cemetery in her Introduction to Archaeology class to widen the scope of the students' community engagement. Through the BCCE's faculty fellows program, Baughan connected with biologist Kristine Grayson who also incorporated the cemetery into her community-based learning course. Together, with support from the BCCE and associate director of faculty engagement Terry Dolson, Baughan and Grayson launched the East End Cemetery Collaboratory in the summer of 2017, bringing together other faculty across disciplines and community partners to collectively engage with the cemetery's past, present, and future.

The East End Cemetery Collaboratory is now an active community of faculty from the departments of biology, archaeology, religion, history, and sociology at the University of Richmond, Virginia Commonwealth University, the College of William & Mary, and members of the Friends of East End.[49] One result of the collaboratory is a digital map, built by the University of Richmond's Digital Scholarship Lab and Spatial Analysis Lab, which reveals the location of headstones for visitors to the site and shares personal histories, gravestone symbolism, ecology, demography, and more. There are countless stories to be told of the individuals buried at East End Cemetery and many graves to uncover behind the overgrowth. The same is true for Evergreen Cemetery whose ownership transferred to Enrichmond Foundation in 2017.[50] Friends of East End was recently awarded 501(c)(3) status, and the documentation efforts of Brian Palmer and Erin Hollaway Palmer continue to gain nationwide attention. In June 2018, HB 284 was signed into law by Governor Ralph Northam, a bill sponsored by Delegate Delores McQuinn (District 70), to help restore historic sites, such as the Evergreen and East End Cemeteries. The work of the campus-community collaboration will continue in an effort to reclaim the hallowed ground and the buried histories of our city's residents.

Challenges

The East End Cemetery Collaboratory's evolution, while generative, reveals a persistent challenge at UR Downtown: how to measure and claim UR Downtown's "success." The collaboratory is fluid, collective, and interdisciplinary—and not UR Downtown's to "own" or "manage." UR Downtown's location and programming served as a spark and a support. This has often been the case as connections, collaborations, conversations, and new partnerships have emerged out of UR Downtown programs and the meetings and events held there. What was UR Downtown's role? Could this all happen on campus? Our experience tells us no. Usage numbers, storytelling, and feedback from stakeholders demonstrate the importance of the University of Richmond having a community engagement hub in the city.[51] Community organizations, from the start, have frequented and valued UR Downtown. Nonetheless, the value proposition and answer to the question on campus—why go downtown?—is one we are continually attentive to. What can happen downtown that cannot happen on campus? How do we work with our University of Richmond community to make the case for going downtown? How do we celebrate the community's consistent space use and feedback on the fruitfulness of the programming at

UR Downtown? For faculty, hosting classes downtown works only when tied to learning opportunities nearby. For students, often eager to get into the city, offering consistent, reliable transportation and conveniences such as using meal swipes at the Richmond on Broad Café is important, as is the vibe of the space. For staff, providing opportunities to see the space opens up new ways of thinking about how to use it, but time to explore and initiate new programs in a unique venue is limited.[52]

The experimental and serendipitous origins of UR Downtown created a number of challenges. The UR Downtown staff had to pilot the new environment while working in a space that at first was not fully recognized across campus units as a University of Richmond facility. The pioneers in the early years had to manage ways to extend the University of Richmond's network, campus mail system, and transportation services off campus and to navigate creating security protocols and building management. We learned by doing. Over time, the challenges of working and growing in a retrofitted building have emerged. The spaces and layout, while used and useful, do not always fit the needs of our staff and stakeholders. Ongoing complaints from campus and community constituents focus on the entrance of the building as being unwelcoming and corporate. Others criticize the interior design as "too UR looking," while some argue it is "not UR enough." Parking is also a persistent and common complaint, as it is for other institutions and businesses downtown.

While operational issues around transportation, parking, and design can be addressed over time if there are resources, the greatest imperative for UR Downtown is leadership. UR Downtown, like other large-scale institutional initiatives, needs many champions. Since opening, UR Downtown has been through a presidential transition, four provosts, and the restructuring of the university hierarchy. While typical in higher education, this leadership churn has underscored the importance of having a network of active supporters in top-down and grassroots leadership positions who value UR Downtown's distinctive role in a Richmond education and in community development. Champions distributed across units and institutional locations from the President's Office, Business Affairs, and Academic Affairs to Student Development, Enrollment Management, the Faculty Senate, and University Staff Advisory Council are critical for building on

UR Downtown's strengths and forging new initiatives that align with the university's changing strategic goals and ongoing commitment to community engagement. These champions, along with faculty, staff, student, and community supporters, understand that UR Downtown furthers the University of Richmond's mission to prepare students "for lives of purpose, thoughtful inquiry, and responsible leadership in a diverse world" through community engagement in the heart of our city.

Back to the Future

Over the past decade, UR Downtown has grown its footprint and programming, moving away from the early "one-stop shop for services" model toward a purpose-driven hub aimed at transformational learning and regional impact. Beginning in 2017, the BCCE facilitated an inclusive yearlong effort to imagine UR Downtown's future.[53] Led by a Strategy Council with faculty from our five schools, staff, students, and community partners and based on input from over six hundred people, the process revealed the need for a clearly stated purpose and enthusiasm from all stakeholder groups for a bold, dynamic long-term vision. The importance of UR Downtown as a symbol, space, and set of programs was affirmed—as was the opportunity for broader and deeper campus-community collaborations. UR Downtown shares the mission of the university, amplifies its values of ethical engagement, diversity and inclusion, student growth, and pursuit of knowledge, and now has a clear purpose statement: UR Downtown provides students, faculty, staff, alumni, and community members with a shared learning environment and platform for engaging together in the heart of a diverse metropolitan area. The long-term vision calls for three goals tied to the themes of *learn, create, and connect with the city.* Supporting each goal are an array of strategic priorities that build on successful existing programs and imagine new endeavors such as an urban semester, a Richmond research hub, a social innovation program, and well-designed spaces and programming to bring together faculty, staff, students, community organizations, and community members to collaboratively address the region's pressing issues. The proposed goals of the long-term vision are to:

- Provide access to applied place-based learning experiences that promote student growth and the creation of new knowledge that builds capacity in the region.
- Leverage UR's distinctive strengths with Richmond's arts and culture, entrepreneurial, legal, and government hubs downtown to facilitate new learning opportunities, creativity and innovation, and collaboration that contributes to the region.
- Support cross-sector collaboration, respectful engagement, and economic impact in the heart of the city.[54]

In 2018 and 2019, faculty and staff groups undertook feasibility planning to assess and recommend which tactics of the long-term vision are doable, fundable, sustainable, and most meaningful at UR Downtown. At the same time, the city of Richmond was wrestling with an ambitious plan to develop a ten block area downtown, close to UR Downtown, to include a new hotel, coliseum, and bus transfer station.[55] The opportunity for the University of Richmond to meaningfully matter in the city whose name we share is urgent, considering that Richmond has a 40 percent child poverty rate, struggling schools, and an affordable housing crisis. In our next decade, we aim to center community voices, expertise, and needs as we galvanize sustained partnerships and possibilities toward a region where all thrive.[56]

NOTES

1. New Orleans was the largest slave market in the "New World." Between 1800 and 1861, approximately three hundred thousand to five hundred thousand enslaved Africans were sold and transported from Virginia. By 1850, the slave trade was the single largest part of Richmond's economy. Benjamin Campbell, *Richmond's Unhealed History* (Richmond, VA: Brandywine, 2012), 109.

2. President Edward L. Ayers, remarks for the Bonner Center for Civic Engagement Tenth Anniversary panel, April 17, 2015.

3. The first seminary classes were held at the Dunlora Plantation in Powhatan in 1830. In 1832, the Virginia Baptist Seminary was founded at a rural site north of Richmond called Spring Farm. The school moved, in 1834, to the Haxall Mansion in Richmond. John Reuben Alley, *University of Richmond: The Campus History Series* (Charleston, SC: Arcadia, 2010), 9.

4. Reuben E. Alley, *History of the University of Richmond 1830–1971* (Charlottesville: University Press of Virginia, 1977), 24.

5. Campbell, *Richmond's Unhealed History*, 109.

6. J. R. Alley, *University of Richmond*, 21. The Law School of Richmond College opened in 1870, but classes were suspended twice due to financial troubles. In 1890, the school received a $25,000 endowment from T. C. Williams's family that secured the law school's future. The School of Law moved with Richmond College to the new suburban campus in 1914. J. R. Alley, *University of Richmond*, 21. While named the T.C. Williams School of Law, the University uses the School of Law in referencing the school.

7. Campbell, *Richmond's Unhealed History*, 134–135. By 1907, monuments of Jefferson Davis and General J.E.B. Stuart had been added to Monument Avenue, which later included statues of Stonewall Jackson (1919), Matthew Fontaine Maury (1929), and Arthur Ashe (1996). Monument Avenue is a National Historic Landmark in the city of Richmond. In 2017, Mayor Levar Stoney charged a newly formed Monument Avenue Commission to consider the future of the monuments. The commission issued a report in July 2018 recommending the removal of Jefferson Davis and the contextualization of the other Confederate monuments. The next steps were unclear as a state law limits localities' power to remove or modify war memorials. The final report was accessed on October 1, 2018, and is available at https://static1.squarespace.com/static/594bdfc3ff7c502289dd13b3/t/5b3a8217 88251b63fef735f7/1530561059506/MonumentAvenueCommissionFINAL.pdf.

8. Following protests, four of the bronze statues representing J. E. B. Stuart, Stonewall Jackson, Jefferson Davis, and Matthew Fontaine Maury were removed in July 2020. The Robert E. Lee monument was removed September 8, 2021.

9. With the future addition of a woman's college, more space was needed. At first the trustees were not keen to move to that "old malarial duck pond" in Westham. Claire Millhiser Rosenbaum's *A Gem of a College: The History of Westhampton College, 1914–2007* (1989; repr. Midlothian, VA: American Book Company, 2007), 17. A fire on campus in 1910 sped up the need for a new campus. J. R. Alley, *University of Richmond*, 25.

10. J. R. Alley, *University of Richmond*, 12, 27. For a comprehensive history of the development of Westhampton College and the importance of women's education as part of the University of Richmond, see Rosenbaum's *A Gem of a College*. For information on the history of enslavement, including an enslaved burial ground, and the African American mutual benefit association that predate the University of Richmond's current location, see Lauranett L. Lee and Shelby M. Driskill's "Knowledge of This Cannot Be Hidden": A Report on the Westham Burying Ground at the University of Richmond, December 28, 2019, accessed on March 5, 2020, available at https://equity.richmond.edu/about/foundational-work/inclusive-excellence/report-pdfs/burying-ground-report.pdf.

11. See Boatwright Memorial Library Digital Collections, accessed on November 13, 2018, available at http://centuries.richmond.edu/files/original/2ae03 ac4f9ddd7f5d6616add286ec39b.pdf and http://centuries.richmond.edu/files/or iginal/6e83598ee49b414ddd8e655c1c5a0d16.pdf.

12. Between 1906 and 1914, the city of Richmond increased its physical dimensions by 400 percent and grew to a population of 155,000 largely due to an-

nexation. Christopher Silver, *Twentieth Century Richmond: Planning, Politics, and Race* (Knoxville: University of Tennessee Press, 1984), 62.

13. Silver, *Twentieth Century Richmond*, 93.

14. Silver, *Twentieth Century Richmond*, 143. See the University of Richmond's Digital Scholarship Lab's "Mapping Inequality: Redlining in New Deal America" web page for the Home Owners' Loan Corporation maps and comments on Richmond neighborhoods and hundreds of other cities, accessed on November 13, 2018, available at https://dsl.richmond.edu/panorama/redlining /#loc=4/36.71/-96.93&opacity=0.8.

15. The tobacco workers strike was one of twenty-six protests explored by the associate professor of history and American Studies Dr. Nicole Sackley's American Studies Seminar students in their 2018 exhibition, *PROTEST! A Richmond History,* which opened in the Wilton Companies Gallery at UR Downtown as part of the RVA First Fridays art walk. More information is on the exhibition website, accessed on November 13, 2018, available at http://blog.richmond.edu /rvaprotest/about-our-exhibition/.

16. J. R. Alley, *University of Richmond*, 65.

17. In 1969, E. Claiborne Robins and his family gave a gift of $50 million to the University of Richmond, the largest amount a living benefactor had ever given an American university. Robins School of Business "Alumni Hall of Fame," accessed on November 13, 2018, available at https://robins.richmond.edu/faculty -staff/hall-of-fame.html.

18. The law firm changed names several times before it closed in 2011. Margaret Edds, "Closing Statement," *Style Weekly*, December 20, 2011, accessed September 1, 2018, available at https://www.styleweekly.com/richmond/closing-state ment/Content?oid=1646015.

19. Campbell, *Richmond's Unhealed History*, 152. In razing Apostle Town, nearly two hundred houses were demolished. The first phase of Gilpin Court opened with 297 units of public housing: only twenty-five applicants were from the former Apostle Town. Campbell, *Richmond's Unhealed History*, 152.

20. Campbell, *Richmond's Unhealed History*, 157. For more information on the history of public housing in Richmond, see Thad Williamson and Amy L. Howard, "Reframing Public Housing in Richmond, Virginia: Segregation, Resident Resistance, and the Future of Redevelopment," *Cities* 57 (September 2016): 33–39.

21. Julian Maxwell Hayter, *The Dream Is Lost: Voting Rights and the Politics of Race in Richmond, Virginia* (Lexington: University of Kentucky Press, 2017), 52–54.

22. The Maggie L. Walker Memorial located in Jackson Ward was dedicated in 2017.

23. The Tea Room was a who's who of white Richmond, the "cultural epicenter" of Richmond in the 1950s. More information is available via Style Weekly, accessed September 1, 2018, available at https://www.styleweekly.com/richmond /tearoom-returns-minus-the-segregation/Content?oid=1387966.

24. Raymond Pierre Hylton, "The Barriers They Broke," *Style Weekly*, November 5, 2008, accessed August 10, 2018, available at https://www.styleweekly .com/richmond/the-barriers-they-broke/Content?oid=1368704.

25. Amy Biegelsen, "Requiem for a Dream," *Style Weekly*, June 27, 2007.

26. Richmond artist Caryl Burtner presented work that explored the demolition of downtown landmarks, including the Sixth Street Marketplace bridge, in UR Downtown's 2014 exhibition *Missing Richmond*.

27. Robert A. Pratt, "A Promise Unfulfilled: School Desegregation in Richmond, Virginia, 1956–1986." *Virginia Magazine of History and Biography* 99, no. 4 (1991): 415–448, available at http://www.jstor.org/stable/4249244. Pratt examines "passive resistance" strategies in Richmond that ended with court-ordered busing in 1970.

28. For more information, visit the University of Richmond Race and Racism Project web page, accessed on September 1, 2018, available at http://memory.rich mond.edu/. The *Race and Racism at the University of Richmond Project* is an interdisciplinary initiative that "documents, interrogates, and catalyzes community discussions on the history of race and racism at the university. Focused around student-centered research and community-based learning, this project contributes to broader conversations surrounding the role of the university in the local, regional, and national community."

29. For more on the School of Professional and Continuing Studies, see "The History of SPCS," accessed on September 1, 2018, available at https://spcs.rich mond.edu/about/school-history/index.html.

30. "Proposal, The Center for Civic Engagement," submitted to the Bonner Foundation for approval by the board of trustees, October 10, 2003.

31. The university's strategic plan, "The Richmond Promise, 2009–2014," named community engagement as one of its five principles: "Principle IV: The University will be intentionally engaged with the city of Richmond and the wider region. Community engagement will be both a method to shape students within a civic-minded campus culture and a means to contribute the intellectual capital and skills of faculty, staff, students, and alumni to the identified needs of the larger community," accessed on September 6, 2018, available at https://strategic plan.richmond.edu/common/the-richmond-promise_final.pdf.

32. This is the current mission of the BCCE, adopted in 2017 after a yearlong strategic planning process. It reflects the work and direction that the BCCE has been doing since its founding in 2004 by Director Dr. Douglas A. Hicks, accessed August 30, 2019, available at https://engage.richmond.edu/about/history/index .html.

33. In 2006, the School of Law received a three-year grant from the Jeanette S. Lipman Foundation to establish the multidisciplinary Jeanette S. Lipman Family Clinic to be located in and to serve clients from the city of Richmond. In 2007, the School of Law partnered with the Virginia Commonwealth University's School of Social Work and Department of Psychology to develop the clinic, which could

provide wraparound legal, mental health, and case management services to its clients. The clinic began accepting clients in 2009 under clinical faculty Professor Dale Margolin. Also in 2006, Theodore and Laura Lee Chandler, with David Baldacci, pledged funds toward the creation of the Harry L. Carrico Center for Pro Bono and Public Service. The Carrico Center created a needed centralized pro bono system, managing multiple programs, and facilitating placements for law students under the leadership of Tara Casey. The BCCE received university funds, in a joint request with the School of Law in 2006, for the creation of the Richmond Families Initiative, to connect undergraduate students in academically grounded partnerships with Richmond nonprofits serving children and families in the city. Judy Pryor-Ramirez began overseeing the program in 2007. University of Richmond Downtown, A Year in Review, 2009–2010, copy available by request to the authors.

34. Rich Johnson and The Wilton Companies generously donated and rehabilitated the space.

35. University of Richmond Downtown, A Year in Review, 2009–2010.

36. Harry L. Carrico Center for Pro Bono and Public Service, accessed on September 1, 2018, available at https://law.richmond.edu/public-service/pro-bono/index.html.

37. The Lipman Family Law Clinic moved back to main campus in response to client and faculty feedback in 2013. At the same time, other clinical faculty and their students at the School of Law began using UR Downtown as needed to meet with clients and prepare for court nearby.

38. Partners in the Arts, accessed on September 1, 2018, available at https://spcs.richmond.edu/professional-education/areas/teaching-instruction/partners-arts/index.html#:~:text=Partners%20in%20the%20Arts%20(PIA,the%20Arts%20Integrated%20Learning%20Certificate.

39. In 2017, the BCCE completed a five-year strategic plan that called for the reorganization of our work into stakeholder groups (faculty, students, community relations) rather than programs, like the Richmond Families Initiative. While Richmond Families Initiative as a program was dissolved, our long-standing relationships with community organizations and commitment to our collective work has continued.

40. Many of the VITA volunteers were enrolled in federal tax courses with Dr. Ray Slaughter, associate professor of accounting, and accounting courses with Dr. Joyce Van Der Laan Smith, associate dean for undergraduate business programs and associate professor of accounting.

41. Thad Williamson, "Justice, the Public Sector, and Cities: Relegitimating the Activist State," in *Justice and the Contemporary American Metropolis*, edited by Clarissa Hayward and Todd Swanstrom (Minneapolis: University of Minnesota Press, 2011), 177–197. According to Williamson, at least eight hundred residents out of approximately one hundred ninety-five thousand participated in the planning process, exceeding the expectations of Rachel Flynn, the community

planning director who spearheaded the participatory planning process (188). Richmond Downtown Plan, July 2009: accessed on September 19, 2018, available at https://www.rva.gov/planning-development-review/downtown-plan.

42. More about the Arts District is available at http://www.rvaartsdistrict.com/about.

43. RVA First Fridays is downtown Richmond's long-standing monthly art walk and happens year-round on the first Friday of every month.

44. Dr. John Moeser, senior fellow with the BCCE from 2005 to 2016, also served on the commission and took up one of the swing office spaces at UR Downtown in 2015.

45. *The Community Voice* engaged students and faculty from the Virginia Commonwealth University Departments of Health Administration, Art Education, and Social and Behavioral Health, Virginia Commonwealth University Health System administrators from the Virginia Coordinated Care program, Hands Up Ministries, a nonprofit focused on addressing poverty in the city and providing affordable housing, and residents from Richmond's largely underserved Highland Park community.

46. *Mapping RVA: Where You Live Makes All the Difference*, an exhibition of Housing Opportunities Made Equal of Virginia, Inc., with research support from Dillon Massey, '15, was on view from April 5 to August 23, 2013; *Transportation Today and Tomorrow: Envisioning a Greater Richmond*, curated by Emily Onufer, '17, and featuring portraits by Dean Whitbeck, was on view from September 1, 2016, to January 13, 2017; *UncoveRVA: Archaeology for Our Past, Present, and Future*, curated by students in the course, Archaeology in the City, taught by Derek Miller, University of Richmond visiting lecturer of anthropology, was on view from April 7 to August 4, 2017; and *PROTEST! A Richmond History*, curated by students in the American Studies Seminar, taught by Nicole Sackley, associate professor of history and American Studies, was on view from April 5 to September 1, 2018.

47. The University of Richmond is a key sponsor for this signature event in the city's Arts District.

48. See Brian and Erin Hollaway Palmers' *The Afterlife of Jim Crow: East End and Evergreen Cemeteries in Photographs* (Richmond, VA: Brian and Erin Palmer, 2018).

49. See Friends of East End, accessed on September 15, 2018, available at https://friendsofeastend.com/.

50. Jeremy Lazaras, "Evergreen Cemetery Sold to Enrichmond Foundation," *Richmond Free Press*, June 2, 2017, accessed on September 15, 2018 available at http://richmondfreepress.com/news/2017/jun/02/evergreen-cemetery-sold-enrichmond-foundation/.

51. In 2017–2018, there were 201 university-sponsored events and 224 community-sponsored events at UR Downtown.

52. UR Downtown launched a Summer in the City program in 2012 to provide opportunities for faculty and staff to explore the city outside of the academic year.

53. The Spark Mill served as the consultants for the process and the long-term vision. For copies, contact Amy Howard at ahoward3@richmond.edu.

54. UR Downtown: Long-Term Vision, 2018, accessed January10, 2019, available at https://downtown.richmond.edu/about/vision.html.

55. For more on the city's aspirations for the redevelopment of downtown in 2018, see the Request for Proposal for the North of Broad Development, accessed on September 15, 2018, available at https://www.rva.gov/sites/default/files/2019-09/RFP-North-of-Broad-Downtown-Development.pdf.

56. During COVID-19, UR Downtown was closed down. The programs and partnerships that grew out of the space have continued as UR looks for new ways to deepen campus-community partnerships, including a possible new space in the city.

2

Toward Creating the Democratic, Engaged Urban University

Penn's Partnership with West Philadelphia
as an Experiment in Progress

IRA HARKAVY, RITA A. HODGES,
JOHN L. PUCKETT, AND JOANN WEEKS

The true starting point of history is always some
present situation with its problems.

—JOHN DEWEY, *Democracy and Education*

If you want truly to understand something,
try to change it.

—Maxim widely attributed to KURT LEWIN

Introduction

The extreme poverty, persistent deprivation, and pernicious racism afflicting communities in the shadows of powerful and wealthy (and relatively wealthy) urban universities raise troubling moral issues as well as questions about higher education's contribution to the public good.[1] It is essential that universities as key anchor institutions significantly contribute to radically reducing the pervasive, ongoing, seemingly intractable problems of our inner cities.[2]

Conditions in Philadelphia, the city where the University of Pennsylvania is located, are an example of a more general phenomenon of urban distress. With approximately 25 percent of its population living in poverty, Philadelphia has had the highest poverty rate among the nation's ten largest cities for the past decade. Over 12 percent of Philadelphians live in deep poverty (an income of $12,150 or less for a family of four in 2016).[3] At the same time, Philadelphia is home to educational and medical institutions that should and could help change these conditions. It has one of the highest concentrations of "eds and meds," which represent twelve of the fifteen largest private employers;[4] and the Philadelphia metropolitan area contains more than fifty colleges and universities. Simply put, the revitalization of Philadelphia, and of American cities in general, depends on the effective and thorough engagement of higher education.

A simple typology helps illustrate our assessment of the current state of university-community engagement and points to what could and should be done. An urban university's interaction with its local community might usefully be placed within the following four categories:

1. Gentrification and displacement of low-income residents
2. Disregard and neglect
3. Partially engaged (frequently indicated by involvement of the academic *or* the institutional/corporate component of the university, but not both)
4. Truly engaged (involving comprehensive, significant, serious, and sustained involvement of *all* aspects of the university with the community, including integration of intellectual and institutional resources)

We argue for the development of truly engaged universities, in which a very high priority is given not only to markedly improving the quality of life in the local community but also to working *with* the community respectfully, collaboratively, and democratically. In addition, helping develop and implement solutions to strategic and community-identified local problems functions as a curriculum, text, *and* performance test for a truly engaged university's research, teaching, and learning activities. No urban university, as far as we can tell, presently meets these criteria. Nonetheless, progress has occurred over the past thirty or so years with an increasing number of universities taking meaningful, if insufficient, steps in the right direction.

Fortunately, a burgeoning democratic civic and community engagement movement has developed across higher education in the

United States and around the world to better educate students for democratic citizenship and to improve schooling and the quality of life in communities. Service learning, engaged scholarship, community-based participatory research, volunteer projects, and community economic development initiatives are some of the means that have been used to create mutually beneficial partnerships designed to make a positive difference in the community and on the campus.[5]

Over the past three decades, the academic benefits of community engagement have also been illustrated in practice—and the intellectual case for engagement effectively made by leading scholars and educators, including Ernest Boyer and Derek Bok, as well as current and recent university presidents such as Nancy Cantor, James Harris, and Eduardo Padrón. That case can be briefly summarized as follows: When institutions of higher education give very high priority to actively solving real-world problems in and with their communities, a much greater likelihood exists that they will significantly advance learning, research, teaching, and service and thereby simultaneously reduce barriers to the development of mutually beneficial higher education–community partnerships. More specifically, by focusing on solving universal problems that are manifested in their local communities, institutions of higher education will generate knowledge that is both nationally and globally significant and be better able to realize their primary mission of contributing to a healthy democratic society.

Some of the most promising initiatives today are built on deep ongoing partnerships between colleges and universities and their local communities. These partnerships also involve the development of substantive efforts that draw together faculty, students, and community members to address community-identified real-world problems. They provide rich opportunities for students to develop the skills they need to be effective democratic-minded citizens. They give rise to research activities that link the expertise within the university with the expertise outside its walls—that is, the expertise embodied in community members who deeply understand the local context in which problems are situated. Sustained partnerships of this kind not only foster the civic development of students; they also strengthen democracy at the local level. It is worth noting that on these campuses, a serious commitment to such partnerships has led to changes in the colleges and universities themselves—altering assumptions about how we should teach and whose knowledge counts, and encouraging new and broader understandings about what faculty work is important and what kind of research matters.[6] A powerful commitment to the democratic ideal moves institutions from a commitment to promoting civic education among its students to a commitment to advancing democratic civic engagement by means of university-community partnerships. These partnerships, while incorporating and, in part, built on individual faculty research projects, are often based on the assumption that individual projects are insufficient to produce the far-reaching transformation needed in the university and the quality of life in communities and society.[7] We now discuss the significance of genuine democratic engagement for the university and the community in fuller detail.

The Inclusion of Community Voice

Our argument, simply put, is that an inclusive epistemology that involves the knowledge possessed "on the ground" by community members is required for the effective solution of locally manifested universal problems, such as poor schooling, educational attainment gaps, eroding environments, inadequate health care, poverty, and high levels of economic inequality. This epistemology expands the definition of expertise and knowing to include other voices—those steeped not necessarily in professional credentials or academic knowledge but in lived experience of the conditions and actualities under examination. What is called for is a movement away from a narrow definition of "expert" to a "community of experts," a broadening of context to include indigenous place-based knowledge.[8] Community members with that knowledge must also be *actively* involved when the problem is defined, and they must remain involved through the development and implementation of solutions.[9]

In describing the set of assumptions involved in participatory action research (PAR), a form of research particularly appropriate for place-based academic-community partnerships, William Foote Whyte argues that "the standard model does not represent the one and only way to advance scientific knowledge." Instead, he encourages a "research strategy that maximizes the possibility of encountering creative surprises [which] are most likely to occur if we get out of our academic morass and seek to work with practitioners whose knowledge and experience is [sic] quite different from our own."[10] Furthermore, there is a major difference between researching as a detached observer and researching as an active participant, whose work genuinely matters to the local population. As participants, researchers are much more likely to develop trusting relationships with community members, which is a requisite for having access to insider knowledge.[11]

Although involving diverse community voices in research projects, especially place-based research projects, has numerous benefits, it is not easy to do. It requires doing research differently than usual and rejecting the assumption that applied and theoretical research should be distinct. Understanding that application and theory are necessarily interconnected and mutually enhancing in place-based problem-solving projects is fundamental. This integrative approach can be usefully described as implementation research, which we illustrate when we discuss anthropologist Francis Johnston's work on the Agatston Urban Nutrition Initiative (AUNI).

Implementation research, as stated, involves the integration of theory and practice.[12] The primary test of the effectiveness of *place-based* implementation research is whether it contributes to the solution of locally manifested universal problems. This approach assumes that human beings "learn by doing," and from and through implementation. It also assumes that research designed to realize large societal goals through developing and implementing programs on the ground with community partners, refining these programs, and engaging in an iterative process leads to significant learning, high-level theoretical advances, and improved practice. The core rationale for implementation research is perhaps best expressed in a well-known maxim attributed to psychologist Kurt Lewin: "If you want to truly understand something, try to change it."

To briefly summarize our argument:

1. Locally manifested universal problems cannot be solved without the inclusion and active involvement of community members residing in the locality that is the focus of engagement and study.

2. The inclusion and active engagement of community members, in turn, will result in better, more innovative and trans-

formative research, and better, more decent and just communities and societies.

3. Developing place-based implementation research projects that are carried out with community members and focus on locally manifested universal problems is a promising strategy to help achieve the advancement of knowledge and the continuous improvement of the human condition.[13]

To illustrate these claims, we now turn to the case we know best, the University of Pennsylvania's Netter Center for Community Partnerships' ongoing partnership with Penn's local geographic community of West Philadelphia.

Penn, the Netter Center, and the West Philadelphia Community

Admittedly, the history of the Netter Center's work with West Philadelphia has been a process of painful organizational learning and conflict; we cannot overemphasize that we have made many mistakes and our understanding and activities have continually changed over time. Penn is only now beginning to tap its extraordinary resources in ways that could mutually benefit both Penn and its neighbors and result in truly radical school, community, and university change. To better understand the work, it is useful to provide a brief history and current description of West Philadelphia as well as Penn's relationship to the community.

A Snapshot of Philadelphia and West Philadelphia over Time

Penn education professor John Puckett (one of the authors) and Penn archivist Mark Lloyd outline the post–World War II demographic changes in Philadelphia, particularly the trends that adversely affected its growing African American population. In *Becoming Penn*, they note that "between 1940 and 1950, Philadelphia's black population grew by 50 percent, from 250,000 to 375,000." But postwar loss of factory jobs and the migration of Philadelphia's textile industry to the South, in their words, "signaled the decline of Philadelphia manufacturing, with dire ramifications for blacks and working-class whites with insufficient means to leave their ethnic enclaves." Out-migration of white families to the suburbs in the 1950s "accounted for a loss of 69,000 people, or 3 percent, in the general population, a diminution that was never recouped."[14]

These trends continued unabated to the end of the millennium, intensifying as Philadelphia became more impoverished and more segregated, as was the case in Penn's local community of West Philadelphia (whose current population is nearly two hundred twenty thousand). The citywide population declined 18.6 percent between 1970 and 1990; the population in West Philadelphia decreased 20.3 percent during this period. The U.S. censuses for 1970, 1980, and 1990 confirm that West Philadelphia became more racially segregated and poorer, increasing from 67 percent African American in 1970 to 72 percent in 1990, with families below the poverty line rising from 12.5 percent to 18.21 percent overall and many neighborhoods surpassing 35 percent poverty levels.

Penn and West Philadelphia from Conflict to Increasing Collaboration

In the middle decades of the twentieth century, Philadelphia, like New York and Chicago, looked to its universities to play key roles in the city's urban renewal plans. Universities, in turn, enlisted the city's help to achieve their goals to expand. The University of Pennsylvania built its modern campus through the instrumentality of Redevelopment Authority Units 1B, 2, and 4. Dedicated to Penn for urban renewal, these three planning units represented the lion's share of an eighty-block area that was designated the University Redevelopment Area by the City Planning Commission. Here, Penn exercised a legal writ for academic, residential, and commercial expansion, supported by millions of federal dollars released under Section 112 of the 1959 Housing Act.[15]

Penn had no such writ in the Market Street corridor, an area two blocks north of the campus designated by the Philadelphia City Council and City Planning Commission as "blighted," where Penn desired a sphere of influence. Mindful of Penn's interests, the Redevelopment Authority announced in 1960 the creation of Unit 3, an eighty-two-acre urban renewal zone. The properties were to be redeveloped under the auspices of the West Philadelphia Corporation, an institutional coalition that included the University of Pennsylvania as the senior partner and Drexel Institute of Technology (now Drexel University), Philadelphia College of Pharmacy and Science (now University of the Sciences in Philadelphia), Presbyterian Hospital (now Penn Presbyterian Medical Center), and Osteopathic Medical School (now Philadelphia College of Osteopathic Medicine) as the junior partners.[16] (See Figures 2.1 and 2.2.)

The planners envisaged a science center as a catalyst for the economic, cultural, and scholarly flowering of "University City," the name they gave to the neighborhoods that bounded the corporation's member institutions. As recruitment magnets for the University City Science Center and the scientists and scholars they hoped to attract, the West Philadelphia Corporation dedicated dollars and human capital across University City to school-improvement initiatives, residential planning, housing conservation and condominium developments, a guaranteed mortgage plan for Penn faculty and staff, historical preservation, arts and culture, beautification, recreation, and retail development in the Walnut Street corridor.[17]

The University City Science Center along Market Street was to be distinctively urban, and the planners hoped to lure the research units of major technology industries such as IBM to West Philadelphia. They denied charges that they conspired to construct a buffer zone between Penn and working-poor Black people in Mantua and Belmont, neighborhoods north of Unit 3. Yet, there was no denying that the professionals the science center hoped to recruit would be overwhelmingly white, simply by virtue of the racial demographics of higher education and the learned professions in the 1960s. Unit 3 redevelopment, with the science center at its core, effectively created a barrier between Penn and its neighbors to the north.[18]

As demolitions instigated the displacement of working-poor Black people in the Market Street corridor, a neighborhood known locally as the Black Bottom, racial politics flared. Of the 2,653 people displaced in Unit 3, roughly 2,070 (78 percent) were Black. Protests by displaced residents and their allies, including student demonstrators at Penn, fell on deaf ears at the Redevelopment Authority and the West Philadelphia Corporation, which managed the affair with hubris and insensitivity as to the probable consequences of the removals, one of which was to be long-lasting damage to Penn's community relations.[19]

Figure 2.1 Map of West District from the Philadelphia 2035 West District Plan. (Courtesy of the Philadelphia City Planning Commission, 2018)

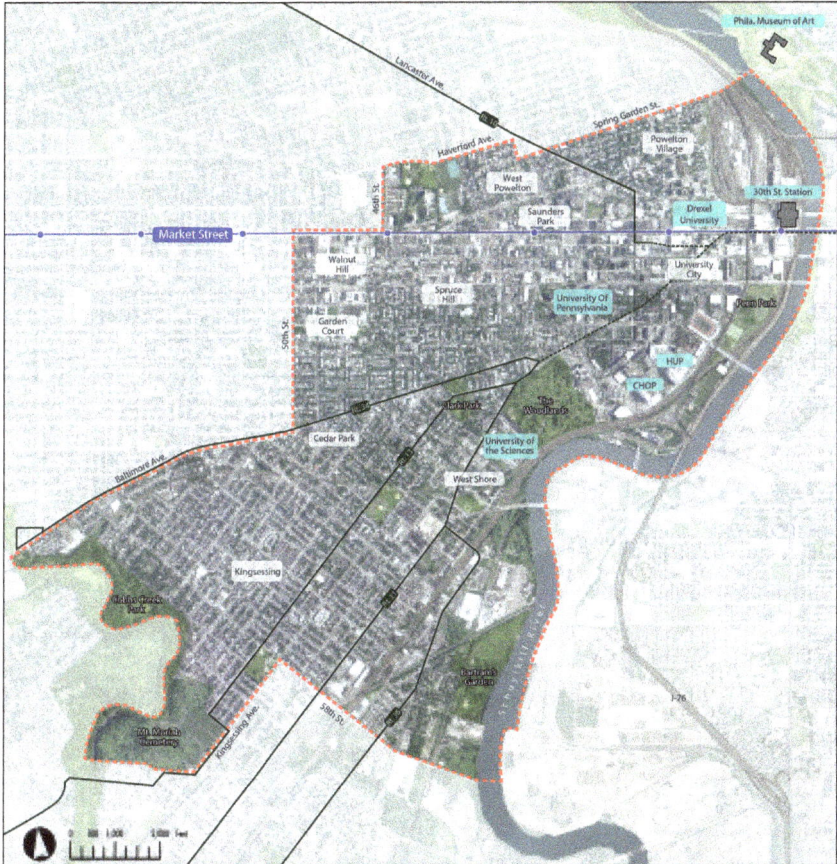

Figure 2.2 Map of University Southwest District from the Philadelphia 2035 University Southwest District Plan. (Courtesy of the Philadelphia City Planning Commission, 2013)

By the mid-1960s, at least in some quarters of the Penn campus, students and faculty had awoken to changing times with a newfound sense of civic purpose. An activist minority opposed the university's complicity in military research at the science center and, by implication, its support for the Vietnam War; they also decried the displacement of working-poor Black people in Unit 3, the paucity of low-income housing in West Philadelphia, and the absence of democracy in all of these developments.[20] In February 1969, a student protest at a science center construction site escalated into a six-day sit-in at College Hall, which was supported by area-wide college and university students and local Black activists. This highly publicized, nonviolent sit-in, controlled in the end by moderate student activists led by Ira Harkavy (then a Penn undergraduate), concluded with an agreement drafted by community and student leaders between the "community of demonstrators" and the Penn trustees. The trustees agreed to establish a "Quadripartite Commission" of students, faculty, administrators, and Black leaders from West Philadelphia as a nonprofit watchdog that would guarantee equity in the university's future land dealings west and north of the campus. When they created the Quadripartite Commission, the trustees promised, albeit ambiguously, to establish a $10 million community development fund to build affordable housing in West Philadelphia's poorer neighborhoods. The fund never materialized. After two years, the Quadripartite Commission broke apart over irreconcilable interpretations of the trustees' vaguely phrased intentions.[21]

Alienation and drift characterized Penn's community relations in the 1970s. Penn students were fearful of venturing into West Philadelphia, which was increasingly a high-crime, drug-plagued district. Penn expanded its security apparatus, adding campus police, high-intensity lights, dormitory guards, and an escort service.[22] Drug-related crime, school failure, joblessness, widespread anomie, marauding youth gangs, and other social maladies—this was the situation that confronted Sheldon Hackney when he became president in 1981. Puckett and Lloyd, in their history of Penn in the postwar era, describe Hackney's "policy of reconciliation," which aimed to restore relations with the community and support a neo-Progressive proactive strategy inaugurated by activist faculty members to help solve West Philadelphia's numerous social problems.[23] As ex officio chairman of the West Philadelphia Corporation, Hackney restructured the corporation as the West Philadelphia Partnership. This was more than a symbolic change: The new partnership, unlike its predecessor, accorded equal voting rights on the board of directors to West Philadelphia's neighborhood associations. The greatest local impact stemmed, in our judgment, from Hackney's support for programs that provided direct assistance to the disinvested public schools of West Philadelphia. The most comprehensive of these was the West Philadelphia Improvement Corps, which originated in an undergraduate seminar in 1985 (described further below). The growth and expansion of the West Philadelphia Improvement Corps from a youth corps to a comprehensive university-assisted community school–based neighborhood revitalization program would ultimately lead to the founding, in 1992, of the Netter Center for Community Partnerships.[24]

Penn's involvement in West Philadelphia before the 1980s, with respect to urban renewal, displaced residents, and the creation of the University City Science Center, had decidedly harmful effects. Developing an effective response to the urban crisis was made all the more daunting and complex by the profound distrust with which the university was regarded by African Americans in West Philadelphia.

The Origins of the Netter Center
for Community Partnerships

The West Philadelphia Improvement Corps' and the Netter Center's work (which largely emerged from the research of one of the authors, Ira Harkavy, and the distinguished Penn historian Lee Benson) was particularly inspired by Benjamin Franklin's founding vision for Penn, which promoted the pursuit of learning and knowledge for the betterment of humanity, seeking to instill in students "an *Inclination* join'd with an *Ability* to serve Mankind, one's Country, Friends, and Family [emphasis in original]."[25] Franklin's vision was rooted in the Enlightenment idea, powerfully expressed by Francis Bacon, that "knowledge is power" for "the relief of man's estate."[26] Over time, Benson and Harkavy also came to see the Netter Center's work as a concrete example of the educator and pragmatic philosopher John Dewey's general theory of learning by means of action-oriented, collaborative, real-world problem-solving.[27]

What had immediately concerned them in the early years was that West Philadelphia, Penn's local geographic community, was rapidly and visibly deteriorating, with devastating consequences for community residents as well as the university. These consequences included increased blight, crime, and poverty as well as concern about Penn's ability to continue to attract and retain outstanding faculty, staff, and students. Given that "present situation" (as Dewey would have phrased it), they asked, what should the university do?[28] Committed to undergraduate teaching, Harkavy and Benson designed an Honors Seminar aimed at stimulating undergraduates to think critically about what Penn could and should do to remedy its "environmental situation." Intrigued with the concept, President Hackney, also a historian, joined them in teaching that seminar in the spring semester of 1985. The seminar's title suggests its general concerns: "Urban University-Community Relationships: Penn–West Philadelphia, Past, Present, and Future as a Case Study," a class that Harkavy teaches to this day.

We need not recite the process of trial, error, and failure that led Benson and Harkavy, and their students, to see that Penn's best strategy to remedy its rapidly deteriorating environmental situation was to use its enormous internal and external resources to help radically improve both West Philadelphia public schools and the neighborhoods in which they are located. Most unwittingly, as the seminar's work progressed, they reinvented the community school idea. They developed a strategy that can be expressed as the following proposition: Universities can best improve their local environment if they mobilize and integrate their great resources, particularly the "human capital" embodied in their students, to help develop and maintain university-assisted community schools (UACS) that engage, empower, and serve not only students but also all other members of the community and function as focal points for creating healthy urban environments.

Observing the work of the Penn students and their partners in the West Philadelphia community schools over a number of years led Benson and Harkavy and their colleagues to develop a key principle that has guided their thinking and practice in a wide variety of ways and situations. That principle can be formulated as follows: At all levels (K through 16 and above), collaborative, community-based, problem-solving, action-oriented projects, which by their nature innovatively depart from customary teacher-dominated school routines, allow and encourage both teachers and students to participate democratically in school and classroom governance and functioning. Such projects create spaces in which school and classroom democracy can grow and flourish. In our judgment, that general principle can be instrumental in inspiring and developing effective programs for democratic citizenship in a wide variety of schools (at all levels) and communities.

Over time, Benson and Harkavy's seminar stimulated a growing number of Academically Based Community Service (ABCS) courses (described below) in a wide range of Penn schools and departments, developed and implemented under the auspices of the Netter Center for Community Partnerships. These courses comprise a core component of a communal PAR project involving the center and its community partners in West Philadelphia.

The Netter Center and Communal PAR

The Center for Community Partnerships (renamed, in 2007, the Netter Center for Community Partnerships) was established in 1992 by then Penn president Sheldon Hackney as a university-wide center that would identify, mobilize, and integrate Penn's vast resources to work with partners to help transform West Philadelphia, particularly by improving the public schools while helping transform teaching, research, learning, and service at the university.

The center's work was building on faculty efforts begun in the 1980s, including the development of two core concepts: ABCS and UACS. Through ABCS courses, service is rooted in and intrinsically tied to research, teaching, and learning, with a primary goal of contributing to community improvement. UACS, as discussed above, educate and engage students, their family members, and other members of the community, providing an organizing framework for bringing university resources, including ABCS courses, to West Philadelphia schools. ABCS courses, internships, and work-study and volunteer opportunities bring approximately twenty-five hundred Penn students into UACS, where programming occurs during the school day, after school, evenings, and summers. We have come to view ABCS and UACS as core to a comprehensive anchor institution strategy in which universities engage in sustained, mutually beneficial partnerships with their communities.

Over the past few decades, an increasing number of faculty members, from a wide range of Penn schools and departments, have revised existing courses or have created new ABCS courses, providing innovative curricular opportunities for their students to become active learners, creative real-world problem solvers, and active producers (as opposed to passive consumers) of knowledge. In 2020–2021, the Netter Center helped coordinate seventy-eight ABCS courses taught across ten of Penn's twelve schools, including twenty-one departments within the School of Arts and Sciences, engaging approximately eighteen hundred Penn students (undergraduate, graduate, and professional).

The distinguished Cornell sociologist William Foote Whyte, who introduced Benson, Harkavy, and Puckett in the mid-1980s to his PAR projects, influenced the Netter Center's conceptualization of ABCS. Whyte's research focused on labor-management relationships and worker participation at Xerox Corporation and the Fagor cooperative group in Mondragón, a town in Spain's Basque country.[29]

For approximately thirty years, Benson, Harkavy, Puckett, Francis Johnston (professor of anthropology who joined the effort in 1991), and other Netter Center colleagues have been developing a form of PAR that focuses on mobilizing resources and organizing partnership relationships to form a university-wide, community-wide *communal* PAR project. There is a fundamental difference between PAR as usually practiced and communal PAR. Both research processes are directed toward problems in the real world, they are concerned with application and implementation, and they are participatory. They differ in the degree to which they are continuous, comprehensive, beneficial, and necessary to the organization or community being studied and to the university. The effort of Whyte and his associates at Cornell, particularly anthropologist Davydd Greenwood, to advance industrial democracy in the worker cooperatives of Mondragón were not an institutional necessity for Cornell. By contrast, the success of the Netter Center's research efforts in West Philadelphia is in Penn's enlightened self-interest—hence the emphasis on the communal nature of this version of PAR. Proximity and a focus on problems that are institutionally important to the university encourage sustained and continuous research involvement.

The Netter Center's academic leadership also emphasized the need to go beyond individual community-based PAR projects, which they saw as insufficient for the problems at hand in both the community and the university. They proposed and worked to develop a multidisciplinary and multiproject approach that engaged colleagues from across the university working together with the community in deep, thick, and ongoing *local* partnerships, joined with institutional resources (employment, purchasing, real estate, etc.). Simply put, interconnected, complex, very long-term *structural* problems such as poverty, poor schooling, inadequate health care, they believed, required bringing individual projects together and developing an infrastructure that could engage the entire university. Among other things, in 1992, upon the Netter Center's founding, they established a strong community advisory board comprising leaders from West Philadelphia to advise and help design and direct the center's local efforts. Many of these leaders knew Harkavy from the late 1960s when he worked with them and their organizations on civil rights and protests often directed against Penn's treatment of the community, including the 1969 College Hall sit-in.

In October 2004, leaders of the higher education democratic civic and community engagement movement, including Harkavy, attended the third in a series of conferences sponsored by the Kellogg Forum on Higher Education for the Public Good at the Johnson Foundation's Wingspread Conference Center in Racine, Wisconsin. The conference, Higher Education Collaboratives for Community Engagement and Improvement, assigned participants to one of several working groups. The "faculty and researcher working group" echoed many of the themes identified in this chapter.[30] Its report, with Harkavy serving as lead author, identified *democratic purpose, process, and product* as crucial for successful university partnerships with schools and communities.

The principles of democratic purpose, process, and product are succinctly phrased as follows:

1. *Purpose*: An abiding democratic and civic purpose is the rightly placed goal if higher education is to truly contribute to the public good. In our estimation, higher education's core purposes are education for democratic citizenship and the creation of knowledge to advance the human condition, which involves developing and maintaining a democratic society. We argue for a participatory democracy, not just democracy as defined by voting or a system of government. We see democracy as the pragmatic philosopher John Dewey (1939) wrote, "a way of life,"[31] in which all citizens actively participate in all the communal, societal, educational, and institutional decisions that significantly shape their lives.[32]
2. *Process*: In a democratic process, the higher education institution and the community, as well as members of both communities, treat each other as ends in themselves rather than

as means to an end.[33] The relationship itself and welfare of the various partners are the preeminent value, not developing a specified program or completing a research project. We also see democratic processes as involving inclusivity, transparency, and openness. These are the types of collaborations that tend to be significant, serious, and sustained, lead to a relationship of genuine respect and trust, and most benefit the partners and society.

3. *Product*: A successful partnership also strives to make a positive difference for all partners—this is the democratic product. Contributing to the well-being of people in the community (both now and in the future) through structural community improvement should be a central goal of a truly democratic partnership for the public good. Research, teaching, and service should also be strengthened as a result of a successful partnership. Indeed, working with the community to improve the quality of life in the community may be one of the best ways to improve the quality of life and learning within a higher education institution.[34]

These are guiding principles of communal PAR. Not every research project undertaken under the Netter Center's auspices involves this kind of PAR, but the term "communal PAR" designates the overarching goal of the Netter Center, its university affiliates, and the center's community partners. Center-affiliated research undertaken at a school or community site is participatory in the sense that it is commensurate with the Wingspread principles of democratic purpose, process, and product and works to involve school and community members, including the Netter Center's Community Advisory Board, from planning through implementation of the project. Though it has a long way to go before it ultimately achieves its goal, the center's overall effort has been consciously democratic and participatory—to genuinely work *with* the community, not merely *in* it.

Democratic Faculty-Community Partnerships in Action

The Netter Center's most comprehensive example of communal PAR and place-based implementation research is anthropology professor

Francis Johnston's work that led to the Agatston Urban Nutrition Initiative (AUNI), originally called the Turner Nutritional Awareness Project.

In 1991, Professor Francis Johnston, a renowned expert on nutritional anthropology decided to redesign a course, Anthropology 210, to focus on helping solve the community-identified problem of poor nutrition. Johnston began work with the community through an approach that embodied democratic purpose, process, and product from its inception. The work began at Turner Middle School, located about 2.5 miles from Penn's campus, where the teachers had recognized that the standard snack of potato chips and colored sugar water was not contributing to their students' health or academic success. Johnston's redesigned course, "Anthropology 310: Nutrition, Health, and Community Schools," became the prototype for ABCS courses.

The initial class of eighteen Penn students worked with Turner teachers led by Marie Bogle, an extraordinary educator and organizer, and sixth-grade students as partners on a range of small-scale PAR projects dealing with healthy foods, physical growth, dietary intake, and obesity status. The results were used in planning subsequent activities. Anthropology 310's success not only influenced the Anthropology Department (which went on to develop an academic track on Public Interest Anthropology) but also inspired other Penn departments and schools to become involved.[35] Over the next few years, a widening circle of Penn faculty and students worked with Johnston in collaboration with local middle school teachers and students to understand the nutritional practices in the community and to address the problem through a series of jointly developed projects. These included an educational program, an in-school market that provided healthy snacks, a school-based garden, and a nutritional outreach program for the community. Ultimately, Johnston's course led to the development of the AUNI—a central Netter Center program that works with approximately six thousand Philadelphia public school students as well as hundreds of adult community members at West Philadelphia community and senior centers.

Professor Terri Lipman in Penn's School of Nursing has offered ABCS opportunities with AUNI for nurse practitioner students. Since 1989, Lipman's research has focused on identifying children with diabetes and increasing the physical activity of underserved populations. In 2005, Lipman began teaching her clinical practicum for nurse practitioner (NP) students, Nursing 723: "Nursing of Children II," as an ABCS course. The NP students received classroom content on diabetes in children, racial disparities in children with endocrine disorders, and key aspects of community engagement. In the clinical component of the course, NP students trained and mentored Sayre High School students on obtaining accurate assessments of height and weight, evaluating growth disorders, and identifying diabetes risk factors. NP and high school students together assessed the growth and risk factors in elementary school–aged children from the community. From 2005 to 2009, they assessed 240 elementary school children, found 30 percent to be at risk for type-2 diabetes, and made recommendations for follow-up care.[36]

In 2012, as a component of her ABCS teaching and research, Lipman partnered with a local dance program, *Inthedance*, to launch Dance for Health at the Sayre Recreation Center. Dance for Health aims to increase physical activity by engaging multiple generations in dance in a safe indoor environment at no cost to participants. NP students in Lipman's ABCS course, now called Nursing 735: "Pediatric Acute Care Nurse Practitioner: Professional Role and Intermediate Clinical Practice: Dance for Health," and Sayre High School students evaluate the participants' height, weight, heart rate, and pedometer readings and survey their perception of endurance and enjoyment of activity. To date, Dance for Health has engaged over seven hundred participants at Sayre, expanded to four additional sites in West Philadelphia, and demonstrated a positive impact on cardiovascular health, memory, social support, and anxiety reduction. Teams of Penn nursing students and Sayre High School students have also jointly given scientific presentations and received awards at national pediatric nursing conferences across the United States.[37] Professor Lipman and her community partners, *Inthedance* cofounders David Earley and Selena Williams Earley, were named recipients of the Provost/Netter Center Faculty-Community Partnership Award in the spring of 2019. This annual award, chosen by the provost and the Netter Center director based on the recommendations of a review committee composed of faculty and a community member, recognizes sustained and productive university-community partnerships with a $10,000 prize split between the faculty member and the community partner.

The inaugural award winner of the then named Netter Center Faculty-Community Partnership Award (prior to joint sponsorship from the Provost's Office) was Herman Beavers, professor of English in the School of Arts and Sciences and the undergraduate and graduate chair in the Department of Africana Studies, and his partners at the West Philadelphia Cultural Alliance (WPCA), particularly WPCA executive and Netter Center Community Advisory Board member Vernoca Michael. Beavers began teaching "August Wilson and Beyond" in 2013 with instructor Suzana Berger. In the course, students from Penn and WPCA members discuss a series of ten works by the playwright August Wilson, who focused on African American experiences of the twentieth century through the lens of a Pittsburgh neighborhood. Through the conversations, they explore the topics of race and class. The Penn students and WPCA members then work together to create original "Community Monologues," inspired by the words of West Philadelphia residents and the works of Wilson, which are shared through live dramatic performances each semester. The course is designed to help students of multiple generations gain a deeper understanding of Wilson's writing and of the multifaceted community surrounding Penn's campus.

UACS, Anchor Institutions, and Movement Building

The Netter Center's work has grown in recent years to include children and families at eight UACS in West Philadelphia. All UACS have a full-time site director who collaborates closely with each school and its community to determine the activities that best serve their specific needs and interests. In addition to coordinating the programs, UACS site directors serve as liaisons between the university and the school as well as between school day teachers and the afterschool program. Staff from the center's thematic-based programs such as the AUNI, Moelis Access Science (STEM outreach), and our College Access/ Career Readiness programs are also regularly working in the schools.

Not to minimize the accomplishments described above, academic engagement alone is insufficient to make meaningful change. The involvement of the entire university is called for if genuine progress is to be made. The Netter Center currently closely partners with the Office of Executive Vice President on issues of community economic development that help advance Penn's role as an anchor institution that works with its community in positive and mutually beneficial ways. Among Penn's strategies is working with the University City District, which was created in 1997. Penn's executive vice president is its chair. A key component of the University City District is the West Philadelphia Skills Initiative, which began in 2011 following a proposal by the Netter Center. An employer-driven job training program, West Philadelphia Skills Initiative trained approximately 1,312 local residents for jobs at Penn and other local anchor institutions between 2011 and 2021, with 83 percent of participants retaining employment for at least twelve months, generating $63.4 million in wages for previously unemployed West Philadelphians.[38]

Netter Center strategies, including ABCS and UACS, as well as the university's community economic development activities (like West Philadelphia Skills Initiative) have helped Penn become an increasingly engaged anchor institution, but they remain insufficient. Indeed, the data illustrate that much more remains to be done. According to the U.S. Census Bureau's American Community Survey Five-Year Estimate, median household incomes for the years 2014–2018 in three of the neighborhoods where the Netter Center works—Mantua, Kingsessing, and Cobbs Creek—were $20,424, $29,656, and $33,275, respectively.[39] (See Figures 2.1 and 2.2.) By comparison, Philadelphia's average median household income in 2018 was $46,116. The federal poverty level in 2018 for a family of three was $20,780 and $25,100 for a family of four.[40] School District of Philadelphia data on the percentage of "economically disadvantaged" students in the eight publicly funded UACS that partner with the Netter Center paint a similar picture—all are classified as 100 percent "economically disadvantaged," and all but one school has percentages of students over 91 percent African American.[41] Significant change clearly needs to occur to effectively engage all aspects of the university with the community as well as to better integrate currently siloed, unintegrated efforts.

For universities and colleges to fulfill their great potential as democratic anchor institutions and really contribute to developing an inclusive, antiracist, just democratic society, they will have to do things very differently than they do now. To begin with, changes in "doing" will require recognition by higher education institutions that as they now function, they—particularly research universities (including

Penn)—constitute a major part of the problem, not a significant part of the solution. To become part of the solution, they must give full-hearted and full-minded devotion to the painfully difficult task of transforming themselves into socially responsible *civic* universities and colleges. To do so, they will also have to radically change their institutional cultures and structures, democratically realign and integrate themselves, and develop a comprehensive and realistic strategy.

Local changes cannot be sustained if they remain only local and unconnected to broader developments. Systemic change must be not only, therefore, locally rooted and generated but also part of a national/global movement for change. For that to occur, an agent is needed that can simultaneously function on the local, national, and global levels. Universities are, in our judgment, that agent. They are simultaneously the preeminent local (embedded anchors in their communities) and national/global (part of an increasingly interactive worldwide network) institutions.

Since the Netter Center's inception, one of its objectives has been to cultivate regional, national, and international networks of individuals and institutions of higher education committed to democratic civic engagement with their communities. This has included, for example, the Philadelphia Higher Education Network for Neighborhood Development; the UACS Network and UACS Regional Training Centers; the Anchor Institutions Task Force; and the International Consortium for Higher Education, Civic Responsibility, and Democracy.[42] The Netter Center builds these networks to learn from and work with others, to stimulate change in other localities, and to help develop a higher education democratic civic and community engagement movement, which in our judgment, is necessary to transform communities and universities for the better.

Conclusion

In summary, we contend that American universities should give a very high priority—arguably their highest priority—to solving locally manifested universal problems. If universities were to do so, they would demonstrate in concrete practice their self-professed theoretical ability to simultaneously advance knowledge and learning. They would then satisfy the critical performance test proposed in 1994 by the president of the State University of New York at Buffalo, William R. Greiner, namely, that *"the great universities of the twenty-first century will be judged by their ability to help solve our most urgent social problems* [emphasis added]."[43] By that real-world performance test, American colleges and universities are falling woefully short. What specific step might help engage Penn, as well as other universities, to embrace that democratic vision actively as well as rhetorically?

To help answer that question, we turn to one of John Dewey's most powerful propositions: "Democracy must begin at home, and its home is the neighborly community."[44] Genuine participatory democracy, Dewey emphasized, has to be built on face-to-face interactions in which human beings work together cooperatively to solve the ongoing problems of life.[45]

In effect, we are updating Dewey and advocating the following proposition: *Democracy must begin at home, and its home is the engaged neighborly college or university and its local community partners.* Neighborliness, we contend, is the primary indicator that an institution is working for the public good.

The benefits of a local-community focus for college and university civic engagement programs are manifold. Ongoing and continuous interaction is facilitated through work in an easily accessible location. Relationships of trust, so essential for effective partnerships and effective learning, are also built through day-to-day work on problems and issues of mutual concern. In addition, the local community provides a convenient setting in which a number of service-learning courses, community-based research courses, and related courses in different disciplines can work together on a complex problem to produce substantive results. Work in a university's local community, since it facilitates interaction across schools and disciplines, can also create interdisciplinary learning opportunities. And, finally, the local community is a democratic real-world learning site in which community members and academics can pragmatically determine whether the work is making a real difference, and whether *both* the neighborhood and the higher education institution are better as a result of common efforts.

For Dewey, knowledge and learning are most effectively advanced when human beings work collaboratively to solve specific, strategic, real-world problems. "Thinking," he famously wrote, "begins in . . . a *forked road* situation, a situation that is ambiguous, that presents a dilemma, which poses alternatives."[46] As mentioned above, a focus on universal problems—for example, poverty, poor schooling, and inadequate health care—that are manifested locally are, in our judgment, the best way to apply Dewey's brilliant proposition in practice. We contend that a focus on local engagement is an extraordinarily promising strategy for realizing an institutional mission and purpose. Or, as elegantly expressed by Paul Pribbenow, president of Augsburg College, the "intersections of vocation and location" provide wonderful opportunities for both the institution and the community.[47]

"Only connect!" the powerful and evocative epigraph to E. M. Forster's classic novel *Howard's End* captures the essence of our argument.[48] Namely, the necessary revolutionary transformation of research universities is most likely to occur in the crucible of significant, serious, and sustained engagement with local public schools and their communities. Abstract, solipsistic, contemplative, ivory tower isolation will neither shed intellectual light on our most pressing societal problems nor produce positive democratic change. It simply will not get us where we need to go. To put it more positively, we conclude by calling on active community-engaged academics and their community partners to work together to create and sustain a global movement dedicated to realizing Dewey's vision of neighborly communities and participatory democratic societies.

NOTES

1. This chapter draws heavily from several existing publications written by the authors—most notably *Knowledge for Social Change: Bacon, Dewey and the Revolutionary Transformation of Research Universities in the Twenty-First Century* (2017) by Lee Benson, Ira Harkavy, John Puckett, Matthew Hartley, Rita A. Hodges, Francis E. Johnston, and Joann Weeks (Philadelphia: Temple University Press). It also draws from "Engaging Urban Universities as Anchor Institutions for Health Equity," by Ira Harkavy, in *American Journal for Public Health* 106, no. 12 (December 2016). For Dewey quote in epigraph, see John Dewey, *Democracy and Education* (1916), reprinted in *The Middle Works of John Dewey, 1899–1924*, vol. 9, ed. Jo Ann Boydston (Carbondale: Southern Illinois University Press, 1978), 222; digitally reproduced in *The Collected Works of John Dewey, 1882–1953: The Electronic Edition*, ed. Larry Hickman (Charlottesville: InteLex, 1996).

2. For a discussion of urban universities as anchor institutions, see Ira Harkavy et al., "Anchor Institutions as Partners in Building Successful Communities and Local Economies," in *Retooling HUD for a Catalytic Federal Government: A*

Report to Secretary Shaun Donovan, ed. Paul C. Brophy and Rachel D. Godsil (Philadelphia: Penn Institute for Urban Research, 2009), 147–169, accessed May 23, 2022, available at https://www.margainc.com/wp-content/uploads/2017/05 /Retooling-HUD-Chapter-8.pdf. Also see Harkavy, "Engaging Urban Universities as Anchor Institutions for Health Equity."

3. The Pew Charitable Trusts, "Philadelphia 2017: The State of the City," April 2017, accessed April 9, 2017, available at http://www.pewtrusts.org/~/media/assets /2017/04/pri_philadelphia_2017_state_of_the_city.pdf.

4. The Pew Charitable Trusts, "Philadelphia 2017: The State of the City." http:// www.pewtrusts.org/~/media/assets/2017/04/pri_philadelphia_2017_state_of _the_city.pdf.

5. Community-engaged work is happening at colleges and universities in small towns and rural areas as well as in urban centers. Campus Compact has a membership of over one thousand colleges and universities that are "committed to the public purposes of higher education. We build democracy through civic education and community development" ("Campus Compact Overview," accessed May 23, 2022, available at https://compact.org/who-we-are/). For a more detailed overview of the civic and community engagement movement and its impact across higher education, see Benson et al.'s *Knowledge for Social Change*, chap. 5.

6. For example, see Nancy Cantor, "Anchor Institution–Community Engagement in Newark: Striving Together," in *Anchor Institutions Advancing Local and Global Sustainable Community Development: 2017–2018 Conference Proceedings*, Rutgers University–Camden, Camden, NJ (2018): 89–95, accessed May 23, 2022, https://clc.camden.rutgers.edu/files/CLC-Conference-Proceeding-2018.pdf; Paul Pribbenow, "Lessons on Vocation and Location: The Saga of Augsburg College as Urban Settlement," *Word and World* 34, no. 2 (2014).

7. Lee Benson, Ira Harkavy, and John Puckett, *Dewey's Dream: Universities and Democracies in an Age of Education Reform* (Philadelphia: Temple University Press, 2007); John Saltmarsh and Matthew Hartley, *"To Serve a Larger Purpose": Engagement for Democracy and the Transformation of Higher Education* (Philadelphia: Temple University Press, 2011).

8. Nancy Cantor and Peter Englot, "Beyond the 'Ivory Tower': Restoring the Balance of Private and Public Purposes of General Education," *Journal of General Education: A Curricular Commons of the Humanities and Sciences* 62, nos. 2–3 (2013): 121.

9. William F. Whyte, Davydd J. Greenwood, and Peter Lazes, "Participatory Action Research: Through Practice to Science in Social Research," in *Action Research for the 21st Century: Participation, Reflection, and Practice*, ed. William F. Whyte, special issue, *American Behavioral Scientist* 32, no. 5 (May 1989): 513–551.

10. William F. Whyte, "Advancing Scientific Knowledge through Participatory Action Research," *Sociological Forum* 4, no. 3 (September 1989): 383–384.

11. Eugene J. Webb, Donald T. Campbell, Richard D. Schwartz, and Lee Sechrest, *Unobtrusive Measures*, rev. ed. (Thousand Oaks, CA: Sage, 2000).

12. The intellectual benefit of integrating theory and practice is succinctly captured by Paul Lazarsfeld and Jeffrey Reitz in *An Introduction to Applied Sociology* (New York: Elsevier, 1975), 10: "Nothing is more conducive to innovation in social theory than collaboration on a complex practical problem."

13. For a discussion of the connection between the advancement of knowledge and the continuous improvement of the human condition, see Benson et al., *Knowledge for Social Change*.

14. John L. Puckett and Mark Frazier Lloyd, *Becoming Penn: America's Pragmatic University, 1950–2000* (Philadelphia: University of Pennsylvania Press, 2015), 89–90.

15. Puckett and Lloyd, *Becoming Penn*, 25–87.

16. Puckett and Lloyd, *Becoming Penn*, 92–93.

17. Puckett and Lloyd, *Becoming Penn*, 98–99.

18. Puckett and Lloyd, *Becoming Penn*, 98.

19. Puckett and Lloyd, *Becoming Penn*, 103–139; cf. Margaret Pugh O'Mara, *Cities of Knowledge: Cold War Science and the Search for the Next Silicon Valley* (Princeton, NJ: Princeton University Press, 2005), 142–181.

20. Puckett and Lloyd, *Becoming Penn*, 118–139.

21. Puckett and Lloyd, *Becoming Penn*, 130.

22. Puckett and Lloyd, *Becoming Penn*, 162–164.

23. Puckett and Lloyd, *Becoming Penn*, 177.

24. Puckett and Lloyd, *Becoming Penn*, 219–224.

25. Meyer Reinhold, "Opponents of Classical Learning in America during the Revolutionary Period," *Proceedings of the American Philosophical Society* 112, no. 4 (1968): 224; Benjamin Franklin, "Proposals Relating to the Education of Youth in Pennsilvania [*sic*]" (1749), reprinted in *Benjamin Franklin on Education*, ed. John Hardin Best (New York: Teachers College Press, 1962).

26. Although Bacon actually wrote "knowledge itself is a power," the famous statement "knowledge is power" captures Bacon's meaning and is widely attributed to him. See his *Meditationes Sacrae* (1957), in *The Works of Francis Bacon*, vol. 1, ed. Basil Montagu (New York: R. Worthington, 1984), accessed November 3, 2017, available at https://en.wikisource.org/wiki/Meditationes_sacrae. The phrase for "the relief of man's estate" can be found in *The Advancement of Learning* (1605), ed. Rose-Mary Sargent, *Selected Philosophical Works* (Indianapolis, IN: Hackett, 1999), 29.

27. Lee Benson and Ira Harkavy, "Progressing beyond the Welfare State," *Universities and Community Schools* 2 (1991): 2–28.

28. John Dewey, *Democracy and Education* (1916), reprinted in *The Middle Works of John Dewey, 1899–1924*, vol. 9, ed. Jo Ann Boydston (Carbondale: Southern Illinois University Press, 1978), 222; digitally reproduced in *The Collected Works of John Dewey, 1882–1953: The Electronic Edition*, ed. Larry Hickman (Charlottesville: InteLex, 1996).

29. Whyte, Greenwood, and Lazes, "Participatory Action Research," 513–551; William F. Whyte and Kathleen K. Whyte, *Making Mondragón: The Growth*

and Dynamics of the Worker Cooperative Complex, 2nd ed. (Ithaca, NY: ILR Press, 1991); Davydd Greenwood and José Luis González, *Industrial Democracy as a Process: Participatory Action Research in the Fagor Cooperative Group of Mondragón* (Assen–Maastricht: Van Gorcum, 1992).

30. Faculty and researcher working group participants at the 2004 Kellogg Forum on Higher Education for the Public Good included Tony Chambers, Arthur Dunning, Ed Fogelman, Richard Guarasci, Ira Harkavy, Jeffrey Higgs, Leonard Ortolano, and Jane Rosser.

31. John Dewey, "Creative Democracy—The Task before Us" (1939), in *The Essential Dewey: Volume 1: Pragmatism, Education, Democracy,* ed. Larry Hickman and Thomas Alexander (Bloomington, IN: Indiana University Press, 1998), 341.

32. Benson, Harkavy, and Puckett, *Dewey's Dream.*

33. This approach resonates with Kant's 1797 second categorical imperative: "Act in such a way that you always treat humanity, whether in your own person or in the person of any other, never simply as a means, but always at the same time as an end." See Immanuel Kant, *Grounding for the Metaphysics of Morals,* third ed., translated by J. W. Ellington (Indianapolis/Cambridge: Hackett, 1993), 30.

34. Ira Harkavy, "Higher Education Collaboratives for Community Engagement and Improvement: Faculty and Researchers' Perspectives," in *Higher Education Collaboratives for Community Engagement and Improvement,* ed. Penny A. Pasque et al. (Ann Arbor, MI: National Forum for Higher Education and the Public Good, 2005), 22–23.

35. Francis E. Johnston and Ira Harkavy, *The Obesity Culture: Strategies for Change—Public Health and University-Community Partnerships* (Cambridgeshire, UK: Smith-Gordon, 2009).

36. Terri H. Lipman, Mary McGrath Schucker, Sarah J. Ratcliffe, Tyler Holmberg, Scott Baier, and Janet A. Deatrick, "Diabetes Risk Factors in Children: A Partnership between Nurse Practitioner and High School Students," *American Journal of Maternal Child Nursing* 36, no. 1 (January–February 2011): 56–62, available at doi:10.1097/NMC.0b013e3181fc0d06.

37. Penn NP and Sayre high school students have continued to present their research together each year at the National Pediatric Nursing Conference (a total of twenty poster presentations and two oral presentations), resulting in seven national awards. They have also been honored for their service to the community through citations from Philadelphia City Council and a proclamation from the mayor of Philadelphia.

38. Additional information on University City District and its West Philadelphia Skills Initiative, accessed May 23, 2022, available at https://www.universitycity.org/wpsi.

39. Alfred Lubrano, "Philadelphia a City of Extremes: High Incomes, High Poverty, Report Shows," *Philadelphia Inquirer,* December 19, 2019, accessed May 23, 2022, available at https://www.inquirer.com/news/poverty-median-household-income-philadelphia-temple-university-graduate-hospital-20191219.html.

40. Alfred Lubrano, "New Federal Report Surprises: Philadelphia Poverty Down, Income Up," *Philadelphia Inquirer*, September 26, 2019, accessed May 23, 2022, available at https://www.inquirer.com/news/poverty-median-household -income-philadelphia-pennsylvania-new-jersey-census-american-community -survey-20190926.html.

41. The School District of Philadelphia "School Profiles" accessed May 23, 2022, available at https://schoolprofiles.philasd.org/.

42. More information on these networks is available at www.phennd.org, www.nettercenter.upenn.edu/what-we-do/national-and-global-outreach, www .margainc.com/aitf, and www.internationalconsortium.org, accessed May 23, 2022.

43. William R. Greiner, "In the Total of All These Acts: How Can American Universities Address the Urban Agenda?" *Universities and Community Schools* 4, nos. 1–2 (1994): 12.

44. John Dewey, *The Public and Its Problems*, in *The Later Works of John Dewey, 1925–1953*, vol. 2, ed. Jo Ann Boydston (Carbondale: Southern Illinois University, 1981), 368. Quotations from *Later Works* were verified in Larry Hickman, ed., *The Collected Works of John Dewey, 1882–1953: The Electronic Edition* (Charlottesville, VA: InteLex, 1996).

45. Although he never used the specific term, Dewey's emphasis on and advocacy for participatory democracy are among his most important contributions. See Robert Westbrook, *John Dewey and American Democracy* (Ithaca, NY: Cornell University Press, 1991); Benson, Harkavy, and Puckett, *Dewey's Dream*.

46. John Dewey, *How We Think*, rev. ed., in *The Later Works of John Dewey, 1925–1953*, vol. 8, ed. Jo Ann Boydston (Carbondale: Southern Illinois University, 1981), 122.

47. Pribbenow, "Lessons on Vocation and Location," 158.

48. E. M. Forster, *Howard's End* (Toronto: William Briggs, 1911), front matter.

3

Digital Storytelling and University-Based Community Engagement in Cleveland

> I remember! . . . The heavy stifling sulfur oxide yellow tinted
> smog sometimes left us gasping for a breath of cleaner air. The
> homes and bridges surrounding the valley were ungraciously
> painted with the permeating industrial coal soot. . . . When cross-
> ing the Clark Avenue Bridge, one was forced to close the win-
> dows of the car and use a hanky to cover one's nose. . . . It was
> a way of life that allowed us to dream of moving to the suburbs
> and clean air one day.

Lifelong Clevelander George Lonero's reminiscence was among the
comments that appeared soon after a *Cleveland Historical* project team
member posted on Facebook a 1941 photo of the Cuyahoga River and
Republic Steel Corporation's sprawling mill framed by the downtown
Cleveland skyline beneath a smoke-darkened sky.[1] (See Figure 3.1.)
Cleveland Historical (available at clevelandhistorical.org) is a website
and app developed by the Center for Public History + Digital Humanities (CPHDH) at Cleveland State University (CSU), an urban public
university in downtown Cleveland. (See Figure 3.2.) The picture was

Figure 3.1 Republic Steel mill and yards against a smoke-filled sky over downtown Cleveland, 1941. Photo lede for Sarah Nemeth's Republic Steel story on *Cleveland Historical*. (Courtesy of Cleveland Public Library)

among the media included in a digital story about antipollution activism against Cleveland's onetime leading steel manufacturer. The photo was one of several selected by Sarah Nemeth, the graduate student who curated the Republic Steel story.[2] The story is one of more than seven hundred—each containing an interpretive narrative, historical

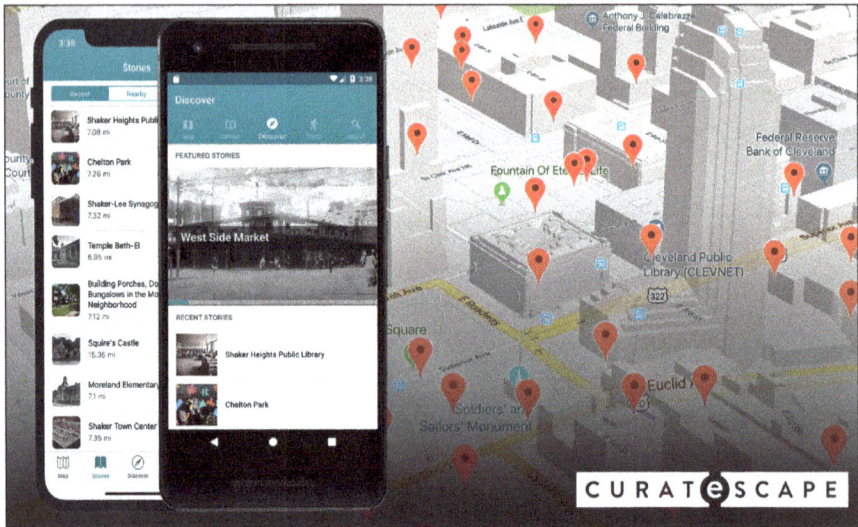

Figure 3.2 *Cleveland Historical*, developed by the CPHDH at CSU, is a website and free mobile app developed at the university using the Curatescape framework for Omeka, a toolset funded by the NEH. (Courtesy of CSU Center for Public History + Digital Humanities)

images, and sometimes audio and video clips—that are accessible from pins on an interactive map as well as through other discovery paths on the website and app.

Struck by the photo, Lonero shared his own story, as did other readers. Nemeth's story stimulated public discussion about the urban environment and elicited insights about one factor in the central city's losses to its suburbs. With more than a half million annual visitors and thousands of followers on its social media channels, *Cleveland Historical* provides a profoundly different and larger audience than a student's writing typically reaches. The project demonstrates the potential for university-based urban history projects to shape public understandings of cities and to foster a sense of place that can influence social relations and community-based activism. This chapter argues that digital storytelling can blur the lines between urban universities and urban communities, especially when it involves meaningful opportunities for public involvement and connects urban history to the contemporary city. Informed by oral history interviews and constructed primarily by students and community members, CPHDH's flagship project creates richly layered, place-based portraits in concert with the public, permitting an ongoing dialogue that epitomizes the more expansive and outward-looking mission of urban universities to nurture multidirectional flows of knowledge. After summarizing the origins, development, and outcomes of the *Cleveland Historical* project, this essay explores the project's deep community engagement in an urban neighborhood and reflects on the challenges and rewards of public-engaged scholarship as they relate to both academic practitioners and urban publics.[3]

Background

The origin of the *Cleveland Historical* project lies partly in a radio project launched in 2002 by Mark Tebeau, then a history professor at CSU. His students interviewed dozens of people about the Cleveland Cultural Gardens, a group of nationality-based sculpture gardens in Rockefeller Park on Cleveland's east side. The work resulted in a series of "sound portraits" produced by Cleveland's public radio station WCPN. The interviews became part of the Cleveland Regional Oral History Collection, now numbering almost twelve hundred oral histories that are showcased on the *Cleveland Voices* website (available at cleveland-voices.org). The location-based stories that these oral histories supported comprised one of the first "tours" (thematic or geographic story collections) on *Cleveland Historical.*

Cleveland Historical is also rooted in a second predecessor project. In 2005, Tebeau and I began our first collaboration together. The Greater Cleveland Regional Transit Authority had selected Cleveland Public Art to coordinate public art installations as part of the Euclid Corridor Transportation Project. The Euclid Corridor, which grew out of decades of unfulfilled efforts to build a subway or light rail line on Euclid Avenue (historically, Cleveland's principal thoroughfare), was ultimately funded as a bus rapid transit line with center median platform stations.[4] What started as a plan to guide students in preparing research papers to inspire public art expanded into a digital storytelling project. Our students curated multimedia stories of places along the Euclid Corridor to place on touch screen kiosks in stations along the route. Steered by the imperative of delivering richly layered content to the most transient of audiences, they produced concise place descriptions combined with historical photos and oral history audio clips—all clustered on an interactive map.[5]

Even before the kiosks debuted in 2008, the concept was practically obsolete. In the previous year Apple had launched the iPhone, and smartphones were rapidly elevating expectations for individualized experiences that stationary touch screens could not match. Additionally, we wanted to expand beyond the confines of the Euclid Corridor and to create the opportunity for people to augment their experience of places by interacting with layered historical presentations. We quickly saw this place-based digital storytelling as a forum for public history engagement that was largely absent in Cleveland. At the time, no local institution had developed online interpretive historical content. The city's leading history organization, Western Reserve Historical Society, had not digitized its outstanding collections, let alone crafted born-digital content. CSU Library Special Collections had spent the past decade digitizing tens of thousands of historic images, but its website, *Cleveland Memory Project*, was largely confined to an image database and an idiosyncratic assemblage of Cleveland-related e-books and other items.[6] The best interpretive online resource was the *Encyclopedia of Cleveland History*, which originated in 1987 as the pioneer city encyclopedia before appearing online in 1998. The *Encyclopedia of Cleveland History* provided comprehensive entries about people, places, organizations, and events, but it lacked images, geolocation, and a storytelling quality. More a reference tool than an exploration of place, it was not set up with community engagement as a primary motive.[7]

Therefore, the door was open wide for a novel resource that departed from the urban encyclopedia model through its emphasis on "the interpretive perspective."[8] Our idea was to tell a story, but not necessarily *the* story, about each place we curated. Informed by Dolores Hayden's *Power of Place* project and early web-based mapping projects like the Los Angeles Conservancy's Getty Foundation–funded *Curating the City: Wilshire Blvd.* and Historical Society of Pennsylvania's National Endowment for the Humanities (NEH)–funded *PhilaPlace*, *Cleveland Historical* sought to reframe public engagement with local history.[9] Our project was unique in that we were adapting Hayden's approach of using places as containers for stories to a digital format, using oral histories to capture multiple perspectives on places, and doing so in collaboration with university students, K-12 teachers, and community organizations.

After we unveiled *Cleveland Historical* in 2010, we continued to work with community partners, embodying CSU's mission (expressed metaphorically in "The City Is Our Campus," a tagline it was then using) to serve the broader metropolitan community. We also used *Cleveland Historical* as an iterative research experience in our classes. The emphasis on building content that was thematic, geographically contextualized, and source-driven made *Cleveland Historical* an ideal vehicle for course assignments. Similarly, *Cleveland Historical* fit the Introduction to Public History course needs well because it emphasized adapting one's writing style for a broad audience, anticipating the potential that student-curated stories would stimulate public discussion and debate. It also mimicked the actions involved in curating a museum or historic site exhibition. More broadly, the project promised to engage the public in imagining the city's and region's history, the power of place in shaping history, and (through oral histories) the perspectives from which people approach, understand, and attach significance to urban places, whether for their physical attributes, associations with events, or ability to serve as vessels for memory.

We undertook development of the mobile apps for *Cleveland Historical* with an eye toward encouraging people to enhance their spatial and historical understandings of the city by interacting with layered media.[10] We also hoped that *Cleveland Historical* might be more than simply a model for assembling, interpreting, and sharing place-based content. With funding from CSU and an NEH grant in 2011–2012, we created a generalizable codebase to scale from one to many projects. The web and mobile framework became what we called Curatescape—a combination of responsive themes, Omeka content management system, plugins created or selected by our team, and mobile apps that permit users to create, publish, and update material. We worked with partners to produce Curatescape projects in Baltimore, New Orleans, and Spokane. Since that time, Curatescape has grown to some sixty projects.[11]

Just as *Cleveland Historical* makes Cleveland a learning laboratory for students by engaging them in researching and connecting to urban places, Curatescape has built capacity for further public and digital humanities innovations that serve many other communities. With the intent to create a hub for coordinating and administering a range of digital public historical work, Tebeau and I cofounded CPHDH in 2008. Expertise accumulated in ongoing Curatescape development (as well as in oral history) provided a foundation for garnering additional external funding that has enabled CPHDH to support community-based projects locally, nationally, and even internationally. While continuing to engage in local public history projects, we built an international collaboration with academic and community partners in Kisumu, Kenya. With funding from two NEH grants (in 2014 and 2017), we developed a Curatescape WordPress version that surmounted logistical, financial, and technological obstacles to doing projects like *Cleveland Historical* in Africa and, by extension, the developing world.[12] Although Curatescape is an open-source toolset that supports easy, low-cost adoption for web users, CPHDH has been able to support its core operating costs by licensing the apps and providing conceptual and technical services related to the use of the framework. CPHDH is committed to empowering people to engage with the intertwined historical and contemporary dimensions of the places they inhabit and navigate on a daily basis. This commitment embodies making the work of urban universities relevant to urban communities.

Place in History, History in Place

A close examination of more than a decade of collaborative digital public history work in the Detroit Shoreway neighborhood reveals how *Cleveland Historical* has become embedded in the community. To be sure, the depth and persistence of this project varies from place to place, a matter addressed later. Nevertheless, this neighborhood-level collaboration shows that even a metropolitan project can be modular, supporting deeper linkages wherever there is a groundswell of interest in collaboration while also connecting the local to the regional.

Detroit Shoreway is a roughly two-square-mile neighborhood located about one to two miles west of downtown Cleveland. In 2010, with more than fourteen thousand residents, it was the tenth most populous among thirty-six neighborhoods in the Cleveland corporate limits. Detroit Shoreway developed in the mid-nineteenth century as large numbers of primarily German and Irish immigrants, later joined by Italians, Romanians, and other eastern and southern Europeans, settled near factories and mills along the shoreline of Lake Erie to the north and in the Walworth Run valley to the south. Ethnic churches and businesses, especially along Detroit Avenue, became community anchors, and, eventually, streetcars linked the area more effectively to downtown Cleveland and other neighborhoods.[13]

After a century of growth, Detroit Shoreway experienced the same problems of deindustrialization, suburban flight, and community disinvestment that afflicted many urban neighborhoods in Cleveland and nationally. By the early 1970s, a group of concerned citizens began to try to reverse the area's fortunes. Raymond L. (Ray) Pianka and Irene Catlin, along with a handful of other residents, coordinated a home painting and repair program on West Seventy-Sixth Street in the summer of 1972. Pianka and others founded the Detroit Shoreway Community Development Organization (DSCDO) the following year. DSCDO worked to revitalize industry, businesses, and housing in the neighborhood while also cultivating a socially diverse community.[14] (See Figure 3.3.) In 1979, the organization purchased the deteriorating Gordon Square Arcade and restored it into low-income second-floor apartments above a mix of old and new street-level businesses and offices. The reopening of the arcade's Capitol Theatre in 2009 was a symbolic reflection of the organization's sustained commitment.[15]

In 2005, Nelson Beckford, a DSCDO community organizer, contacted us after learning of our work with Cleveland Public Art and invited us to collaborate on an oral history project to help foster greater understanding among community residents. Mark Tebeau and I trained our students in oral history methods. At first we interviewed DSCDO staff, along with people who were instrumental in renewing the neighborhood, including Ray Pianka, who was serving as Cleveland Housing Court Judge but still committed to supporting the neighborhood where he had lived his whole life. In addition, we presented the project to meetings of Detroit Shoreway block clubs to build interest and trust. DSCDO also helped us coordinate an oral history recording day at an old schoolhouse.

The initial period of collecting resulted in listening booths featuring short audio stories about neighborhood places in Gypsy Beans Cafe, a coffeeshop at Detroit and West Sixty-Fifth Street, diagonally across from the Gordon Square Arcade. One day in 2010, Pianka, who had observed our work, asked if he might fund a student to research some

Figure 3.3 Detroit Shoreway is a Cleveland neighborhood in which CPHDH has partnered with a community development corporation to collect oral histories and curate location-based stories since 2005. (Courtesy of Cleveland State University Library Special Collections)

historic buildings in Detroit Shoreway and neighboring Ohio City. As we came to learn, Pianka's interest was deeper than that of a local history buff. In 1969, at age eighteen, he learned that a Queen Anne–style house in the neighborhood was to be demolished. He talked to the owner, who said Theodore Roosevelt had reputedly given a speech from the house's porch. Pianka researched the story with the idea of saving the house. Although he failed to stop the demolition, a local newspaper highlighted his research. It was an early lesson in the power of history to raise neighborhood interest and awareness. He had later used history to justify saving the Gordon Square Arcade, and now, late in his career as a housing judge, he added public history to his tool kit for stabilizing and protecting neighborhoods.[16]

At the time, Jim Dubelko was taking Mark Tebeau's U.S. Urban History course, and Tebeau mentioned the opportunity to him. Over the next six and a half years, Dubelko wrote nearly fifty place-based histories for *Cleveland Historical*. Many of these stories unearthed little-known insights about houses and buildings. Pianka used these stories often to foster a sense of place, and, when he knew a significant site was threatened with demolition, he used *Cleveland Historical* as a preservation advocacy tool.

One of Dubelko's first stories explored the house where the 1912 world featherweight boxing champion Johnny Kilbane once lived on Herman Avenue between West Seventy-Fourth and Seventy-Sixth Streets. Pianka understood the potential for Kilbane's story to resonate once more in a neighborhood whose residents were eager to deepen connections with a city in its struggle to remake its identity amid a long decline. After all, when Kilbane returned triumphantly to Cleveland on St. Patrick's Day, in 1912, he became, in effect, the grand marshal for one of the city's largest St. Patrick's Day parades, which wended its way from downtown to his home. The next day, the *Cleveland Leader* dubbed his neighborhood Kilbane Town. Dubelko's story resurrected a long-forgotten tale, inspiring residents to successfully petition Cleveland City Council, in 2012, to landmark Kilbane's house and rename a block of Herman Avenue "Kilbane Town."[17] (See Figure 3.4.)

A second example of the power of public history that emerged from Dubelko's work was when he completed a story about a onetime 1836 mansion on Detroit Avenue known as Needham Castle. Finding no surviving photos of the house, which had been demolished in 1954, he inserted a sentence in the narrative that noted the lack of such a photo. This foray into crowdsourcing paid dividends. A reader who was a descendant of the third owner of the house wrote us that she had family photos taken in and outside the house in the 1910s, along with some old paintings of the mansion. The tale of how the Needham Castle story helped surface previously unknown primary sources became the new closing paragraph in Dubelko's narrative and demonstrates how digital storytelling can foster interaction with the public.[18]

Among the fruits of our labor in Detroit Shoreway were the personal and organizational relationships that brought introductions to additional people and new story ideas. Although we did not sustain a singular focus on Detroit Shoreway, some staff members who were at DSCDO in 2005 remained active in the organization and took special interest in supporting each new phase of public history work in the neighborhood. For example, when Sarah Nemeth embarked on a new round of oral histories in the summer of 2017 that focused on

Figure 3.4 Johnny Kilbane, world featherweight boxing champion from 1912 to 1923, lived on Detroit Shoreway's Herman Avenue. A century after his first title, a *Cleveland Historical* story about him led to the official designation of Herman Avenue as "Kilbane Town," resurrecting a nickname devised by the *Cleveland Leader* in 1912. (Courtesy of Cleveland State University Library Special Collections)

Detroit Shoreway, some of our original collaborators introduced us to DSCDO's current community organizers, who acquainted us with more residents and business owners. Nemeth's new interviews illustrated the revitalization and accompanying challenges of gentrification that Detroit Shoreway saw in the intervening period. She interviewed the owners of Happy Dog and Sweet Moses, two prominent eateries that exemplified the most recent phase of revitalization along Detroit Avenue, but also women—one white, one African American—who lived along the tattered fringes of Detroit Shoreway. Far from the shiny and colorful shops that enticed young professionals to the rebranded Gordon Square Arts District, they worried about reduced bus service, racism, home abandonment, gang violence, and drugs. Their voices remind us that in neighborhoods, let alone entire cities, it is not possible to construct a simplistic narrative that labels a place as declining or revitalizing. Neighborhoods are in constant flux, and they are perceived variously based on individuals' relationship to place.

One of the most exciting moments came when Nemeth was introduced to a Mexican American woman who has been a longtime activist on behalf of migrant workers and the leader of Cleveland's oldest Hispanic organization, which dates to the 1930s. The daughter of a tool-and-die worker and a nurse, both migrants, Ruth Rubio-Pino moved to Cleveland's Near West Side from Edinburg, Texas, in 1964. The family assumed responsibility for an informal social and mutual benefit organization called Club Azteca on Detroit Avenue.[19] Rubio-Pino's story highlights an overlooked thread in the ethnic tapestry of Detroit Shoreway, whose history tends to focus on Germans, Irish, Italians, and Romanians despite a decades-long presence of Latin American residents. The outcomes of our renewed collaboration in Detroit Shoreway included a two-part oral history podcast that Nemeth produced on the historical development and recent gentrification in the neighborhood, and a Club Azteca story is in development for *Cleveland Historical* at the time of this writing.[20]

Our work also helped us establish connections in Stockyards and Clark-Fulton, both of which lie to the south of I-90, isolating these underserved neighborhoods from Detroit Shoreway and Ohio City, two of Cleveland's "hot" neighborhoods. Several years ago DSCDO took charge of a less well-organized counterpart struggling to serve Stockyards, Clark-Fulton, and Brooklyn Centre (located still farther to the south and separated from the other two by I-71) and shepherded its transformation into the Metro West Community Development Organization (MWCDO), which borrows its name from Metropolitan General Hospital. Despite the challenges of trying to unify three neighborhoods in what might be seen as a rather artificial construct, MWCDO has established a stronger connection to the communities it serves.

With MWCDO's help, we made connections that led to new oral histories and app stories. Among the latter were stories that recovered former places, including a vanished waterway, a forgotten earlier neighborhood shaped by that waterway, and the namesake for the Stockyards neighborhood. These places and their identities were passing (or had already passed) from the realm of living memory. Just as Dubelko's Kilbane Town story animated a new sense of place in Detroit

Shoreway, we hoped to reframe understandings of the Stockyards neighborhood, so named for the Union Stockyards that operated there into the 1970s. Long before I-90 formed a mental and physical northern boundary of Stockyards, a nearby pair of steep hills framing a valley provided a similar demarcation. Walworth Run, a meandering brook named for an early settler from New England, flowed through the valley before emptying into the Cuyahoga River. As the nineteenth century progressed, shipping lanes and railroads brought rapid industrialization, transforming Walworth Run and the Cuyahoga River into open sewers from industrial effluent. Public health concerns in the time before bacteriological science prompted plans in the 1870s to encase the stream in an underground pipe. The sewer rendered Walworth Run invisible and, with the exception of a new street tracing its route and bearing its name, all but forgotten. Added to *Cleveland Historical* in 2014, "Where in the World Is Walworth Run?" provides an opportunity to reframe a story of environmental degradation that is too often told only through the 1969 Cuyahoga River Fire, which is marshaled (erroneously) as the symbolic start of the environmental movement and pivot for a narrative of city decline and renewal.[21]

Through another story about a long-forgotten neighborhood named the Isle of Cuba, Walworth Run emerges as an environmental agent with social consequences. Before the sewer hid the stream, periodic flooding along its banks led one newspaperman to conclude, in 1882, that the dry land cut off by the rising waters may have taken a shape resembling the Caribbean island. The environment coupled with and reinforced social reasons for the isolation of "Cuba." As Dubelko writes, sensational stories of drunken revelry, periodic violence, and, in the eyes of native Clevelanders, strange Slavic customs of the area may also have played a role in perpetuating this odd name. That xenophobic view only grew during the Spanish-American War, when neighborhood gangs called the Cubans and the Spaniards warred over turf on either side of Walworth Run. The Cuba name waned in the 1920s as the area's "otherness" faded amid the maturation of Stockyards with established businesses and "durable neighborhood institutions."[22] Perhaps, too, the Immigration Act of 1924 contributed to a sense that "Cuba" was now on the path to being whitened and Americanized— which leads to an interesting connection to a later period in the area's social history. After World War II, as Puerto Ricans migrated to a number of American cities, many of them settled on the Near West Side. As Ohio City began a long gentrification process starting about fifty years ago, many Hispanics moved southward and westward, including into Clark-Fulton and Stockyards.[23] Until recently, language barriers, poverty, discrimination, and the lingering effect of interstate highways that surrounded these communities plunged them into a renewed era of isolation. This isolation, along with an obscure, exotic name, inspired what became Dubelko's "Isle of Cuba" story. Pianka thought that a place identity once linked to a Caribbean island might resonate in what ironically went on to have a sizable Hispanic presence. Of course, behind Pianka's interest in local history was his commitment to strengthening neighborhoods.

The Challenges of Curating the City

Our collaboration in Detroit Shoreway demonstrates the benefits of pairing urban universities and urban communities in place-based digital storytelling activities. Nevertheless, such campus-community collaborations also pose challenges. Among these are justifying the scholarly import of digital public history, choosing from among various interpretive approaches, conveying complex and sometimes controversial narratives, balancing product and process (and, related, sharing authority), and balancing a metropolitan scope and engaging with communities on a more granular level.

University-based public historians who have sought tenure and promotion understand the challenge of justifying the merit of their scholarly production. Part of the problem lies in disagreements over how to approach the study of history. As David Glassberg wrote two decades ago, traditional history graduate education usually prepared students exclusively to (try to) enter the professoriat. It privileged objective, dispassionate study that grew from identifying a historiographical question and frowned on place as a basis for scholarly inquiry.[24] It also tended to value archival documents more than firsthand accounts by living subjects. To a great extent, this bias persists and contributes to the problem of evaluating scholarship that reflects different approaches and creates different products. Tenure and promotion guidelines can inhibit innovations that take unfamiliar forms.[25] They favor peer-reviewed articles and books at a time when an increasing number of historians are undertaking works that should not be judged solely (if at all) by using traditional metrics. Those who develop and implement tenure and promotion guidelines often struggle to assess work that is born digital, iterative, collaborative, and dedicated as much to process as product. Although professional associations have urged policies that fairly evaluate digital and public scholarship, most institutions have not responded with clear and inclusive guidelines.[26] Yet, urban universities also increasingly value innovation and public engagement, and projects such as *Cleveland Historical* can be effective representations of institutional commitments to bridge town-and-gown divides.

A second challenge is one that is more particular to place-based projects like *Cleveland Historical*—that of geolocation and interpretation. Each mapped story on *Cleveland Historical* must have a single location, unlike projects that use tools such as Story Maps and StoryMap JS. *Cleveland Historical* originated with several dozen stories, each of which curated a particular building or site. As the project evolved, we wanted to tell stories about important themes through specific places as well as to recover lost or little-known places and marginalized perspectives. Sometimes it was easy to determine story locations, as in the case of the Cuyahoga River Fire, a story that required little thought to geolocate because the iconic 1969 fire occurred at a known location. In other cases, the choice of location is not so easy. For example, our Cleveland Play House story could have been sited at any of four locations in the vicinity of the Cleveland Clinic main campus three miles east of downtown, but we chose the complex it occupied at the time the story was written. Later, when the playhouse moved to one of the historic downtown Playhouse Square theaters, we decided to move the pin. While doing so left the organization's former space uncurated, it also places the information close at hand for the far larger number of visitors that the city's theater district attracts.[27]

Sometimes, siting a story carries implications not only for the audience but also for the message. Taking up the contentious story of busing to achieve racial integration, Jim Lanese, a retired Cleveland School District administrator and CSU continuing-education student who was active in implementing busing, felt it was important to locate his *Cleveland Historical* story about the debate over busing at a site that did not reinforce the prevalent belief that busing was a wrongheaded policy. Siting it at the Lincoln statue on the Mall outside the Cleveland Board of Education building (now a hotel), Lanese was able to highlight the site where both antibusing protesters and integration backers picketed while sending a subtle message that it is worth revisiting the legacy of busing. The symbolism of Lincoln in the struggle for racial equality hardly needs unpacking. Additionally, the statue was a rallying point for the "Bridgewalk" event in 1980 in which East Siders and West Siders pushed back against the narrative of the Cuyahoga River as a racial barrier by marching across the Detroit-Superior Bridge.[28]

The project also seeks to recover lost or little-known places. In the case of our Kilbane Town story, the surviving Johnny Kilbane home provided a touchstone for amplifying an already-strong Irish American identity in Detroit Shoreway. In contrast, a story about a long gone restaurant in the city's predominantly African American Glenville neighborhood seems less likely to serve a similar role. Although a semester of oral history collecting in Glenville led one student to the fascinating story of Scatter's Barbecue, which connected East 105th Street, once a vibrant stretch of Jewish- and, later, Black-owned businesses, to the Great Migration (Herman "Scatter" Stephens moved to Cleveland from Alabama in 1920), the fact that the business closed fifty years ago and its building was razed limits the story's potential to rekindle a sense of place.[29] Another student's interest in studying civil rights attorney Chester Gillespie's activism to break down Jim Crow in downtown office buildings, in the 1930s and 1940s, led her to pin her story at what is a 1980 office tower. The Hickox Building, which Gillespie's law firm occupied at the height of his struggle against discriminatory leasing, had been demolished twenty-five years earlier. Few of the buildings whose owners had denied Gillespie's attempts to secure space were still standing, and none was as centrally located as this site at Euclid and East Ninth, now a focal point for downtown revitalization. In this case, unlike the vacant lot on a forlorn stretch of East 105th, hollowed out by waves of suburban flight, including by African Americans, the choice of this corner places a marginalized story in one of the city's most central spaces and fosters a sense that downtown belongs to everyone or at least should.[30]

The Curatescape model, specifically *Cleveland Historical*, has embraced a third challenge: creating a broad, accessible platform that balances a range of needs related to both product and process. The project was devised in part to foster engaged learning in university courses, wherein students move from being consumers to producers of knowledge.[31] *Cleveland Historical* content mostly reflects student research and authorship informed by close faculty guidance, although a significant proportion of its stories also derive from community-based contributors. Despite the democratizing potential of empowering students and community partners to "do history" in the public realm, however, no project could be a fully decentered, inclusive, community-based undertaking and also be informed by historical scholarship if professional historians abdicated their role in shaping a project.

Perils await even in well-coordinated university-community partnerships. For example, CPHDH worked with teams of neighborhood volunteers as part of one grant-funded history project. These volunteers proved knowledgeable and passionate about their communities' histories, but sometimes their zeal to capture every detail threatened to obscure the broader contexts that professional historians could contribute. In particular, one volunteer took the lead in writing a story of how the Cleveland area came to have so many places with the name Brooklyn, including the city neighborhoods of Brooklyn Centre, Old Brooklyn, and Brooklyn Heights, and the separate municipality of Brooklyn. She became so fixated on relating the intricacies of how each place developed that she felt incensed when a member of our team suggested framing her story in a way that could illustrate the history of annexation as a tool for capturing urban growth. Unfortunately, the two approaches proved irreconcilable, and the volunteer declared that she would only publish on *Cleveland Historical* if she were permitted to complete the story alone.[32] Albeit an extreme example, it suggests why many academics find it more comfortable to present papers to fellow academics at conferences than to negotiate the rocky terrain of the public sphere, where their expertise may not be embraced or recognized.

Cleveland Historical also grapples with a fourth challenge, one that is perhaps the most difficult.[33] Notwithstanding the fact that deep, sustained, collaborative engagement with a specific community can often be the most rewarding and powerful way to conceive university-based urban history projects, our work reflects a somewhat different approach, one that carries pros and cons. Choosing to curate a large metropolitan area leads to challenges, as achieving deep and sustained collaboration throughout such an area is difficult. Although *Cleveland Historical* focuses primarily on Cuyahoga County, even that area numbers approximately 1.25 million people in thirty-six city neighborhoods and sixty-one suburban municipalities and townships. Such a project risks becoming an assemblage of individual hyperlocal narratives. It also risks privileging broad and shallow historical exploration and short-term collaborations over focused, deep, and sustained partnerships. With a metropolitan focus, there is so much ground to cover that it is necessary to be selective. We have been selective in a number of ways: by allowing our students to choose their research topics and by prioritizing places where a community organization can support content creation. Doing so has resulted in uneven coverage, which can be seen in an examination of the project's map. The largest clusters of story pins correspond to places where it has been possible to arrange sponsored research. Slightly over half are in areas that have enjoyed the highest degree of upkeep or revitalization of landmarks of historical importance, the strongest sense of place, and a surfeit of civic attention: Downtown, University Circle, Detroit Shoreway, Tremont, Ohio City, Cleveland Heights, and Shaker Heights. One might assume that our project reinforces inequities in the metropolitan community by design. What should we make of the fact that most of the city's African American and Latinx neighborhoods are underserved by the project?[34] How can we address this gap in ways that are sensitive to these communities and to process?

The project team continues to address these questions, however imperfectly. Underserved neighborhoods struggle with issues of a much more pressing nature than those of placemaking. Working in such settings requires a heightened attentiveness to building trust, which, in turn, demands patience and persistence. In addition, it can be extraordinarily difficult for a student to complete even a single story in the confines of a semester because such places tend to be underrepresented in the available photographic collections in libraries and archives and in the mainstream press. To be sure, community members may possess old photos, but it is hard to locate and obtain permission to use them in a short time frame. Also, there are newspapers specific to the concerns of African Americans, Latinxs, other ethnic groups, and neighborhoods, but, even if they are accessible, these tend to be weekly at best, meaning that they offer fewer articles than the city's daily newspapers. Some may be in other languages that students are not equipped to read.

We have worked to ensure greater inclusion of diverse places, peoples, and perspectives. We have become more active in documenting diverse voices on the premise that a stronger oral history base will support more varied app content. For example, we obtained two internal undergraduate summer research grants in recent years that supported students in focused oral history collecting and digital storytelling. In one, we worked with a community activist to interview some five dozen people about the struggle for racial integration in Cleveland's inner-ring suburbs.[35] In another, three students interviewed African Americans in the Glenville and Fairfax neighborhoods, which have received relatively little historical attention despite their proximity to University Circle and the Cleveland Clinic. One of the products was a *Cleveland Historical* story about the Pla-Mor Roller Rink in Fairfax that served the community in the decades when African Americans faced discriminatory treatment at Skateland on Euclid Avenue. This story helps illustrate the social impacts that went along with housing discrimination.[36]

A second approach is placing thematic constraints on course projects. Doing so requires a willingness to subordinate students' existing interests to the needs of the project, not to mention the opportunity to immerse them in an exploration of a historical theme in which their individual efforts contribute to something larger. In my Introduction to Public History course, students researched themes such as "African Americans in Cleveland," and, in the year preceding the fiftieth anniversary of Carl B. Stokes's becoming the nation's first-elected Black mayor of a major American city in 1967, I assigned places connecting in some way to Stokes.[37] Some students utilized previously collected oral histories, including one by Ruth Zeager on the 1969 Haggins Realty bombing in Cleveland Heights, in which Cleveland's first Black-owned suburban real estate office was attacked for breaching the color line. Zeager's story complicates the popular narrative of Cleveland Heights as a racially progressive community, demonstrating how civil rights advances have been punctuated by setbacks and forcing the reader to grapple with whether Isaac Haggins Sr., in facilitating residential integration, was a blockbuster or a civil rights activist.[38] (See Figure 3.5.)

Figure 3.5 Isaac Haggins Sr., whose Haggins Realty office (the first African American–owned real estate office in a Cleveland suburb) was bombed in 1969, received an outpouring of community support. The author interviewed Haggins in 2013, providing a rich source that informed Ruth Zeager's *Cleveland Historical* story about the Haggins Realty bombing. (Courtesy of Cleveland State University Library Special Collections)

A third approach revolves around public outreach. We have experimented with app-enhanced, guided neighborhood tours coordinated with community organizations such as community development corporations or historical societies.[39] Although most participants did not use the app except when prompted to navigate to a particular photo on a story for the sake of visual comparison, the tours provided an opportunity to invite public input, conduct new oral histories, or scan items from personal collections. Moreover, they help us serve as conveners for discussions about the city. In addition to tours, we maintain an active presence on social media. Several years ago, we added Disqus, a third-party comments forum, to each story, but few readers felt moved to comment in this space, preferring to share via their own social media. Our own posts about *Cleveland Historical* stories on Facebook, Twitter, and Instagram have produced far more and richer engagement.

Finally, we have explored ways to solicit story ideas and even stories from the public through social media but in the future should experiment with articles or ads with calls to action that we might place in community-based newsletters or email blasts. These are less likely to yield the rewards that come from working programmatically with an organization that already has close ties in its community, but they may still decenter the project in ways that give voice to members of the public. In collaboration with Aaron Cowan, an urban historian at Slippery Rock University who uses Curatescape with students to curate Butler, Pennsylvania, we developed a *Cleveland Historical* public submission guide, which we share when someone expresses interest in contributing a story.[40]

One such person was Aundra Willis-Carrasco of San Diego, California, who became interested after reading a story that I cowrote with a student about Cleveland's so-called Second Downtown on Euclid Avenue from East 101st to East 107th Streets. As our app story related, her brother Winston Willis was one of Cleveland's most successful yet maligned African American businessmen, whose presence on a lucrative stretch of Euclid Avenue and sometimes provocative actions angered the city's power structure. Willis ultimately lost his business holdings amid controversy and was forced to serve time in prison.[41] Given that his sister makes no secret of her mission to vindicate her brother, I was concerned when she asked to write an app story about Willis's legendary club, the Jazz Temple, which was a nationally known venue in the 1960s until a likely racially motivated bombing led to its closure. However, the author worked cooperatively to utilize suggested scholarly sources to contextualize her story and to tailor her work to our submission guidelines. Moreover, her experience as a server at the club and her possession of unique family photos offered a powerful reminder of the importance of embracing the potential pitfalls of stepping outside the comfortable confines of academia to seek a "shared authority."[42]

When we launched our *Cleveland Historical* Instagram account in 2017, we opened with a photo of Winston Willis and his girlfriend Charlene at the Jazz Temple. A woman named Rebecca Callister left the first comment on this photo: "Thank you for starting out this account the right way! I'm so proud to be from Cleveland and hope you continue to represent our inclusive and diverse community well."[43] Our intent on Instagram is to entice new audiences to *Cleveland Historical*. In one sense, although social media accounts might be one step removed from the project, they are now important facets of *Cleveland Historical*. Put more directly, *Cleveland Historical* is not just available at clevelandhistorical.org and in the app stores; it is also on Facebook, Twitter, and Instagram. The original website and app have become our project's comprehensive collection of stories, from which we have the opportunity to curate our project in ways that better reflect the full metropolitan community. If it will take much time to diversify the project's content, our social media promotion is at least a small step we can take to demonstrate our aspirations.

Conclusion

The memories and perspectives shared in the oral histories that inform many stories on *Cleveland Historical* and the community responses and conversations that those stories prompt remind us of the deep connection between people and place. Place matters, which is why urban public history projects are a natural fit with the larger work that urban universities, especially urban public universities like CSU, seek to engage in with the broader communities they serve. Projects like *Cleveland Historical* remind us that places to which people feel attached can build a sense of history and feelings of connectedness, belonging, and, sometimes, purpose. Such feelings can result when people learn how to see their own perspectives in a historical frame where personal and familial understandings mesh with those of larger urban communities. Such projects also turn cities into learning laboratories—not places that are merely viewed and scrutinized with detachment from the height and distance of proverbial ivory towers but ones whose physical and social presences may blend with those of the university campus. This meshing of urban places and urban universities does not simply happen; it must be cultivated by building rapport and trust. For historians, it requires taking a step further from the "bottom-up" approach that many in the field have employed over the past several decades. It requires moving beyond simply presenting history in places and in a style that will appeal to the public. It entails locating expertise both inside and outside the university, sharing authority, and embracing multidirectional flows of knowledge. In 2008, as CPHDH was forming, we set out to curate Cleveland. A decade later, it is clear that we were not alone in our endeavor. Many in the community share our passion for excavating and bringing to light the stories about place that help us situate our lives in time and place. Going forward, our hope is to forge a greater collaborative spirit around curating the city.

NOTES

1. George Lonero, "In Answer to Your Question," May 15, 2017, comment on *Cleveland Historical*, "There was a time when if you thought of Cleveland you thought of steel."

2. Sarah Nemeth, "Republic Steel Corporation: The Prisoners of Cleveland's War on Air Pollution," *Cleveland Historical*, available at http://clevelandhistorical .org/items/show/790.

3. On the value of university-based and community-embedded urban history projects, see Andrew Hurley, *Beyond Preservation: Using Public History to Revitalize Inner Cities* (Philadelphia: Temple University Press, 2010); Denise D. Meringolo, ed., "Special Section: The Place of the City," *Journal of Urban History* 40, no. 3 (2014): 419–477.

4. J. Mark Souther, "A $35 Million 'Hole in the Ground': Metropolitan Fragmentation and Cleveland's Unbuilt Downtown Subway," *Journal of Planning History* 14, no. 3 (2015): 179–203.

5. Mark Tebeau, "Strategies for Mobile Interpretive Projects for Humanists and Cultural Organizations," NEH white paper, March 3, 2013, 1, available at http:// securegrants.neh.gov/publicquery/main.aspx?f=1&gn=HD-51456-11. A demo video of the touch screen interface is archived and available at http://csudigital humanities.org/2008/05/euclid-corridor-oral-history-project-2/.

6. More information on the *Cleveland Memory Project* is available at http:// www.clevelandmemory.org.

7. David D. Van Tassel and John J. Grabowski, eds., *The Encyclopedia of Cleveland History* (Bloomington: Indiana University Press, 1987), available at http:// case.edu/ech/. In recent years the *Encyclopedia of Cleveland History* has added multimedia content and developed a social media presence; this is part of a growing trend, for example, see "Digital Summer School: The Encyclopedia of Milwaukee," *The Metropole*, June 28, 2018, available at http://themetropole.blog/2018 /06/28/digital-summer-school-the-encyclopedia-of-milwaukee/.

8. Mark Tebeau, "Listening to the City: Oral History and Place in the Digital Era," *Oral History Review* 40, no. 1 (2013): 26–27.

9. Dolores Hayden, *The Power of Place: Urban Landscapes as Public History* (Cambridge, MA: MIT Press, 1995); *Curating the City: Wilshire Blvd.*, available at http://www.laconservancy.org/wilshire; *PhilaPlace*, available at http://www .philaplace.org.

10. Despite this intent, we found that the vast majority of the project's audience actually discovered *Cleveland Historical* via Google searches or social media referrals. Nevertheless, the app's full potential is reached by those who use it while actively exploring the city.

11. Tebeau, "Strategies for Mobile Interpretive Projects"; "Public Projects," *Curatescape*, available at http://curatescape.org/projects/.

12. J. Mark Souther, Meshack Owino, and Erin J. Bell, "Adapting Mobile Humanities Interpretation in East Africa," NEH white paper, March 15, 2016, available at http://securegrants.neh.gov/publicquery/main.aspx?f=1&gn=HD-51912-14; J. Mark Souther and Meshack Owino, "Curating East Africa: A Platform and Process for Location-Based Storytelling in the Developing World," NEH white paper, March 31, 2019, available at http://securegrants.neh.gov/publicquery/main.aspx?f=1&gn=HAA-255990-17.

13. "Neighborhood," *Detroit Shoreway*, available at http://www.dscdo.org/neighborhood.

14. Gerald Meyer, interview by Tiffany Hunter, March 30, 2006, *Cleveland Voices*, available at http://clevelandvoices.org/items/show/2630.

15. Ray Pianka, interview by Becky Solecki, 2005, *Cleveland Voices*, available at http://clevelandvoices.org/items/show/2609; Rich Raponi, "Capitol Theatre," *Cleveland Historical*, available at http://clevelandhistorical.org/items/show/152.

16. Jim Dubelko, "Using History to Preserve and Rebuild Cleveland: Remembering Judge Ray Pianka," CPHDH, available at http://csudigitalhumanities.org/2017/02/using-history-to-preserve-and-rebuild-cleveland-neighborhoods-remembering-judge-ray-pianka/.

17. Dubelko, "Using History"; Jim Dubelko, "Kilbane Town," *Cleveland Historical*, available at http://clevelandhistorical.org/items/show/288.

18. Dubelko, "Using History"; Jim Dubelko, "Needham Castle," *Cleveland Historical*, available at http://clevelandhistorical.org/items/show/324.

19. Ruth Rubio-Pino, interview by Sarah Nemeth, August 11, 2017, *Cleveland Voices*, available at http://clevelandvoices.org/items/show/2939.

20. Sarah Nemeth, "Detroit Shoreway, Part One," *Cleveland Voices*, available at http://clevelandvoices.org/items/show/2978; Sarah Nemeth, "Detroit Shoreway, Part Two," *Cleveland Voices*, available at http://clevelandvoices.org/items/show/2988.

21. Jim Dubelko, "Where in the World Is Walworth Run? Bridged, Culverted, Sewered and Today Largely Forgotten," *Cleveland Historical*, available at http://clevelandhistorical.org/items/show/659.

22. Jim Dubelko, "The Isle of Cuba," *Cleveland Historical*, available at http://clevelandhistorical.org/items/show/646; Dubelko, "Using History."

23. J. Mark Souther, *Believing in Cleveland: Managing Decline in "The Best Location in the Nation"* (Philadelphia: Temple University Press, 2017), chap. 6.

24. David Glassberg, *Sense of History: The Place of the Past in American Life* (Amherst: University of Massachusetts Press, 2001), chap. 1. On the importance of "place," see also Tebeau, "Listening to the City," 27–28.

25. Denise D. Meringolo, "The Place of the City: Collaborative Learning, Urban History, and Transformations in Higher Education," *Journal of Urban History* 40, no. 3 (2014): 423.

26. See, especially, "Guidelines for the Professional Evaluation of Digital Scholarship by Historians," *American Historical Association*, available at http://www.historians.org/teaching-and-learning/digital-history-resources/evaluation-of-digital-scholarship-in-history/guidelines-for-the-professional-evaluation-of-digital-scholarship-by-historians.

27. "Cleveland Play House: From East Side Farmhouse to Playhouse Square Fixture," *Cleveland Historical*, available at http://clevelandhistorical.org/items/show/6.

28. Jim Lanese, "The Desegregation of Cleveland Public Schools: A 40-Year Struggle for Public School Equity," *Cleveland Historical*, available at http://clevelandhistorical.org/items/show/813. For more thoughts on the challenges of geolocation in relation to *Cleveland Historical*, see Tebeau, "Listening to the City," 30.

29. Julie A. Gabb, "Scatter's Barbecue," *Cleveland Historical*, available at http://clevelandhistorical.org/items/show/654.

30. Rhianna Gordon, "Chester K. Gillespie: The Struggle to End 'Jim Crow' in Downtown Cleveland," *Cleveland Historical*, available at http://clevelandhistorical.org/items/show/675.

31. Pushing students to become producers rather than merely consumers of knowledge is a widely shared goal among public historians. See Patricia Mooney-Melvin, "Engaging the Neighborhood: The East Rogers Park Neighborhood History Project and the Possibilities and Challenges of Community-Based Initiatives," *Journal of Urban History* 40, no. 3 (2014): 474.

32. Patricia Mooney-Melvin argues that local history needs to be contextualized more broadly, such as at the metropolitan level; Mooney-Melvin, "Engaging the Neighborhood," 468–469.

33. Here I expand on Mark Tebeau's reflections, in 2013, on the unevenness of representation in the project; see Tebeau, "Listening to the City," 31–32.

34. As of this writing, less than 8 percent of our stories focus substantially on African Americans, who comprise 30 percent of Cuyahoga County.

35. "Racial Integration in the Heights," *Cleveland Voices*, available at http://clevelandvoices.org/collections/show/84.

36. J. Mark Souther and Timothy Klypchak, "Pla-Mor Roller Rink," *Cleveland Historical*, available at http://clevelandhistorical.org/items/show/621.

37. "African Americans in Cleveland," *Cleveland Historical*, available at http://clevelandhistorical.org/tours/show/43.

38. Ruth Zeager, "Haggins Realty Bombing," *Cleveland Historical*, available at http://clevelandhistorical.org/items/show/640; Isaac Haggins Sr., interview by J. Mark Souther, August 6, 2013, *Cleveland Voices*, available at http://clevelandvoices.org/items/show/2378.

39. See, for example, "Father's Day Historic Walking Tour Honors the Late Raymond Pianka," *Plain Press*, July 2, 2017, available at http://plainpress.wordpress.com/2017/07/02/fathers-day-historic-walking-tour-honors-the-late-raymond-pianka/.

40. "Cleveland Historical Project Overview and Public Submission Guidelines," *Curatescape*, available at http://curatescape.org/wp-content/uploads/2018/01/ClevelandHistoricalPublicGuideFINAL-1.pdf.

41. Adonees Sarrouh and J. Mark Souther, "Cleveland's Second Downtown," *Cleveland Historical*, available at http://clevelandhistorical.org/items/show/49; Michael Frisch, *A Shared Authority: Essays on the Craft and Meaning of Oral and Public History* (Albany: State University of New York Press, 1990).

42. Aundra Willis-Carrasco, "The Jazz Temple: When Jazz Came to University Circle in the 1960s," *Cleveland Historical*, available at http://clevelandhistorical.org/items/show/811.

43. *Cleveland Historical*, "With Winston in the out-front managerial role, the Temple took off like wildfire . . . ," Instagram photo, October 25, 2017, available at http://www.instagram.com/p/BasNpwDh7ak/.

4

Mapping Miami

Affordable Housing, Equitable Community Development, and Grassroots Engagement in South Florida

Robin F. Bachin

Introduction: Public Housing, Public History, and Campus-Community Partnerships

On November 12, 2015, twenty-five former residents of the Scott Carver Public Housing Project in the Liberty City neighborhood of Miami, which was razed in 1999, visited the Special Collections Department at the University of Miami (UM) Otto G. Richter Library to learn about the process of collecting and archiving historical documents and begin an oral history project. The visit, organized by the university's Office of Civic and Community Engagement (CCE), was part of an initiative to document the history of housing activism in Miami. (See Figure 4.1.) Over the past decade, the Special Collections Department, through the leadership of Béatrice Skokan and Cristina Favretto, has launched several efforts to increase its grassroots activism holdings, working with local organizations focused on immigration, gender, human rights, social services, housing issues, and environmental and racial justice. One of the goals of the library has been to make history accessible not only to scholars and students but also to community members who have played an active role in shaping the activist tradition in Miami.

Figure 4.1 Scott Carver Residents' Council visit to the University of Miami Otto G. Richter Library Special Collections Division. (Courtesy of the University of Miami Office of Civic and Community Engagement, 2015)

The importance as seeing oneself as a historical actor, whose efforts are significant and worthy of archival documentation, was exhibited during the archive visit when former Scott Carver resident Yvette Norton found her signature on a petition that was part of the records of the Community Justice Project, a Miami-based group of community lawyers that provide legal counseling to grassroots organizations in the areas of racial justice, economic equity, and capacity building.[1] The organization, along with the Low-Income Families Fighting Together (LIFFT) project of the Miami Workers Center, joined forces with Scott Carver residents to protest the county's decision to tear down the housing project. "Here I am," she said, as she held up the petition and pointed to her name. (See Figure 4.2.)

Providing a forum for documenting the stories of public housing residents, and enabling them to see their efforts as part of the larger narrative of Miami's history, has been central to CCE's collaboration with the groups representing displaced residents of public housing in Miami. We have sought to utilize the tools and methodologies of ur-

Figure 4.2 Yvette Norton. (Courtesy of the University of Miami Office of Civic and Community Engagement, 2015)

ban and public history to provide multiple forums for residents to chronicle their history, make it accessible to a wide audience, and capture the personal recollections of those directly affected by federal and local housing policy decisions. Through traditional public history methodologies, like oral history, and innovative technological tools, including data visualization and Geographic Information Systems (GIS) mapping, CCE has created a variety of processes for engagement to bring multiple stakeholders to the table to chronicle their histories, understand current neighborhood housing conditions, and develop policy solutions that are community driven. These processes have involved building trust with various community stakeholders, from community organizations suspicious of university involvement in their neighborhoods to city and county departments with whom we sought to collaborate and share data. Using a community-driven approach to engaging with local stakeholders and providing data and tools in a free, accessible, and transparent way have enabled us to forge close working relationships with these groups to create a large-scale project on affordable housing in Miami that has expanded and iterated based on continuous feedback from multiple partners.

This chapter explores some of the strategies CCE has used to build coalitions across sectors to recover stories of racial displacement in Miami. It highlights the ways we have utilized big data and civic tech alongside narrative storytelling to capture a fuller picture of the history of neighborhood change in cities. It also addresses the challenges of doing this work within the institutional structure of a research university, where research imperatives often do not align with those of grassroots activists. Like the other chapters in this volume, it seeks to provide frameworks for rethinking and reimagining the role of the urban research university in the twenty-first century. It shows how universities can redefine their roles as anchor institutions in cities by being boundary spanners—people or organizations that facilitate collisions across sectors that result in collaboration and dynamic public engagement. As institutions of higher learning seek to redefine their mission amid challenges to their cost, relevance, and accessibility, embracing public scholarship and intentional engagement with community needs can show the potential of collaborative knowledge coproduction to foster transformational change on our campuses and in our communities. It enables us to prepare students to lead lives of continuous learning and active citizenship, so they have both the skills necessary to confront changing cultures of work and shifting methods of democratic engagement and the imperative to promote just, equitable, and inclusive communities.[2]

Forging Lasting Partnerships: The CCE and the Imperative of Institutional Commitment

The multifaceted approach to collaborating with community partners and establishing numerous nodes of connection between the campus and the community that shaped our Scott Carver project reflects a broader commitment to developing sustainable relationships that are mutually beneficial and impactful. Over the past two decades, many institutions of higher education have looked to civic engagement with local communities as the way to revive these broader humanitarian goals of the collegiate experience. This process of rethinking the direction of higher education has had profound implications not only for the structure of the curriculum and the recruitment of students but also for the relationship between universities and their communities. New programs promoting civic engagement, combining community involvement with cross-disciplinary learning, have highlighted how the production and transmission of knowledge are not linear, top-down processes but rather spontaneous and surprising endeavors in which all involved—student, teacher, community resident—have something to contribute and something to learn.

These are the commitments that undergird the CCE, housed in the Office of the Provost at the University of Miami. The creation of the office, in 2011, was the culmination of a faculty- and student-led effort to more fully integrate community-based learning into the curriculum. Moreover, it came at a time when both metropolitan Miami and the state of Florida were cited by numerous surveys as having some of the lowest levels of civic engagement in the nation. A 2010 report by the National Conference on Citizenship, an organization chartered by Congress in 1953 that tracks civic participation across the nation, was titled *A Tale of Two Cities—Civic Health in Miami and Minneapolis-St. Paul*.[3] The report examined various components of civic health, including volunteering, voter turnout, attending public meetings, nonprofit capacity, and one-on-one interactions with neighbors. The findings indicated that cities possessing vibrant nonprofit sectors, and schools and universities deeply engaged with their communities, had the highest levels of civic health nationwide. The authors pointed to the Twin Cities' "culture of civic empowerment," which is "oriented toward enlisting and empowering diverse people—paid employees as well as volunteers—in the common work of shaping the area's future without abandoning their own cultural backgrounds and values."[4] The Twin Cities ranked first in civic engagement nationally; Miami ranked last. In response to this report, former Florida senator and governor Bob Graham argued, "While Miami's unique demographics do not fully explain its low level of civic engagement, the combination of rapid growth and extraordinary diversity define a social, economic, and political context within which citizens and community leaders must find a way to create a culture of engagement. Over the next generation, America will look more like Miami than Minneapolis, and the challenge of empowerment in the face of change and diversity that Miami faces today will be echoed in communities across the nation. The lessons learned here will have important implications for the future."[5]

The University of Miami heeded the call to provide a forum for fostering civic engagement among our students by harnessing our diverse academic resources to solve complex problems through dynamic, collaborative, and multidisciplinary teaching and research. By creating the CCE, the university made a commitment to break down boundaries—between academic disciplines within the university and between the university and the public—to forge a model of the engaged university in a state and metropolitan region in dire need of repairing its civic health. The mission of CCE is to enhance university-community collaborations by engaging the university's academic resources in the enrichment of civic and community life in local, national, and global communities. The foundation of this academic collaboration is "engaged scholarship," that is, scholarship that addresses public problems and is of benefit to the wider community. All our efforts are grounded in a culture of collaboration and an ethic of reciprocity. Our goals include fostering stronger connections between the University of Miami and the South Florida community, developing new courses in which community-based partnerships are central to course learning outcomes, and creating new initiatives that bring multiple disciplines together to work collaboratively with local organizations on shared community-based projects addressing community-identified needs.

Affordable Housing, Scott Carver, and Stories of Displacement

At the time of the founding of CCE, in 2011, one of the most pressing issues facing Miami was the housing crisis, as it continues to be today. The economic recession, housing downturn, and resulting foreclosure crisis laid bare the extent to which government programs, developers, and nonprofit organizations had been unable to adequately address the need for safe, secure, and accessible affordable housing in South Florida. At the time, unemployment rates were at record highs, at 9.1 percent nationally and 10.7 percent in Florida, according to data from the U.S. Bureau of Labor Statistics. The October 2011 report from the U.S. Census Bureau showed that the rate of homeownership during the previous decade decreased by the largest percentage since the Great Depression. Moreover, according to Harvard University's Joint Center for Housing Studies, over the past decade, the Miami metro area has consistently had the highest percentage in the United States of renters spending more than half of their income on housing costs, making them severely cost burdened.[6] CCE aimed to address the housing crisis by bringing together policy experts, nonprofits, grassroots activists, developers, government agencies, and elected officials to identify needs, develop strategies for solutions, and help translate local activism into effective public policy. This initiative examined both the historical and the contemporary context for affordable housing, from both local and national perspectives. It drew from models of what has been done well in the past and sought solutions for best practices from other cities across the country while recognizing the unique elements that shape housing policy and practice in South Florida.

Through our Focus on Affordable Housing Project, we have developed solutions that address the need for safe, accessible, and sustainable housing and community development that are grounded in communities' sense of their history. We also have made the historical process of displacement a centerpiece of our work. Whether through racialized zoning practices like the Home Owners' Loan Corporation redlining maps or the persistent gentrification of neighborhoods of color, Miami's housing landscape has been one defined by racial displacement over the past century. By placing the story of housing displacement at the center of the history of urban development in Miami, we hope to expose a past that often is ignored or forgotten and use these stories to inform and shape present-day planning practices. A central feature of our work is collecting oral histories and archival materials that can provide the framework for helping previously displaced residents reweave the fabric of community by making their stories, and their journeys, a central part of the story of Miami.

Miami's history and growth have been shaped by racial segregation and residential displacement since the time of its official founding. When the city was established in 1896, 162 of the 368 people who voted for incorporation were Black. As historians John A. Stuart and John F. Stack Jr. explain, "The communities of white and black residents were interdependent and yet completely segregated."[7] African American and Bahamian migrants who had settled in the territory that would become Miami lived in a section of the city called "Colored Town" (later Overtown), adjacent to the Central Business District, as well as in West Coconut Grove and Brownsville. They were forbidden from renting or owning property, or even staying at hotels, in most sections of the city of Miami, Miami Beach, and suburban Coral Gables. Indeed, privately negotiated restrictive covenants that made it impossible for Black people to rent or own property in these neighborhoods gave way to government policies and planning practices that enshrined segregation as a fixture of life in Miami, and urban America more broadly. As urban planning became more formalized and integrated into public policy in Miami, the impact it has had on the physical landscape of Black neighborhoods, and on the cohesiveness of communities within them, has been profound.[8]

In the 1930s, the Dade County Planning Board made zoning a tool for enforcing segregation in urban planning decisions. Developer George Merrick, founder of the City Beautiful suburb of Coral Gables, and the University of Miami that was its centerpiece, served on both the Dade County Planning Board and the County Zoning Commission. The planning board's 1936 "Negro Resettlement Plan" sought to "remove every negro family from the city limits."[9] As the Central Business District expanded, it encroached on Colored Town, and Miami leaders sought to move Black residents out to make way for new (white) businesses and residents. Merrick also was an investor in Black neighborhoods across Miami. As historians Raymond Mohl and N.D.B. Connolly point out, Merrick, along with other white developers, used his investments in Black rental property to keep himself financially afloat during the Great Depression. Merrick and other developers used funding from the New Deal's Federal Housing Administration to at once clear "slums" and develop new rental housing specifically targeted to Black residents. Merrick explained to other white developers,

"Personally I have handled several Negro towns and I know there is money in it!"[10]

Merrick also was the original developer of the Railroad Shops Colored Addition, where he sold the first lots to Black homeowners after World War I.[11] Railroad Shops represented the promise of homeownership for African American railroad workers in the early twentieth century. Yet, the fate of the Railroad Shops in the 1930s and 1940s shows how the private real estate market and white developers worked directly in tandem with civic, business, and political leaders to drive Black residents out of increasingly desirable areas for white people. City of Miami Commission Meeting Minutes from a Special Session held on August 1, 1939, illustrate how blatant racism structured the planning and zoning decisions, making Black displacement the official policy. In the meeting, white residents requested that the City Commission "cooperate in eliminating Railroad Shops Addition as a negro section." At the time, there were eighty-two Black families in the area and 75 percent of them owned their own homes. The mayor explained that the City Commission had "refused additional permits to colored people in Railroad Shop Addition" and would "make every effort to eliminate colored people in that area."[12]

That meeting also addressed the petition to erect a six-foot wall separating the Liberty Square public housing project from white property to the east. When the federal government built Liberty Square, the first public housing project exclusively for African Americans in Miami, in 1937, they located that development adjacent to the existing Black neighborhood of Liberty City after other proposed locations drew fierce opposition from white property owners. Black people began moving to Liberty City, northwest of Miami's Central Business District, after being forced out of Colored Town to make room for the Central Business District expansion. The construction of Liberty Square, and the displacement of many Black people from the thriving Colored Town neighborhood and from Railroad Shops, inaugurated a pattern of residential segregation that continues to the present.[13]

These examples highlight the decades-long strategies used by planners and elected officials to codify segregation and displace Black residents. Urban renewal projects in the 1940s and 1950s, as well as the construction of Interstate 95 in the 1960s directly through the heart of Overtown, have had devastating effects on the cohesiveness of Black communities. I-95 decimated dozens of blocks of the densely populated neighborhood, destroyed businesses, displaced over ten thousand residents, and forever altered the nature of community life there. The historic fabric of the neighborhood as well as its commercial core were irreparably damaged, and decades of disinvestment added to its challenges.[14]

The story of the Scott Carver Housing Project fits squarely within this historic pattern of disinvestment and displacement. The James E. Scott and Carver homes were erected by 1954 and 1964, respectively. Initially built as two separate projects, the combined housing complex was made up of 850 two-story walk-up units in 76 barracks-style buildings, housing over 1,150 residents. The homes covered close to 43 acres of land located on NW Twenty-Second Avenue in Liberty City, just northwest of Liberty Square. (See Figure 4.3.) While these projects were built as segregated housing for Black families, and many claimed the construction was substandard, the units were much needed as the Black population faced the many institutional barriers to acquiring housing in Miami cited above.[15] Decades of neglect and disinvestment at these projects, similar to conditions faced at housing projects such as Cabrini Green in Chicago and Pruitt-Igoe in St. Louis, dramatically affected the livability of the housing development. By the 1980s, overcrowding and structural design deficiencies at Scott Carver, combined with the lack of proper maintenance and air-conditioning, led to increased deterioration of the development and its classification of being "severely distressed."[16]

Miami-Dade County's housing agency, which had long been cited for its maintenance problems and poor management of its properties, announced its plan to replace the deteriorating Scott Carver homes in 1999 when it received a $35 million grant from the Clinton administration's HOPE VI initiative. HOPE VI was intended to replace severely distressed housing projects, like Scott Carver, that were criticized for housing the poorest people in deteriorating, crime-ridden communities, with new housing designed to create sustainable, mixed-income communities.[17] The redevelopment would bring 354 new townhouse and single-family units to the site. The housing authority's plan to achieve this reconstruction included relocating all of the current residents, then demolishing all of the public housing units and replacing them with a mix of public, subsidized, and market-rate suburban-style

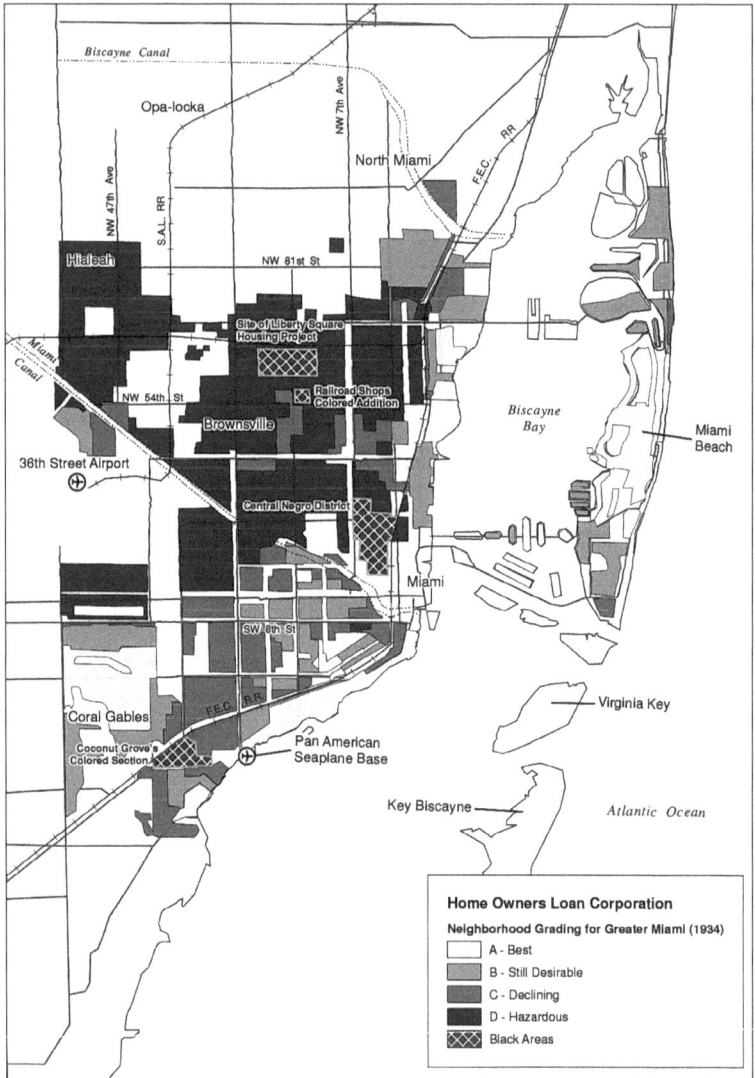

Figure 4.3 Home Owners' Loan Corporation grading and map of Black districts in Miami. (Map by Gordie Thompson. Courtesy of the University of Chicago Press, 2014)

townhouses and apartments. The housing agency offered residents the option to either move into other public housing units or use Section 8 Housing Choice vouchers to relocate to private rentals throughout the county.[18]

With the $35 million grant from the U.S. Department of Housing and Urban Development, the Miami-Dade Housing Agency, which was supposed to use the funds to transform one of Miami's most distressed neighborhoods, instead spent millions of dollars on architects, project managers, and consultants, who ran up staggering costs. In six years, they had spent half the money, displaced over eight hundred families, and built only three homes. A Pulitzer Prize–winning investigation by the *Miami Herald*, called "House of Lie$," revealed gross misman-agement on the part of the housing agency as well as double billing by contractors and consultants.[19] Moreover, the housing agency lost track of hundreds of residents who were displaced as a result of the demoli-tion. Former resident Yvette Norton, who found her name on the peti-tion, recalls, "We were scattered all over, some people as far as Geor-gia. Some people were homeless and living in their cars. But the county had no answers for us."[20]

The *Miami Herald* traced 250 families and discovered that more than one-third of them no longer lived at the current address known by the Miami-Dade Housing Agency.[21] Some of the former tenants staged protests, sued the county for discrimination, and launched a campaign to locate former residents.[22] The Community Justice Pro-ject, in collaboration with the Miami Workers Center, engaged in civil rights lawsuits, direct action, coalition work, and community aware-ness building to restore promised affordable units to displaced resi-dents. Through LIFFT, residents fought for the replacement of those housing units and kept the community together by organizing the "Find Our People" campaign, in which hundreds of former residents returned to the site to write their names at the "Last Building Stand-ing," the only remaining building of the housing project that the com-munity used as a site of organizing and gathering. After consistent prodding from activists, the county housing agency added 590 subsi-dized off-site rental units and affordable homes in the surrounding neighborhood specifically for the Scott Carver tenants.[23] After ten years of community activism, many Scott Carver residents returned to live in the new North Park at Scott Carver site and were successful in having the county designate the "last building standing" as a historic site.[24]

The Scott Carver resident visit to the UM archives was one part of a larger initiative to provide forums for residents to tell their stories. In the Spring 2016 semester, my Introduction to Urban America class collaborated with the Scott Carver Residents' Council, the Community Justice Project, the Miami Workers Center, and UM Otto G. Richter Library's Special Collections Department to enhance the oral history project. Students in the class came from a variety of majors, including History, English, Business, and Broadcast Journalism. We devised a community-based learning project designed around the students' interests and skills as well as the desires of the residents to create a lasting product that would document their stories. The result was a brief documentary film, *Scott Carver: Then and Now*, created by students and community residents. In order to get material for the film, we cohosted a Community Reunion at Gwen Cherry Park in Liberty City, with students conducting oral histories and library staff documenting and archiving historic photos, protest flyers and brochures, petitions, and letters to public officials.[25] The film incorporated a narrative history of public housing and racial segregation in Miami, the oral histories of residents and activists conducted by the students, and ephemera donated to Special Collections.[26] The latter material is now part of the permanent archival collection on housing activism in Miami.

Focus on Affordable Housing: Addressing Pressing Community Needs through Campus-Community Collaboration

The Scott Carver Project was part of a larger initiative at the University of Miami to connect campus and community through faculty and student engagement with residents and activist groups on the front lines of the affordability crisis. In addition to organizing public programs, stakeholder meetings, and courses related to the housing affordability and the history of displacement, CCE also embarked on a neighborhood-focused initiative in the Overtown section of Miami to illustrate how community history could be a potent force in its redevelopment. CCE launched its Overtown Initiative, funded by JPMorgan Chase, to simultaneously address the need for affordable housing and preserve as many of the extant historic structures as possible, thereby helping reestablish a cohesive community fabric in the neighborhood once dubbed "the Harlem of the South." During the Spring 2015 semester, CCE partnered with the University of Miami Center for Urban and Community Design and the Masters in Real Estate Development and Urbanism program in the School of Architecture, and the School of Business Administration, to provide research and technical assistance to preserve and honor the rich history and culture of the neighborhood. Led by CCE program manager Emily Eisenhauer, we worked with community development corporations, elected officials, historic preservationists, the Overtown Community Redevelopment Agency, and local youth organizations to create a historic map of the community and identify historic buildings that could be rehabilitated for adaptive reuse to foster economic revitalization. We brought together UM colleagues in GIS, Architecture, Historic Preservation, and Computational Science to create an app that enables researchers to collect data related to historic designation and streamline the process. Students from our architecture school and computational science program then worked with youths in an Overtown after-school program to research the historic properties in the neighborhood.

Bounded by the Florida East Coast Railroad tracks to the east, NW Tenth Avenue to the west, NW Fifth Street to the south, and NW Twentieth Street to the north, Overtown has been one of the most significant communities in Miami's history from its incorporation as a city in 1896 to the present day. Yet, the numerous attempts throughout the twentieth century to remove Black people from this neighborhood bordering the Central Business District, as well as the construction of I-95 in the 1960s discussed above, had hollowed out the commercial core of the community and displaced tens of thousands of residents. By the time of the economic recession of 2008, Overtown continued to face significant challenges, as the median income was $21,696 and the poverty rate was 53 percent. Because of their limited household income, most of Overtown's renters (66 percent) were cost burdened, paying more than 30 percent of their income toward housing costs. Because Overtown also faced significant redevelopment pressures as the real estate market recovered, residents feared higher rents and the loss of affordable units. This increased development activity also put Overtown's historic sites at risk.

The goal of the Overtown project was to work in collaboration with community groups to propose revitalization ideas that respected the neighborhood's history and incorporated it into design plans. The effort in the School of Architecture was led by faculty including Chuck Bohl, Sonia Chao, Jorge Hernandez, Ricardo Lopez, and Armando Montero. Students in historic preservation and real estate development courses consulted with neighborhood stakeholders—including the Southeast/Overtown-Park West Community Redevelopment Agency, Urban Philanthropies, and the Overtown Children and Youth Coalition as well as the city of Miami Historic Preservation Office—to conduct case studies on the adaptive reuse of historic buildings on three blocks in Overtown. Students created development scenarios that would allow historic buildings to be preserved through rehabilitation and conversion to new uses that would meet the needs of the community and would be financially viable. The student groups performed zoning and market analyses to identify potential adaptive reuses for historic sites and complete a development plan and financial feasibility study for each case study. Three teams of students studied different sections of the neighborhood to redesign blocks to infuse commercial activity into the streetscape and also provide additional units of affordable housing, all the while focusing on preserving the remaining historic structures and working them into the design plans.[27]

One team, for example, created a proposal for the Overtown Folklife Village, in the southeast quadrant of Overtown, which has the largest collection of preserved historic structures, including the Ward Rooming House, which had served African American performers during segregation, and the Providence Lodge, a Masonic Temple. This team proposed combining new mixed-income rental units on vacant land owned by the Overtown-Park West Community Redevelopment Agency with retail, commercial, and entertainment venues to recall the thriving entertainment history of the area. All three teams combined new affordable housing with market-rate units, commercial corridors, and historic preservation to knit the community together in ways that recapture the heyday of neighborhood life in Overtown.[28]

The student case studies relied on public-private partnerships to preserve historic structures and create new affordable housing and commercial corridors. The students considered subsidies that would be available to property owners to help preserve historic structures, including tax benefits for properties designated historic, Transfer of Development Rights available from the city of Miami, and the ad valorem tax exemption available from Miami-Dade County.[29] The case studies also showed how local policies could support preservation by creating tax incentives and using strategies like Neighborhood Conservation Districts, already part of the city of Miami's zoning code Miami 21, to protect the remaining historic fabric of a neighborhood.[30]

CCE also initiated the process of securing historic designation status from the city of Miami for qualified properties in the Overtown neighborhood. CCE's program manager for Affordable Housing and Community Development, Jorge Damian de la Paz, worked in collaboration with historic preservation consultant Alexander Adams to complete a Historic Designation Report for Lawson Edward Thomas's Overtown Law Office (1021 NW Second Avenue). Thomas made significant contributions to Miami as a community activist, lawyer, and judge. He was engaged in a variety of groundbreaking civil rights campaigns and lawsuits throughout South Florida, including organizing a protest against the exclusion of Black people from Miami's beaches. His Overtown law office was the location of various civil rights organizing meetings with community and national leaders. As a result of his significant legal achievements, Thomas was appointed judge of Miami's Negro Municipal Court in 1950, becoming the first Black judge in the South since Reconstruction (the Negro Municipal Court is currently preserved in Overtown as the Black Police Precinct and Courthouse Museum).[31] In addition, CCE worked with Alexander Adams to add additional historic properties in Overtown to the Florida Master Site File, the state's official inventory of historic structures.

The historic preservation initiative was designed to promote urban revitalization in a historically Black neighborhood facing intense development pressures, as it has since its founding over a hundred years ago. Our efforts in collaboration with local stakeholders were aimed at securing protections for the undesignated buildings and the physical form of the neighborhood as downtown building pressures increasingly encroach on the neighborhood. Through this multidisciplinary campus-community collaboration, we sought to preserve historic buildings in the neighborhood, enhance the opportunities for promoting heritage tourism, and work with the youths of the community to document its vibrant history.

Miami Housing Solutions Lab: Mapping, "Civic Tech," and the Accessibility of Big Data

In addition to drawing together students and faculty from across the university to work collaboratively with community organizations, we also launched a series of online mapping tools that uses big data and innovative mapping technology to visualize the landscape of housing affordability in South Florida and present a range of policy solutions. The Miami Housing Solutions Lab, a suite of interactive online tools, utilizes technologies like GIS and interactive media design to address core aspects of urban planning in South Florida. The platform serves as a research tool for planners, developers, community organizations, grassroots advocates, and scholars of urban issues. In creating these tools and making them free and publicly accessible, our goal has been to democratize data that previously was available to only the few with resources to track it down from disparate sources. By putting the data in the hands of community residents, we aim to help facilitate equitable and inclusive community development. All of our housing mapping tools are available at affordablehousing.miami.edu.

The centerpiece of this work is the Miami Affordability Project, or MAP. Funded by JPMorgan Chase and the Jessie Ball duPont Fund, MAP is a publicly accessible mapping technology for visualizing neighborhood-level housing market dynamics and informing data-driven strategies for housing and community development. Created in partnership with the Center for Computational Science at the University of Miami, the tool contains over three hundred data filters that facilitate the analysis of local funding programs, affordability preservation risks, the supply and demand of housing, and opportunities for policy solutions to promote affordability. The goal of MAP is to increase community capacity for engaging with development. The MAP combines data on affordable housing units from local, state, and federal sources to show the location of existing subsidized units. The MAP can help communities develop data-driven strategies for housing, making it easier for community stakeholders to understand and implement policies that prevent displacement, promote fair housing, and create stronger mixed-income communities in South Florida.

MAP overlays housing data on top of census data to help users understand the geography of cost burden and the areas where need is not being met.[32] We utilize data from the American Community Survey (ACS), for example, to understand the basic demographic features of census tracts across Miami-Dade County. We also include housing data from the ACS, including the percentage of overcrowded units, vacancy rates, year built, median monthly renter costs, and percentage of cost-burdened units. The Housing Development layer on MAP includes data on both public housing (housing projects owned by a housing authority) and assisted housing (a housing project developed by a private or nonprofit developer with federal, state, or local funding assistance). We obtained this data from a range of sources, including the Shimberg Center for Housing Studies at the University of Florida, the Miami-Dade County Public Housing and Community Development Department, the Miami-Dade County Property Appraiser, and the City of Miami Community and Economic Development Department.

Figure 4.4 is a screenshot of MAP that shows the cost burden by census tract as well as the inventory of public (magenta dot) and assisted (purple) housing developments. Census tracts that are shaded red are those in which 75–100 percent of renters are cost burdened (paying more than 30 percent of their income on housing). What we see quickly from looking at the map is that the assisted and public housing is concentrated in the urban core, though there is a great deal of need throughout the county, to the south and west of the city of Miami. Users can click on any of the census tracts to get all of the demographic and housing data for that tract and also on the magenta and purple dots to obtain all of the data related to that housing development. Users can find out the name of the development, who owns it, what financing programs were used to subsidize it, what groups it serves (elderly or families, for example), how many units it has, what its inspection scores are, and, perhaps most importantly, what year its affordability restrictions expire. This latter data point is especially significant because it is anticipated that Miami-Dade County will lose thousands of units of affordable housing in the next few years as a result of subsidized affordable housing developments potentially becoming

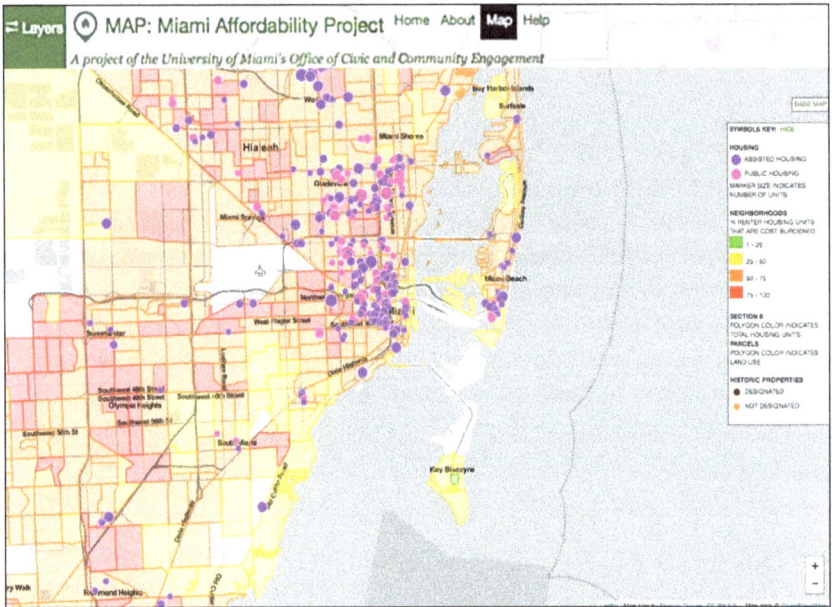

Figure 4.4 Cost burden and location of assisted and public housing. MAP: Miami Affordability Project. (Courtesy of the University of Miami Office of Civic and Community Engagement, 2016)

market-rate properties and, therefore, those units being removed from the affordable housing inventory.

The process of creating these tools involved extensive community engagement, collaborating with grassroots organizations to understand the kind of data they needed and asking how to make the research more accessible. Our community partners in this project included nonprofit advocacy organizations such as Catalyst Miami, Miami Homes for All, Neighborhood Housing Services of South Florida, and Urgent Inc. We also developed a close working relationship with numerous public agencies, including the Housing Finance Authority of Miami-Dade County, the city of Miami Community and Economic Development Department, the Florida Housing Finance Corporation, and, most importantly, the Miami-Dade County Department of Public Housing and Community Development, headed by Michael Liu, a former assistant secretary of Housing and Urban Development. We conducted interactive neighborhood workshops in conjunction with the South Florida Community Development Coalition's Shekeria Brown and Susan Jacobs so that community organizations could use the tools most effectively to meet their goals. Training workshops on how to utilize the MAP took place with community groups all across the county, including in Little Haiti, Overtown, Liberty City, Brownsville, South Dade, and Little Havana.

Numerous local and national agencies and advocacy groups have utilized MAP to make policy recommendations for the future of affordable housing and community development in South Florida. The Urban Institute used data from MAP in its 2017 report, *Miami and the State of Low- and Middle-Income Housing: Strategies to Preserve Affordability and Opportunities for the Future*, which included policy recommendations for the city of Miami and Miami-Dade County. The Florida Legislature's Office of Program Policy Analysis and Government Accountability utilized MAP for its audit of the use of County Housing Surtax funds and recommendations for policy changes, *Miami-Dade's Discretionary Surtax Supports Affordable Housing for Low-Income Residents; Recent Changes Will Improve the Program*. And both the city of Miami and Miami-Dade County have used data from MAP to create their consolidated housing plans.[33]

In addition to MAP, CCE created a Housing Policy Timeline, tracing developments in local, state, and national housing policy from the 1930s to the present. Placing the historical time line alongside the MAP project allows community activists, policy makers, elected officials, and scholars to understand the ways in which policy changes have influenced the physical geography of housing affordability in Miami. The time line is modeled after the "Boston Fair Housing Timeline" and University of Iowa historian Colin Gordon's "Mapping Decline: St. Louis and the American City" platforms.[34] It covers over eighty years of housing policy, ranging from a landmark U.S. Supreme Court case on zoning in 1926 to Miami's condo boom and growing affordability gap following the 2008 recession. The time line includes text summaries, photos, period maps, and other archival resources on major housing-related events and their impact on Miami's neighborhoods. It also features digitized versions of Historic Tax Card photos (including Muhammad Ali's house in Liberty City) that the city of Miami collected to document all buildings in the city beginning in the 1940s. The Miami Historic and Environmental Preservation Board provided CCE access to these photos to digitize and incorporate on the time line. This publicly accessible online tool helps practitioners and advocates better understand the lasting historical legacies of housing policies and urban development initiatives on Miami's neighborhoods.

To inform local housing policy, CCE also developed a comprehensive Housing Policy Toolkit in collaboration with the Metropolitan Center at Florida International University that provides information on best practices in affordable housing policy and practice across the country and then tailors those strategies to the legislative landscape in Miami-Dade County. The Housing Policy Toolkit is designed to give policy makers, housing advocates, and developers the tools to utilize the most effective methods for expanding housing access in the county. We focused on six affordable housing strategies: the preservation of Naturally Occurring Affordable Housing (NOAH), which are market-rate units that are affordable to households (meaning that they would not pay more than 30 percent of their income on housing); the preservation of existing subsidized housing (discussed above); the promotion of transit-oriented development, which gives tax incentives for housing projects developed along transit corridors; the creation of community land trusts, which secure the affordability of land in perpetuity; the use of publicly owned vacant or underutilized land for housing; and expedited permitting, whereby private developers would be able to take advantage of streamlined permitting processes to enable developments to come online more quickly. For each of these strategies, we looked at examples of best practices nationwide and then addressed how the strategy could be deployed in the Miami market. We also suggested specific neighborhoods where each strategy would be most effective given the housing needs and land use in that community.

For example, the preservation of NOAH is an important strategy for many neighborhoods given that these units already exist and do not rely on public subsidy. Property owners in hot real estate markets often require incentives to keep their units affordable and not significantly raise rents given the overall rise in real estate value. Chicago's Community Investment Corporation created a Rental Redevelopment Loan Program to provide flexible financing for the rehabilitation of unsubsidized affordable rental housing. Cook County provides a reduction in property taxes to developers who complete a substantial rehab on multifamily buildings and set aside a percentage of the units for low- and moderate-income tenants. Programs like this could encourage the preservation of NOAH units in Miami as well. Interactive charts on the Housing Policy Toolkit show the number of NOAH units lost over the past decade in various neighborhoods in Miami. Miami-Dade County's surtax program, the local funding program that subsidizes affordable housing, recently added set-asides for small multi-family rental developments in Little Haiti and Liberty City. This set-aside for small developments with forty units or less is an effective way to upgrade NOAH properties to expand the supply of quality affordable housing.

Our current work involves addressing housing affordability and environmental sustainability in tandem, two of South Florida's most pressing challenges, to promote urban resilience. Miami's affordable housing challenges are exacerbated by its coastal geography, bringing increasing risks associated with climate change and sea level rise, including flooding during seasonal high tides and storms. The South Florida region has been identified as one of the most vulnerable to climate risks by the World Economic Forum, with estimated potential financial losses of $278 billion due to rising sea levels. In Miami Beach, flooding has increased by 400 percent in the past ten years.[35] For this *Housing Resiliency and a Sustainable South Florida* project, funded by JPMorgan Chase, CCE is collaborating with local stakeholders to identify creative design and policy solutions to increase Miami's adaptive capacity, while building new networks to strengthen urban resiliency. We are studying solutions to develop comprehensive resilience strategies for retrofitting existing housing in low-income areas and taking into account their relative costs for implementation. The team, led by CCE Housing Resiliency program manager Jennifer Posner, also will engage in advocacy for housing policy and practice in South Florida that encourages the maintenance and development of affordable and resilient housing.[36]

We have developed a new mapping tool to present the intersections of housing affordability and climate change, showing elevation levels across the county, projected sea level rise, projected storm surge, and how these conditions will affect our affordable housing stock. We also have created a Resilience Policy Toolkit that features adaptation, mitigation, and resilience measures and provides a cost-benefit analysis to determine the most effective adaptation and mitigation strategies for different types of affordable housing typologies, including duplex, garden style, midrise, and high-rise structures. We have worked with a broad coalition of stakeholders that includes the chief resilience officers for Miami-Dade County, the city of Miami, and the city of Miami Beach as well as grassroots groups such as Catalyst Miami, the CLEO Institute, and Miami Waterkeeper. The project expands upon MAP; we combined data collection and analysis with mapping to provide a visual picture of sea level rise and flood risk and are working collaboratively with local stakeholders through our ongoing partnership with the South Florida Community Development Coalition to develop innovative and community-informed solutions for adaptation, mitigation, and resilience of the affordable housing stock in Miami. This effort is especially significant since, as the sea rises, the historically more expensive property along the coast will lose its value and neighborhoods situated further inland on the coastal ridge—with the highest elevations in the county—will see their property values rise. This shift in value will have a dramatic impact on the most economically vulnerable neighborhoods, which also happen to be historic communities of color. Our goal for the housing resiliency project is at once to develop mapping tools that allow users to see the impacts of sea level rise and flooding on the affordable housing stock and to suggest policy solutions that provide adaptation and mitigation strategies that help prevent the destabilization of traditional neighborhoods through climate gentrification.[37]

Another feature of the Miami Housing Solutions Lab is LAND: Land Access for Neighborhood Development, a free, interactive online map for visualizing the distribution of local institutional and government-owned vacant and underused properties. The tool, funded by Citi Community Development, includes parcel-level property data and public transit information to encourage the development of affordable housing alongside transit corridors. Our goal is to provide an accessible and innovative platform for neighborhood organizations to promote equitable community development in Miami. LAND represents the first mechanism for showing the total amount of public and institution-owned, underutilized, or unused land across the entirety of the county and its municipalities, including information about where lots are located, who owns them, and how they could be aggregated into larger parcels. By being able to visualize this land, policy

makers can more easily create evidence-based strategies for conveying land to promote housing affordability and equitable community
development.[38]

Like MAP, LAND contains a wide range of data from public sources that we have aggregated to make it easily accessible to planners, policy makers, and grassroots advocacy groups. We used Department of
Revenue codes to identify vacant land and then manually sorted it to
identify to the best of our ability the land that would be suitable for
affordable housing. That does not mean that all the land identified on
the site is suitable for immediate development; it means that the potential exists for developing them into housing. In assembling this information, we identified several interesting and useful data and in-
sight points. Perhaps the most surprising was that, as of the spring of
2019, there was a total of over five hundred million square feet of public, vacant, or underutilized land in Miami-Dade County. Of that land,
some eight hundred thousand square feet were considered "surplus,"
which means that the county identified the lots as not being needed
for governing purposes. It also means these lands have the potential
to be conveyed, sold, or auctioned.

We found various cases where vacant lots that are contiguous to one
another are owned by different public agencies. These parcels represent opportunities for aggregation to create a larger space for the development of affordable housing or other community-focused uses. We
developed a method for selecting the type of landownership by color
so you can easily identify ownership information. Figure 4.5 shows
publicly owned lots adjacent to one another that belong to different
entities. The pink lots are owned by the county, teal are city and county surplus, and green are school board. Another unique feature of the
tool is its lot size calculator. Users can click on adjacent parcels of vacant land to add up the square footage; in the case of the lots shown
in Figure 4.5, the total square footage is 54,362.

The LAND platform also maps unused or vacant lands owned by
faith-based organizations and large anchor institutions, such as hos-
pitals and universities, showing the full range of lots that could be aggregated. In mapping this data, we found that faith-based institutions
form one of the largest categories of institutional owners: they own sev-
en hundred lots of vacant or underused land—or 13 million square feet.
This is significant because many examples across the country exist in

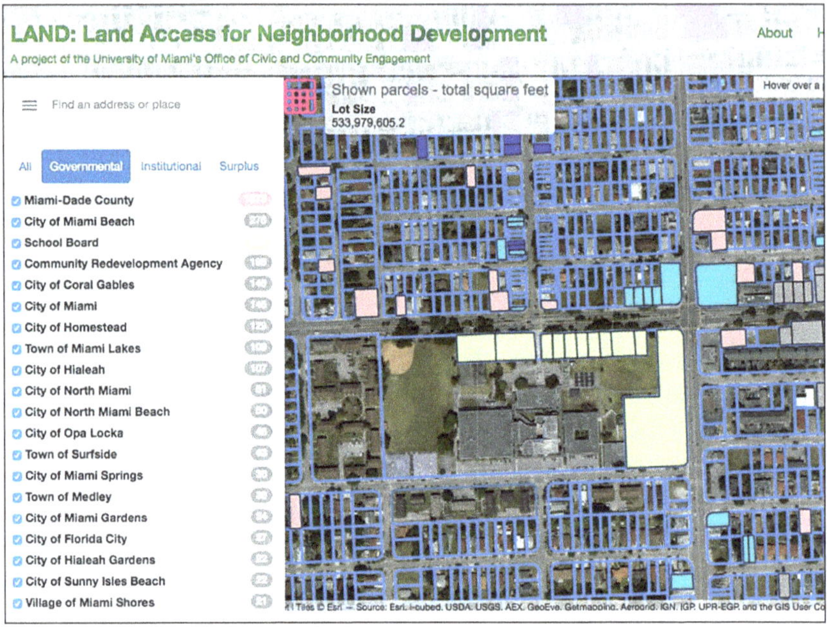

Figure 4.5 Adjacent publicly owned lots. LAND: Land Access for Neighborhood Development. (Courtesy of the University of Miami Office of Civic and Community Engagement, 2019)

which faith-based organizations are key players in developing affordable housing, like the pastor in Brooklyn who is using church-owned land to build twenty-one hundred apartments.[39] In addition, LAND highlights the SMART Plan, the county's transit expansion plan, which is overlaid on the mapping tool; this is the first time a method for visualizing the locations of vacant or underutilized land near transit hubs and corridors has been developed. This means we can more easily see where transit-oriented development can take place utilizing vacant land.

These publicly owned lands present a unique opportunity for community leaders and organizations because the land can be removed from speculative market forces that would normally drive up the cost of acquisition. This tool can be used for creating community land trusts, for example, to stabilize land values and ensure future affordability. Ultimately, this tool is meant to be used for the public good—to identify lots owned by public entities, faith-based organizations, or other large institutions that can be deployed for the overarching needs of the community, such as housing, activity centers, parks, or other community needs.[40]

Community groups throughout South Florida have used the tool to address local housing needs more effectively, and the county's public housing office is relying on the tool to develop its long-term strategic plan for spending federal housing resources. For example, the local advocacy group Miami Homes for All worked in conjunction with Enterprise Community Partners to create a plan for preserving affordable housing in Miami-Dade County and used LAND to identify properties suitable for community land trusts and other affordable housing solutions.[41] LAND also became the basis for a values statement, Public Land for Public Good, that called for "the prioritization of legislation focused on equitable development, environmental justice and a systematic restorative rights framework." The statement, signed by over twenty-five grassroots organizations and published in the *Miami Herald*, demanded "more consistent and strategic public land disposition processes . . . [to] better serve all our communities while reducing vacancy and blight, and adding to our tax rolls."[42] In July 2020, Miami-Dade County passed legislation that required the use of LAND to develop potential property assemblages and explore new types of ownership models so that vacant or underutilized land could be put in service of the public good.[43]

At the national level, Fannie Mae, Enterprise Community Partners, the Urban Institute, the Federal Reserve Bank of Atlanta, and the National Association for Latino Community Asset Builders, among others, have consulted with CCE on data analysis and mapping strategies for utilizing the framework of the LAND tool in other markets. The immediate impact LAND is having on informing policy and strategy decisions among policy makers at the city and county, and among grassroots advocacy groups, highlights the importance of making big data available to multiple stakeholders in a user-friendly format. Communities across South Florida and around the nation are facing significant development and gentrification pressures and having interactive online tools that make land use, ownership, and vacancy data easily accessible allows local leaders to identify actionable and effective solutions for promoting greater access to affordable housing.

Conclusion: Opportunities and Challenges

These projects highlight the important role urban historians can play in making their work matter within their local contexts. As faculty in fields like urban history colloborate with communities, working *with* rather than for community partners, they can create lasting change-oriented projects that involve multiple publics and perspectives through thoughtful civic engagement. These projects showcase the role public history plays in shaping historical understanding and sense of place and serves as a foundation for informing present-day practice in urban revitalization and community development. As historian Robin Kelley explains, students often differentiate between social activism and intellectual work. "They speak of the 'real' world as some concrete wilderness overrun with violence and despair, and the university as if it were some sanitized sanctuary distant from actual people's lives and struggles." What we can help students recognize, he argues, is that "the most radical ideas often grow out of a concrete intellectual engagement with the problems of aggrieved populations confronting systems of oppression."[44] Indeed, universities now have a central role to play in linking critical analysis with community engagement to promote social justice, just as they have at various moments in the past.

The housing initiatives I discussed show how coalition building across sectors can serve as a foundation for shaping present-day practices in urban revitalization and community development. These projects help forge civic identity, shared meaning, and respect for groups that have come before and, at the same time, allow new groups to feel a part of a city's history by reconnecting fragments of its past. These links to the past, and the process of including multiple voices within the narrative of place, can help forge a stronger sense of place attachment and civic identity at a time when transience and disengagement define much of our urban culture. Recognizing the variety of ideas, skills, and traditions that different groups bring to the urban development process allows for a cooperative model of knowledge building and community enrichment. And only through concerted efforts to form coalitions can meaningful change happen in public policy. Scholars of urban history can play a role in building those bridges so that we reconnect the activist tradition with the planning process to shape an urban policy agenda whose overarching goals are the promotion of social justice, racial equity, and environmental sustainability in the United States.

At the same time, there are challenges to doing this work of public scholarship and engagement in an effective and collaborative way. The urgency of addressing today's complex problems in real time means that faculty often feel forced to choose between developing projects that are solution driven and engage with the imperatives of immediate problem-solving and those that result in peer-reviewed publication in specialized journals that often take months or years to go to print. I am not suggesting that this is an either/or choice; clearly both options are possible and desirable. But there often is a misalignment between the values associated with engaged scholarship and public history, on one hand, and those that are rewarded by the academy, on the other. Where public scholarship seeks relevance and accessibility of its research to a wide audience, the academy most often rewards specialized, discipline-based knowledge production. Where public scholarship calls for collaborative, interdisciplinary work to address pressing social problems, the academy, and the field of history, in particular, privilege research conducted by an individual scholar engaging with the literature of the discipline that results in the production of a single-authored book targeted to other scholars in the field. Where public scholarship mandates accountability to diverse groups of community stakeholders, the academy calls for accountability to department chairs and promotion and tenure boards. As Robin DiAngelo and Özlem Sensoy explain, "The modern university—in its knowledge generation, research, and social and material sciences and with its 'experts' and its privileging of particular forms of knowledge over others (e.g., written over oral, history over memory, rationalism over wisdom) . . . has validated and elevated positivistic, White Eurocentric knowledge."[45] If our goal is to make universities relevant in the twenty-first century, then we ought to be using our resources to promote cutting-edge research and teaching that enable faculty and students to apply their skills and knowledge to pressing real-world problems that have the most impact on our communities and shape a more just and inclusive society.

NOTES

1. Andres Viglucci, "A Decade Later, Residents of the Demolished Scott Carver Projects Get to Move Back Home," *Miami Herald*, September 2, 2012, accessed January 9, 2019, available at https://www.miamiherald.com/latest-news/article 1942411.html.

2. For further discussion of the impacts of public scholarship on campuses and communities, see Harry C. Boyte, ed. *Democracy's Education: Public Work, Citizenship, and the Future of Colleges and Universities* (Nashville, TN: Vanderbilt University Press, 2015); Andrew Delbanco, *College: What It Was, Is, and Should Be* (Princeton, NJ: Princeton University Press, 2012); Ira Harvaky et al. *Knowledge for Social Change: Bacon, Dewey and the Revolutionary Transformation of Research Universities in the Twenty-First Century* (Philadelphia: Temple University Press, 2017). For a discussion of the academy privileging certain forms of knowledge over others and the racial implications, see Özlem Sensoy and Robin DiAngelo, "'We Are All for Diversity, but . . .': How Faculty Hiring Committees Reproduce Whiteness and Practical Suggestions for How They Can Change," *Harvard Educational Review* 87, no. 4 (Winter 2017): 557–580, 593–595.

3. Harry C. Boyte, L. Douglas Dobson, Kei Kawashama-Ginsburg, Jonathan Knuckey, and Peter Levine, *A Tale of Two Cities: Civic Health in Miami and Minneapolis-St. Paul*, National Conference on Citizenship, 2010, accessed January 10, 2019, available at http://floridacivichealth.org/files/tale-two-cities.pdf.

4. Boyte et al., *Tale of Two Cities*.

5. *Why Miami's Civic Health Is Lowest in the Nation—And Twin Cities Is Tops*, National Conference on Citizenship, January 24, 2011, accessed January 10, 2019, available at https://ncoc.org/why-miamis-civic-health-is-lowest-in-nation-and -the-twin-cities-is-tops/.

6. *The State of the Nation's Housing*, Joint Center for Housing Studies at Harvard University (Cambridge, MA: President and Fellows of Harvard College, 2012–2018). Harvard has been producing this report since 1988, analyzing housing trends including access, affordability, and policy. The report looks at homeownership, conditions for renters, and overall housing challenges. Consistently, throughout the past decade, the report has ranked Miami as the top metropolitan region for severe cost burden for renters.

7. John A. Stuart and John F. Stack Jr., "The New Deal in South Florida," in *The New Deal in South Florida: Design, Policy, and Community Building, 1933–1940, ed.* John A. Stuart and John F. Stack Jr. (Gainesville: University Press of Florida, 2008), 1–30, 17.

8. N.D.B. Connolly, *A World More Concrete: Real Estate and the Remaking of Jim Crow South Florida* (Chicago: University of Chicago Press, 2014), chronicles the history of these real estate practices though the 1960s. See also Marvin Dunn, *Black Miami in the Twentieth Century* (1997; repr., Gainesville: University Press of Florida, 2016); Paul S. George, "Colored Town: Miami's Black Community, 1896–1930," *Florida Historical Quarterly* 56, no. 4 (April 1978): 434–450; Raymond A. Mohl, "Making the Second Ghetto in Metropolitan Miami, 1940–

1960," in *The New African American Urban History*, ed. Kenneth W. Goings and Raymond A. Mohl (Thousand Oaks, CA: Sage, 1996); Raymond A. Mohl, "Race and Space in the Modern City: Interstate-95 and the Black Community in Miami," in *Urban Policy in Twentieth-Century America*, ed. Arnold Hirsch and Raymond Mohl (New Brunswick, NJ: Rutgers University Press, 1993); Raymond A. Mohl, "Whitening Miami: Race, Housing, and Government Policy in Twentieth-Century Dade County," *Florida Historical Quarterly* 79, no. 3 (Winter 2001): 319–345; Melanie Shell-Weiss, *Coming to Miami: A Social History* (Gainesville: University Press of Florida, 2009), chaps. 7, 8, and epilogue.

9. George Merrick, "Planning the Greater Miami for Tomorrow," transcript of address to the Miami Realty Board, May 27, 1937, NARA, RG 196, Box 298, cited in John A. Stuart, "Liberty City: Florida's First Public Housing Project," in *The New Deal in South Florida*, ed. John A. Stuart and John F. Stack Jr. (Gainesville: University Press of Florida, 2008), 186–222, 212. On Merrick's role on the planning and zoning boards, see Mohl, "Whitening Miami," 320; Mohl, "Making the Second Ghetto," 398.

10. George Merrick, "Real Estate Development Past and Future," transcript of address to the Southeastern Convention of Realty Boards, November 29, 1937, NARA, RG 196, Box 298, cited in Stuart, "Liberty City," 212.

11. Arva Moore Parks, *George Merrick: Son of the South Wind, Visionary Creator of Coral Gables* (Gainesville: University of Florida Press, 2015), 115.

12. "Minutes of Special Meeting of the City Commission of the City of Miami," August 1, 1939, City of Miami Commission Minutes, Office of the City Clerk. For further discussion of the Railroad Shop Colored Addition and evictions, see Connolly, *World More Concrete*, 144–149.

13. Connolly, *World More Concrete*, 86–87. In 1939, the Miami Housing Authority opened another public housing project a few blocks from Liberty Square, this one for white people, Edison Courts. Because of the increasing demand for housing for Black people, given that they continued to be forced out of other neighborhoods, Liberty Square was expanded and soon encroached on the buffer zone that had been created to separate the Black from the white housing developments. As a result, the county erected a concrete wall to clearly separate and demarcate the Black and the white projects. The "race wall," as it was called, has been preserved as a symbol of the history of segregation in Miami.

14. Connolly, *World More Concrete*; Dunn, *Black Miami*; Mohl, "Making the Second Ghetto"; Mohl, "Race and Space."

15. Connolly, *World More Concrete*; Dunn, *Black Miami*; Mohl, "Race and Space"; Stuart and Stack, *New Deal in South Florida*.

16. See Miami-Dade Housing Agency, *PHA Plan, 5-Year Plan for Fiscal Years 2005–2009, Annual Plan for Fiscal Year 2007–2008* (Miami-Dade County, 2007), 31–32. See also Reese v. Miami-Dade County, U.S. District Court for the Southern District of Florida, 242 F. Supp. 2d 1292 (S.D. Fla. 2002), December 5, 2002. The case was argued on behalf of plaintiff Mary Reese and other residents displaced from Scott Carver by Charles F. Elsesser Jr. of Florida Legal Services (among other

attorneys). The case summary states: "According to the County's 1999 HOPE VI grant application to the United States Department of Housing and Urban Development ('HUD'), both developments are antiquated, the units too small, and the density too high. Additionally, there are serious structural, site and infrastructure defects, which render Scott-Carver homes overdue for demolition and redevelopment through the HOPE VI program." Elsesser is cofounder of the Community Justice Project, whose papers are archived at the University of Miami Libraries.

17. See Harry J. Wexler, "HOPE VI: Market Means/Public Ends—The Goals, Strategies, and Midterm Lessons of HUD's Urban Revitalization Demonstration Program," *Journal of Affordable Housing* 10, no. 3 (2001): 195–233; Susan J. Popkin et al., *A Decade of HOPE VI: Research Findings and Policy Challenges* (Washington, DC: Urban Institute, May 2004), accessed February 18, 2019, available at https://www.urban.org/sites/default/files/alfresco/publication-pdfs/411002-A-Decade-of-HOPE-VI.PDF.

18. Marcos Feldman, "How Are the Displaced Scott-Carver Residents Faring? The Aftermath of HOPE VI Public Housing in Miami," research report, Research Institute on Social and Economic Policy, Florida International University, February 2007; Robin Ivery, "Residents Sue to Block Scott Carver Demolition," *Miami Times*, September 12–18, 2001.

19. Debbie Cenziper, "House of Lie$: In Liberty-City, the Miami-Dade Housing Agency Has Left a Wasteland Where Families Once Lived," *Miami Herald*, July 25, 2006, accessed February 10, 2019, available at http://communityjusticeproject.com/media/2014/9/29/house-of-lie-in-liberty-city-the-miami-dade-housing-agency-has-left-a-wasteland-where-families-once-lived.

20. Viglucci, "A Decade Later."

21. Cenziper, "House of Lie$."

22. Reese v. Miami-Dade County; Joseph Phelan, "The Struggle and Victory for Scott Carver Homes," *People's Tribune*, August 2007, accessed February 10, 2019, available at http://www.peoplestribune.org/PT.2007.08/PT.2007.08.8.html; Ivery, "Residents Sue."

23. Cenziper, "House of Lie$."

24. The relocation of residents began in September 2001 with a report from the Miami-Dade Housing Agency claiming that 70 percent of households opted for Section 8 vouchers while the remaining 30 percent moved to other public housing. Out of a study of eighty-two heads of households that had claimed a Section 8 voucher, 52.4 percent had lost it, 36.3 percent moved two or more times, 23.8 percent were homeless, and the remaining were either evicted or foreclosed on. Feldman, "How Are the Displaced Scott-Carver Residents Faring?" 6. The North Park at Scott Carver move-in phase began in 2008 after Habitat for Humanity built 57 new homes; phase 2 was completed in 2012 and provided a total of 354 rental units composed of 177 public housing units, 107 low- and moderate-income (tax credit) units, and 70 market-rate units. See Housing Opportunities Project for Excellence Inc. (HOPE), *Analysis of Impediments to Fair Housing* (Miami-Dade County, 2015), 33.

25. Alex Biencowe, "The Scott Carver Files: Residents Gather to Memorialize the Past," *Miami Times*, April 27, 2016.

26. *Scott Carver: Then and Now*, produced as part of the Scott-Carver Oral History Project at the University of Miami, available at https://www.youtube.com/watch?v=jKdtErgJTuU.

27. *Housing and Historic Preservation in Overtown* (Office of Civic and Community Engagement, University of Miami, Spring 2015), 3, available at https://civic.miami.edu/housing-initiatives/housing-reports/housing-and-historic-preservation-overtown-report/index.html.

28. *Housing and Historic Preservation in Overtown*, 13–16.

29. More information is available at www.Miami2.org. The "Historic Preservation FAQ" is available at http://www.miami21.org/pdfs/Miami21_FAQ_HistoricPreservation_080820.pdf; Miami-Dade County "Ad-Valorem Tax Exemption" information is available at https://www.miamidade.gov/planning/tax-exemption-ad-valorem.asp. See also the National Park Service's information, "Tax Incentives for Preserving Historic Properties," available at http://www.nps.gov/tps/tax-incentives.htm.

30. *Housing and Historic Preservation in Overtown*.

31. "Preliminary Designation Report, Lawson Edward Thomas Overtown Law Office" (Office of Civic and Community Engagement and ALPHA Plan, University of Miami, 2015); Connolly, *World More Concrete*, 127.

32. *MAP: Miami Affordability Project* (Office of Civic and Community Engagement, University of Miami, 2015), available at http://dx.doi.org/10.17604/M6159M.

33. Diana Elliott, Tanaya Srini, Shiva Kooragayala, and Carl Hedman, *Miami and the State of Low- and Middle-Income Housing: Strategies to Preserve Affordability and Opportunities for the Future*, research report (Washington, DC: Urban Institute, March 2017); *Miami-Dade's Discretionary Surtax Supports Affordable Housing for Low-Income Residents; Recent Changes Will Improve the Program* (Florida Legislature, Office of Program Policy Analysis and Government Accountability, June 2017).

34. More information on "Mapping Decline: St. Louis and the American City" is available at http://mappingdecline.lib.uiowa.edu/map/; more information on "Boston Fair Housing Timeline" is available at https://www.bostonfairhousing.org/timeline/.

35. World Economic Forum, *Global Risks Report 2018*, 13th ed. (Geneva: World Economic Forum, January 17, 2018), accessed January 9, 2019, available at http://www3.weforum.org/docs/WEF_GRR18_Report.pdf; Shimon Wdnowinski, Ronald Bray, Ben P. Kirtman, and Zhaohua Wu, "Increasing Flooding Hazard in Coastal Communities Due to Rising Sea Level: Case Study of Miami Beach, Florida," *Ocean and Coastal Management* 126 (June 2016): 1–8; Union of Concerned Scientists, *Underwater: Rising Seas, Chronic Floods, and the Implications of US Coastal Real Estate*, June 18, 2018, accessed January 9, 2019, available at https://www.ucsusa.org/sites/default/files/attach/2018/06/underwater-analysis-full

-report.pdf; Alex Harris, "Federal Report Says What Florida Already Knows—Climate Change Is Affecting Us Now," *Miami Herald*, November 27, 2018, accessed January 10, 2019, available at https://www.miamiherald.com/news/local/environment/article222086110.html.

36. Pamela Giganti, "Sea Level Rise and Affordable Housing," aired December 16, 2018, on WPBT2 South Florida PBS—Your South Florida; Alex Harris, "Climate Gentrification: Is Sea Rise Turning Miami High Ground into a Hot Commodity?" *Miami Herald*, December 18, 2018, accessed December 20, 2018, available at https://www.miamiherald.com/news/local/environment/article222547640.html?mc_cid=8f0b558f92&mc_eid=%5BUNIQID%5D; Richard Luscombe, "Will Florida Be Lost Forever to the Climate Crisis?" *The Guardian*, April 21, 2020, accessed April 26, 2020, available at https://www.theguardian.com/environment/2020/apr/21/florida-climate-crisis-sea-level-habitat-loss; Patrick Sisson, "As Sea Levels Rise, Miami Neighborhoods Feel Rising Tide of Gentrification," *Curbed*, February 10, 2020, accessed February 15, 2020, available at https://www.curbed.com/2020/2/10/21128496/miami-real-estate-climate-change-gentrification.

37. For discussion of sea level rise, climate gentrification, and their impacts on poor neighborhoods, see Maya Earls, "Extreme Weather: Climate Change Exacerbates Housing Shortage—Report," *E&E News*, August 2019, accessed September 15, 2019, available at www.eenews.net/climatewire/2019/08/06/stories/1060859179; Nadege Green, "As Seas Rise, Miami's Black Communities Fear Displacement from the High Ground," *WLRN*, November 4, 2019, available at www.wlrn.org/post/seas-rise-miami-s-black-communities-fear-displacement-high-ground. Accessed November 15, 2019; Sigrun Kabisch, "Urban Transformations to Pursue Sustainability through Resource Efficiency, Quality of Life and Resilience: A Conceptual Approach," special issue, *Geographia Technica* 14 (2019): 98–107; Jesse M. Keenan, Thomas Hill, and Anurag Gumber, "Climate Gentrification: From Theory to Empiricism in Miami-Dade County, Florida," *Environmental Research Letters* 13, no. 5 (2018), available at iopscience.iop.org/article/10.1088/1748-9326/aabb32; Denise Lu and Christopher Flavelle, "Rising Seas Will Erase More Cities by 2050, New Research Shows," *New York Times*, October 29, 2019; Jenny Staletovich, "Flood Gates, Flood Walls and Home Buyouts: Coming Soon to Miami?" *WLRN*, September 23, 2019, accessed September 25, 2019, available at www.wlrn.org/post/flood-gates-flood-walls-and-home-buyouts-coming-soon-miami#stream/0; Galen Treuer, Kenneth Broad, and Robert Meyer, "Using Simulations to Forecast Homeowner Response to Sea Level Rise in South Florida: Will They Stay or Will They Go?" *Global Environmental Change* 48 (January 2018): 108–118, available at https://doi.org/10.1016/j.gloenvcha.2017.10.008; Bill Weir, "Miami's Little Haiti wasn't a target for developers. Until the seas started to rise," *CNN*, July 12, 2019, accessed July 25, 2019, available at https://www.cnn.com/2019/07/11/us/miami-little-haiti-climate-gentrification-weir-wxc/index.html; Teresa Wiltz, "Climate Change Is Making the Affordable Housing Crunch Worse," Pew Charitable Trusts, August 30, 2019, accessed September 15, 2019,

available at www.pewtrusts.org/en/research-and-analysis/blogs/stateline
/2019/08/30/climate-change-is-making-the-affordable-housing-crunch-worse.

38. After the launch of LAND, the program officer from Citi Community
Development and I wrote an Op-Ed in the *Miami Herald* to encourage elected
officials to use the tool to aggregate vacant and underutilized lots for affordable
housing. Ines Hernandez and Robin F. Bachin, "Vacant Land in Miami-Dade
Could Help Ease Affordable-Housing Crisis," *Miami Herald*, Op-Ed, July 1, 2019,
available at https://www.miamiherald.com/opinion/op-ed/article231061808.html.

39. "To Fight Gentrification, a Brooklyn Pastor Plans to Build 2,100 Apartments," *New York Times*, December 10, 2018, accessed December 15, 2018, available at https://www.nytimes.com/2018/12/10/nyregion/christian-cultural-center
-parking-lot.html.

40. "New Tool Shows Vacant Land across Miami Available for Affordable
Housing," *WLRN Sundial*, April 4, 2019, available at https://www.wlrn.org/post
/new-tool-shows-vacant-land-across-miami-available-affordable-housing; "The
Latest on Vacant, Abandoned, and Deteriorated Properties," *Center for Commun-
ity Progress Newsletter*, April 2019; "Identifying Vacant Land in Miami-Dade
County," CBS 4 This Morning, March 23, 2019; Jared Brey, "Who Will Use the
New Tool Mapping Vacant Land in Miami?" *NextCity*, April 23, 2019; Ben Levine
and Stefania di Mauro-Nava, "Mapping Tool IDs Potential Land for Affordable
Housing," GovTech/MetroLab, November 14, 2019; Rene Rodriguez and Sarah
Moreno, "Developers Say There's No Vacant Land in Miami. This Tool Shows Half
a Billion Square Feet," *Miami Herald*, March 15, 2019.

41. The Center for Community Progress is dedicated to working with local
governments to create land banks that can be used to promote affordable housing, environmental conservation districts, and other equitable public uses of vacant land. See their report, *Vacant Land Stewardship*, accessed May 25, 2022,
available at https://communityprogress.org/resources/vacant-land/.

42. Alana Greer, Gretchen Beesing, and Mileyka Burgos, "New Coalition Takes
Multifaceted Approach to Creating Affordable Housing in Miami—Opinion,"
Miami Herald, August 21, 2019, accessed August 22, 2019, available at https://
www.miamiherald.com/opinion/op-ed/article234232662.html.

43. "Directing the County Mayor or County Mayor's designee to draw upon
the work of the University of Miami's Office of Civic and Community Engagement
and that office's Land Access for Neighborhood Development tool." Miami-Dade
County, *Resolution to Aggregate Land and Create Affordable Housing*, File no.
201204, August 31, 2020, accessed September 15, 2021, available at https://www
.miamidade.gov/govaction/matter.asp?matter=201204&file=true&fileAnalysis
=false&yearFolder=Y2020.

44. Robin D. G. Kelley, *Freedom Dreams: The Black Radical Imagination* (Boston: Beacon, 2002), 8.

45. Sensoy and DiAngelo, "We Are All for Diversity, but . . . ," 561.

5

Engaging Neighborhoods in Climate Change Planning with Public History

Andrew Hurley

An unusually fierce thunderstorm ravaged St. Louis on August 15, 1946, dumping nearly five inches of rain on a city already saturated from two weeks of record-breaking precipitation. Among the unfortunate consequences of the downpour was the death of two boys who were sucked through an open manhole into the Harlem Creek sewer serving the Wells Goodfellow neighborhood on the city's western fringe. The boys had been swimming in the spontaneous river that overtook Ashland Avenue when the subterranean storm and wastewater pipes filled to capacity and overflowed. Their deaths directed citizen protests at public officials for the inadequacy of sewer infrastructure in the area. Thirty-five years earlier, the city had opened this area for residential and industrial development by diverting Harlem Creek, a tributary of the Mississippi River, underground. By the 1940s, urban growth had exceeded the original expectations of engineers, producing sewer backups and flash floods during heavy storms. Local agitation for sewer improvements, however, came to naught; St. Louis voters in the 1950s repeatedly rejected ballot measures to increase sewer capacity in the city's northwest quadrant.[1]

Seventy years later, the site of the 1946 drowning showed little visible change, aside from the wear and tear on aging buildings. But the earlier chain of events—the draining of Harlem Creek, the deaths, the citizen protests—had vanished from public memory. During the 1960s, the neighborhood underwent a demographic transition characterized by the mass flight of white households and the in-migration of African American families.[2] This pattern of dramatic racial succession, which extended to wide swaths of north St. Louis, deprived newly arrived residents of the knowledge necessary for coming to terms with a volatile local hydrology that was becoming increasingly unstable due to climatic changes that brought harsher storms and heavier rains. It also left residents ill-prepared to assess some rather dramatic proposals for the installation of green infrastructure corridors within the Wells Goodfellow neighborhood.

For academic historians searching for ways to participate in public debates and planning related to climate change, the sort of memory repair work called for in St. Louis's Wells Goodfellow neighborhood presents an opportunity for actionable engagement.[3] It also confronts publicly engaged scholars with the challenge of mobilizing citizens around a threat that many dismiss as inconsequential. In interior parts of the United States, skepticism about climate change remains high, and, even where it is accepted as fact, its dangers seem remote. Within distressed urban quarters, climate change typically ranks well below crime, employment, health care, and housing in priority hierarchies.[4] Impoverished historical consciousness constitutes another impediment to serious and sustained civic deliberation, not just in neighborhoods where dramatic population turnover has shortened the reach of collective memory; in older districts close to the urban core, what counts as history is the story of the built environment—its growth, its deterioration, and, in some cases, its regeneration. Historic preservation has valorized vintage architecture as the preeminent expression of local heritage, credentialing the urban form as it took shape in the period of formative growth as the benchmark of authenticity.[5] In this formulation, nature is something that gets displaced by the real forces of history and weather is likewise held apart from history as either ambience or temporary disturbance. To the extent that St. Louis has witnessed renewed investment since 1970, it has occurred primarily in white-majority areas where intact assemblages of nineteenth-century architecture have acquired the appeal of historical authenticity. Conversely, nature's resurgence in the form of overgrown foliage and opportunistic wildlife amid abandoned lots in lower-income African American neighborhoods have foreclosed opportunities to claim a material heritage and craft meaningful stories about the past.

With these obstacles in mind, faculty and students in the Department of History at the University of Missouri–St. Louis (UMSL) partnered with neighborhood associations, planning agencies, and ward-based political organizations to build local historical-knowledge foundations more conducive to the consideration of climate change impacts. These university-community collaborations built on relationships that had been established over the previous twenty years. As community engagement became an increasingly important part of the campus mission, faculty associated with the Department of Political Science, the Department of History, and the Public Policy Administration program received encouragement in sharing their academic expertise with community development corporations and other locally based nonprofits in and around the city of St. Louis. A leadership training academy, capacity-building programs for civic organizations, and the incorporation of academic research within several grant-funded urban revitalization initiatives earned UMSL a positive reputation among civic leaders in many, although not all, St. Louis neighborhoods.

This particular project originated as a component of a statewide National Science Foundation–funded research initiative to prepare Missourians for the impacts of climate change. *The Missouri Transect: Climate, Plants, and Community* coordinated a series of interdisciplinary and thematically related inquiries at multiple universities and nonprofit institutions in Missouri and Arkansas.[6] Our program aimed to improve capacities for climate change preparedness in urban neighborhoods, with St. Louis as the primary setting. It was the only project that employed historical methodologies. Research was organized around neighborhood partnerships that joined discrete constellations of local stakeholders—environmental organizations, public officials, community development corporations, civic and religious leaders—with UMSL faculty and students. Each neighborhood initiative linked a collaboratively crafted research agenda with some culminating planning exercise. Over a five-year period, stretching from 2015 through 2019, seven neighborhoods with varying demographic profiles participated.

Despite methodological variations across these collaborations, some general practices pervaded the entire project. For each neighborhood partnership, paid graduate assistants, supervised by faculty in the Department of History, assumed responsibility for compiling historical resource packages that encouraged residents and activists to expand their understanding of local heritage so that it better aligned with the imperatives of sustainability planning. At the core of this historical revisionism lay an acknowledgment that urban places are produced through the perpetual interaction of nature and human action. The concept of a community landscape—a set of evolving relationships among people and the urban environment that are perceived and experienced in the context of shared values and social interactions—guided the selection of historical materials shared with our neighborhood partners as well as the methods we used to engage residents with this material.[7] Our overriding concern for alerting communities to the possible impacts of climate change accounted for the inclusion of historical weather developments in our conceptualization of local landscapes, making our approach particularly distinctive. In addition, our work with local communities combined archival research with lived experience. In several neighborhoods, we employed citizen-produced photo narrations of meaningful local places to illuminate urban neighborhoods as community landscapes.[8] These photo narrations, along with other forms of citizen input, fed a variety of participatory planning processes. While none of these planning processes took climate change as their exclusive focus, the collaborative reinterpretation of urban places as community landscapes created openings for considering climate in discussions about urban development.

Interpreting Neighborhoods as Community Landscapes

The idea of a community landscape flows from a rich academic and professional literature on cultural landscapes, which can be described as a way of seeing and knowing that finds meaning in the multilayered accretion of human adaptations to dynamic natural environments.[9] Within the field of historic preservation, this theoretical construct has been employed to develop protection strategies for sites that juxtapose natural and built elements such as seashores, country estates, parks, and gardens. The concept has rarely found application in urban districts, and, in several crucial aspects, the term is inappropriate for places where social diversity and demographic volatility preclude a unified culture or a traditional way of life. The term "community landscape" preserves the emphasis on commingled natural and built environments while simultaneously highlighting the contingent social and environmental relationships that foster informal social cooperation, collective civic enterprise, and environmental stewardship in cities. Much like a cultural landscape then, a community landscape accommodates the inclusion of nature in the manufacture of local heritage, thereby providing neighborhoods with a more expansive historical palette to draw from in devising preservation and design guidelines. Along with leading cultural landscape theorists, we believe that its features can best be discerned through the eyes and voices of those who inhabit its spaces.

In our overtures to prospective partners and in conversations with local participants, we presented project goals and methods through a community-landscapes framework, eschewing academic terminology. We explained our intention to not simply recover and document local observations and sentiments about place but foster a more environmentally and socially inclusive understanding of how neighborhoods functioned in the past and how they might enlarge their capacities for resilience in the face of external disruptions, including those caused by global warming.

Making a Place for Weather in Community Landscapes

Weather, like other facets of the natural environment, must figure prominently in articulations of community landscapes if urban stakeholders are to anticipate the local impacts of climate change. Unfortunately, with an emphasis on catastrophic, planetary-scale, and long-range scenarios, climate science and derived media coverage have elicited skepticism or indifference among segments of the U.S. population. Educating communities about weather patterns and events that have altered their immediate surroundings can make climate change a more meaningful and relevant concept.[10] Climate scientists acknowledge that the buildup of atmospheric carbon, while forcing an overall hike in world temperatures, will have widely different impacts on regional weather systems. Some places will get much hotter, while others will experience only modest increases in average temperatures. For some people, the critical issue will be water shortages and drought, while others will contend with more frequent and more devastating floods.[11] Cynicism about climate science becomes harder to sustain when confronted with historical data confirming meteorological instability, especially when the data emanates from indigenous and trusted sources.

To this end, student researchers distilled and disseminated rainfall and temperature readings that had been collected by weather stations at scattered locations across the St. Louis metropolitan area since the 1870s. This data was sufficiently voluminous and fine grained to capture trends spanning multiple decades. Drawing conclusions from the charts and graphs we constructed was not always a straightforward matter. Significant variations in the average temperature and precipitation from year to year along with El Niño and La Niña cycles complicated the discernment of smooth linear trends. Nonetheless, a reasonable reading of meteorological evidence from St. Louis area weather stations suggested a historical trend toward warmer and wetter weather. It also suggested increasing weather volatility. Looking at the incidence of very hot weather (days above one hundred degrees Fahrenheit), one detects a notable uptick in the most recent decade (2007–2016) compared with the previous thirty years. (See Figure 5.1.) Likewise, heavy rainfalls, measured by the number of days with an excess of 2.5 inches of precipitation, indicate an increase of heavy storm activity in recent decades. (See Figure 5.2.)

Meteorological patterns offer little guidance for community planning unless their impact on people's lives becomes apparent. A more environmentally inclusive historical consciousness is helpful in this regard. Probing the historical record for weather anomalies, for example, offers historians a set of episodes through which to explore the intersection between natural phenomena and social behavior. Investigating social responses to extreme weather events may be particularly instructive when those episodes have receded from public memory. By incorporating extreme weather events into local historical narratives, public historians can assist local planning efforts by alerting communities to vulnerabilities and helping them understand the dynamic relationship between environmental change and urban development. Ideally, an enlightened citizenry will be better equipped

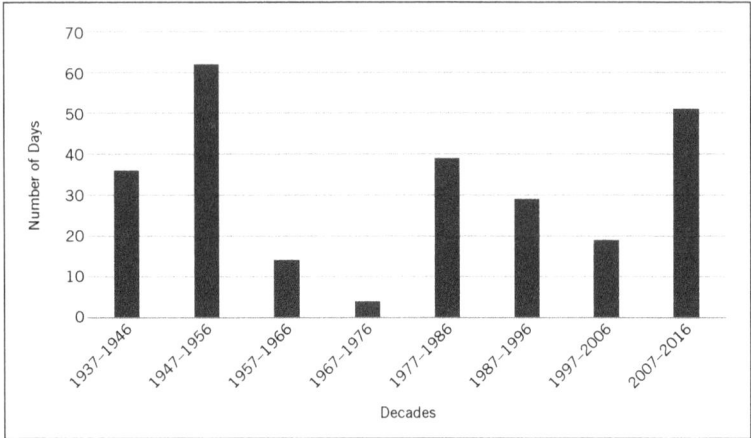

Figure 5.1 Number of days maximum temperature of 100 degrees F or over, Lambert Airport Weather Station, St. Louis, Missouri, 1937–2016. (Midwest Regional Climate Center, cli-MATE web tool, available at https://mrcc .purdue.edu/CLIMATE/)

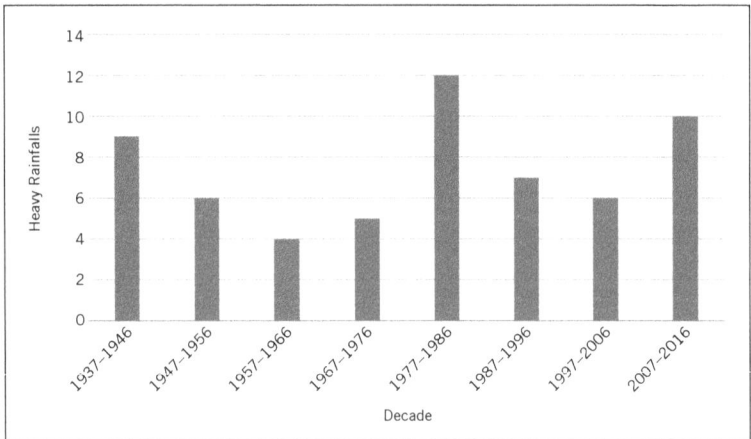

Figure 5.2 Number of one day rainfall events, 2.5 inches and above, per decade, Lambert Airport Weather Station, St. Louis, Missouri, 1937–2016. (Midwest Regional Climate Center, cli-MATE web tool, available at https://mrcc.purdue.edu/CLIMATE/)

to identify profitable points of proactive intervention. Recognizing the limitations of bureaucratic-technological responses to climate change threats, proponents of urban resilience increasingly emphasize the necessity for communities to strategize and act on their own behalf. The application of historical research suggested here aligns with emerging understandings of resilience by building social capital at the neighborhood scale.[12]

Like most cities, St. Louis has had its share of extreme weather episodes with tragic and destructive effects on sizable segments of the population. Most of these, such as the 1946 rainstorm recalled at the start of this essay, have disappeared from local historical narratives, which tend to chart changes that have resulted from deliberate alterations to the built environment. One factor contributing to their omission from the historical record is their perceived irrelevance to contemporary urban conditions. Since the early twentieth century, successful risk mitigation strategies have lessened the human suffering and physical destruction associated with violent weather episodes. A variety of adaptive innovations—protective levees, sewer systems, insurance programs, medical advances, efficient heating and cooling technologies, and advances in meteorology—have immunized large sectors of the population against severe impacts. A closer look at the social consequences of extreme environmental disturbances, however, reveals persistent and emergent vulnerabilities lurking beneath a veneer of safety and security.[13]

Aggregate reductions in damage and mortality have masked the perpetuation and, in some cases, the amplification of more selective and localized patterns of destruction. Heat waves offer a case in point. Prior to the advent of air-conditioning, excessive heat was an equal opportunity killer; during the first half of the twentieth century atypically hot summers consumed hundreds of lives, with no discernible socioeconomic bias. From the 1970s onward, households fortunate enough to enjoy artificially cooled air have thus benefited compared to those either too poor to afford it or unwilling to use it. This distinction shows up clearly in data on heat wave mortality. Since the widespread adoption of mechanical air-conditioning, in the 1970s and 1980s, heat wave deaths have skewed disproportionately toward poor, elderly, and African American populations. This disturbing phenomenon was brought to national attention during a 1995 heat wave in Chicago

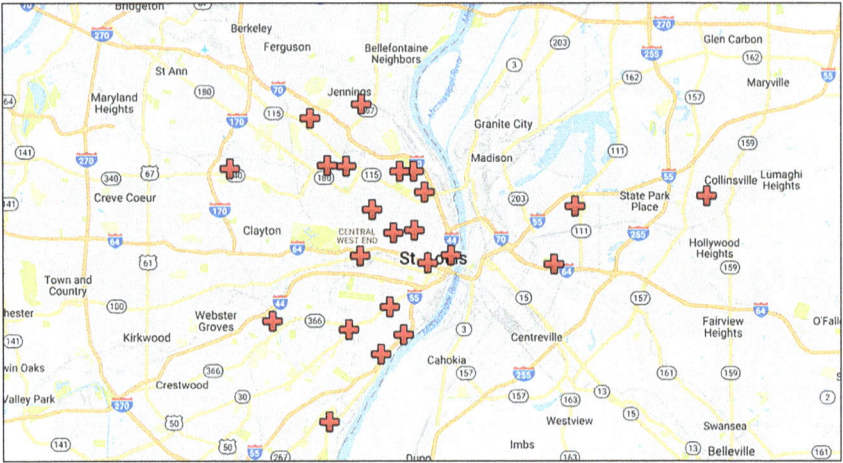

Figure 5.3 Distribution of St. Louis area heat wave deaths, in the summer of 2012. (*St. Louis Post Dispatch*)

that claimed over seven hundred victims, but it was no less evident in outbreaks of intense heat in other cities, including St. Louis.[14] A map of St. Louis depicting the geographic distribution of deaths attributed to heatstroke in 2012 provided visual confirmation of these inequities, with most of the casualties appearing in predominantly African American and low-income districts of north St. Louis city and north St. Louis County. (See Figure 5.3.) When working with communities within this corridor we used this map as a way to initiate discussions about the health risks associated with warming trends.

A slightly different pattern of social harm arises from the malfunction of protective technologies. Postmortem investigations of Hurricane Katrina in New Orleans quickly arrived at the conclusion that the tremendous loss of life and property was not solely the result of the heavy rains and storm surge but rather the failure of levees to withstand the intense pressure of water coursing through confined channels.[15] Infrastructure failure conspired with racially segregated settlement patterns to concentrate the damage in the low-lying, low-income neighborhoods of the Ninth Ward. The poor grades assigned to a multitude of U.S. cities on a series of infrastructure report cards extend the potential for tragedy far beyond New Orleans.[16] St. Louis has thus far averted catastrophic damage on the scale of Katrina, but the frequency of localized infrastructure breakdown in the form of storm-induced power outages, road washouts, and sewer overflows gives cause for alarm. Since 1993, the metropolitan area has suffered eleven summer storm-related blackouts affecting at least fifty thousand customers.[17] To bring this information down to the neighborhood scale we developed a weather-event archive with historical documents and images mapped to specific locations in the city of St. Louis. This digital repository invited residents to learn how extreme weather events have interrupted critical services such as transportation, communication, and electric power. Although much has been made about the utility of GIS mapping for graphically exposing significant relationships and patterns within massive data sets, our application highlights another benefit for public historians—allowing users to quickly locate information about their particular neighborhoods.

Vital to the enterprise of informed neighborhood planning is an understanding of how drastically shifting land uses have mediated the impact of weather and climate on urban communities. Urban history narratives privileging changes in the built environment have deprived communities of vital information about aspects of their natural heritage and contributed to widespread ignorance about critical ecological services that have been lost to time. Environmentally inclusive maps, drawings, and written observations, from the early and mid-nineteenth century, depict much of St. Louis as filled with streams, ponds, fields, farms, orchards, and groves that coexisted with the artifacts of human settlement—country roads, roadside inns, country estates, quarries, brickworks, and rail depots. These natural features were rarely, if ever, remnants of untouched wilderness. Indeed, the grassy prairies encountered by the area's first European settlers were products of regular burning and clearing undertaken by previous generations of Native Americans. The establishment of truck farms, the planting of residential street trees, and the creation of bucolic parks continued the process of reconfiguring nature as an accessory of human settlement. In presenting these lost landscapes to current residents, we hoped to provide a more expansive foundation for the construction of local heritage. We also took special care to demonstrate how landscape change altered the social impacts of extreme weather disturbances.

Public swimming and outdoor sleeping were two popular strategies for moderating the effects of exceedingly hot weather that became less viable during the latter part of the twentieth century. Starting in the nineteenth century and proceeding more systematically in the twentieth century, urban development eliminated many of the natural water bodies that once offered respite from blistering temperatures. Engineers converted free flowing rivers into piped sewers and real estate developers drained ponds and sloughs that stood in the way of new construction. To some extent the creation of neighborhood playgrounds and parks with free swimming pools in the early twentieth century compensated for the disappearance of natural water. Yet, budgetary constraints and problems of civil disorder led to the closing of many of these pools in the final decades of the century.[18]

During the early decades of the twentieth century, St. Louisans seeking relief from scorching temperatures at night routinely ventured from their homes to nearby swaths of comfortable vegetation that served as bedding. City parks filled with throngs of drowsy men, women, and children who sought the regenerative effects of vegetation cooled by evapotranspiration. Those who lacked nearby parks sought whatever green space they could find. Newspapers from the 1930s reported dozens of people sleeping on the planted strips abutting recently constructed automobile parkways. By the 1980s, however, fear of crime, abetted by diminishing numbers of sleepers, eliminated this practice. Indeed, some households without air-conditioning reportedly shut their windows at night during an intense hot spell in the summer of 1980 to prevent the entry of burglars.[19]

The incremental replacement of vegetation and natural hydrology with buildings, pavement, and engineered infrastructure also magnified the impact of excessive heat and heavy storms. As scientists have known for many years, the materials used in constructing the built urban environment—concrete, steel, glass, asphalt—absorb solar radiation and store it as heat that slowly dissipates into the surrounding surface atmosphere, raising temperatures several degrees above those in the surrounding countryside.[20] For each neighborhood in which we worked, we compiled maps and aerial images to show changes in the percentage of acreage covered with vegetation along with visualizations showing the urban heat island effect. These visualizations, along with other materials on landscape change, pushed our audiences to reassess a dominant narrative in urban history that charts progress through additions to the built environment.

Neighborhood Place Stories

For public historians working with specific communities in specific places, oral history has proven to be a powerful tool for giving collaborators agency in the production of usable pasts. New digital technologies have enabled researchers to supplement spoken narration with other media, including photographs.[21] Applied to the enterprise of climate change planning, such multimedia forms of documentation can be useful for capturing local knowledge and sorting out the myriad concerns, desires, and circumstances that shape people's relationship to the environment. Through the sharing of local perspectives, communities may begin the process of revaluing places to better align collective goals with the potential impacts of highly variable weather. Where resources and time allowed, we used our accumulated meteorological and archival data to encourage personal reflections on landscape change. Our Neighborhood Place Stories exercise invited participants to review prepared packets of local historical information and then record photo narrations about meaningful places in their neighborhood with the PixStori mobile app. A series of open-ended cues guided residents in the selection of locations that spoke to matters of heritage, ecology, community identity, and neighborhood transformation. We archived over four hundred of these Place Stories on a website, where they map community landscapes of vulnerability, accomplishment, pride, and hope.[22] A brief selection of these contributions reveals linkages among weather, landscape, and social behavior that shape community responses to the prospect of climate change and incline communities toward certain adaptive interventions.

On a hot August morning in 2016, D'Vion Harris trained his iPad on a fire hydrant near his home in the Wells Goodfellow neighborhood to highlight the lengths to which children in the neighborhood went to find relief from scorching temperatures in the aftermath of swimming pool and community center closures:

> Sometimes when it's hot they cut the fire hydrants on to give the kids somewhere to play or cool off. Because there's no boys or

girls clubs or programs where the kids can go to cool off or play games, so they just play in the streets and cut the fire hydrants on, and that's how the kids cool off . . . the streets fill up with water and then the kids come out and play in their trunks as if they're at a swimming pool.[23]

Unplugging fire hydrants is illegal in the city of St. Louis and the St. Louis Fire Department strongly discourages such behavior because it reduces the water pressure that firefighters rely on to produce powerful hose spray.[24] Harris's comments, however, were not intended as a rebuke to the youngsters. Rather, he wanted to underscore the dire need for safe and reliable cooling amenities, especially for youths. His narration could thus be read as both descriptive and aspirational. Indeed, a variety of Place Stories alluding to the cooling properties of water proved useful in jump-starting community conversations about the local impact of warming temperatures. In one such forum, Harris's Place Story sparked discussion about creative ways to bring water features to neighborhood youths, including temporary waterslides and portable wading pools retrofitted into pickup trucks.

Alerted to the ecological services provided by urban vegetation, many Place Stories participants wanted to talk about green spaces in their neighborhood. What emerged powerfully from the compilation of recordings was their overwhelming tendency to assess these green spaces in terms of the social behavior they nurtured. The perceived social value of green space ranged widely depending on the type of green space selected (e.g., park, garden, prairie planting, lawn) and the neighborhood context. Anxiety about green space was most notable in neighborhoods where economic disinvestment led to a profusion of abandoned and unkempt lots. Paul Brown described one such parcel across the street from his house. Like many residents of the Wells Goodfellow neighborhood, he filtered his landscape impressions through a preoccupation with crime and safety.

There used to be houses in that area in that empty lot all the way up to the [existing] building. Now there's just an empty lot with a lot of overgrowth that comes. And the city will come out and cut it down maybe once or twice a year because the overgrowth grows taller than I am. And all you'll see is the rodents come out and the possums and big rats and the dogs and stuff and people tend to come and throw their unwanted stuff there. . . . It's really kind of scary at night to be just sitting out here because you can't see nothing if you're not watching. People can walk right up on you and come out of the bushes. My girls don't come out at night.[25]

Place Stories like the one authored by Brown reminded green space designers that characteristics of vegetation like the density and height of foliage were just as important to communities as their aesthetic or ecological attributes. They also underscored the critical issue of maintenance and upkeep in the aftermath of cultivation.

Some of the most revealing Place Stories demonstrated how the acquisition of new historical information altered people's perceptions of landscape features by embedding them in adjusted narratives. For Edna Sanford, the revelation about Harlem Creek's previous presence in Wells Goodfellow prompted a reassessment of urban green space. In a Place Story recorded in the summer of 2016, she spoke about a detention basin recently installed along the former creek bed to capture excess stormwater runoff.

Ten years ago there was a major flood down in this area where it washed out a lot of people's homes, cars, and killed many animals back in the days and to learn now what I know that it was back in those days we didn't know at that time that there was a creek back in that area. We always thought that Metropolitan Sewer thought that it was backed, that they didn't ever clean it. And it was backed up rugs and old sewage things that they needed to have cleaned and never got around to it. And now to learn that that's what it used to be, that it was a creek that washed us away ten years ago down here and now look how beautiful it is.[26]

One of the goals of the Place Stories exercise was to see how the presentation of neighborhood landscape histories might expose places where heritage and sustainability assets converged. In the Walnut Park East neighborhood, memory and local identity added complementary layers of value to the perceived cooling benefits of street trees. John W mused:

> The best thing I love about my street . . . is to keep cool in the summertime, we have a lot of trees on the block and thank God for them. Just don't cut them all down because when it's hot that's where we go to get shelter and a little peace of mind. Some say it's oak trees, maple trees. In my yard I had two pine trees but we cut one down. I didn't see any walnut trees, which is what this neighborhood was named from, walnut for Walnut Park, but a lot of different trees . . . (pauses to reflect) . . . we do have walnut trees in my neighborhood because we used to take the walnuts that were in the hull and throw them at each other for fun.[27]

Jacque Foster, the pastor of a socially diverse congregation in the Shaw neighborhood, provided another example of a cherished green space that simultaneously strengthened community identity and provided critical ecological services. (See Figure 5.4.)

> This is the lot attached to Compton Heights Christian Church at Flora and Grand. This lot is always green space and will always be green space because of the agreement when Compton Heights built at this place. I think this is significant space for the community as over the years it has become a place where people gather when they come to receive food and assistance at the food pantry here. It's a place where people gather and sometimes find shade under the trees on the benches in the heat of summer when they're waiting at the bus stop down by the sidewalk. It's a place where the congregation and others in the community have held picnics and ice cream socials and game times where Isaiah 58 ministries gathers with those who have family fun days for children in the community. So this is a significant space that will always be open and green space and I believe it's valuable as that.[28]

Some of the most valuable Place Stories for planning purposes articulated explicit proposals for community action. After photographing

Figure 5.4 Church lot. (Missouri Place Stories project)

a garbage-strewn alley, Antwan Pope recommended the deployment
of cleanup brigades throughout the Wells Goodfellow neighborhood
following heavy storms:

> One of the things that needs to take place over here and we were
> talking about the alleys. Maybe that would help with some of
> the sewer districts and the water flow. For example, if you go
> up the alleys and see a lot of the weeds and trees and trash and
> all of the stuff washes down and it ends up going into the sewers.

And what happens with the sewers is that MSD has to constantly keep cleaning them out. If we would just have alley clean ups, like a team sweep, or something like that, that would be great. I think that the alleys need to be cleaned; trash, weeds, and stuff like that need to picked up. After these bad storms we get all these branches and leaves that eventually run down into the sewer system and it clogs up a lot of stuff. So, that's why a lot of stuff is getting flooded around here and we just need to be better at keeping the alleys a little cleaner than what they are.[29]

From Public History to Community Planning

Translating historically informed insights into more durable urban interventions required a set of skills that we lacked as public historians, thus necessitating more formalized collaborations with civic activists and planning professionals in the final stages of each neighborhood project. From the outset, we understood that our chances of producing tangible outcomes hinged on the quality of the relationships we built with community leaders and organizations. Initially, we targeted neighborhood associations as potential partners, believing that they were best equipped to mobilize large numbers of residents and develop action plans based on the collective analysis of our findings. Our collaboration with the Shaw Neighborhood Improvement Association (SNIA), beginning in the summer of 2015, suggested some of the ways that collaboratively produced landscape histories might prod communities to mitigate the destructive impacts of climate change. At a meeting with SNIA officers and members in May 2016, several hours were devoted to the discussion of the Place Stories recorded in the Shaw neighborhood. One surprising revelation was the extent to which neighborhood identity and heritage revolved around trees. Street trees, meticulously planted by the neighborhood's original developers, created impressive canopies that gave the Shaw neighborhood a distinctive appearance and simultaneously offered cooling services that enabled people to spend time outdoors socializing in hot weather. Many of these trees, however, were threatened by the scourge of the emerald ash borer that was relentlessly making its way across the continent toward St. Louis. To mitigate the loss of an asset whose value would only increase with hotter temperatures, SNIA leadership decided to launch an inventory of vulnerable trees and encourage their replacement with more sturdy species.

The difficulty in getting our partner organization in an adjacent neighborhood to sponsor a similar community forum and the lack of follow-through on the part of SNIA convinced us that voluntary neighborhood associations lacking an urgent incentive to grapple with climate change threats made for uninspired partners. Subsequently, we sought out community partners that were already involved in planning exercises likely to benefit from a consideration of climate change impacts. Beginning in the spring of 2016, we teamed up with the city of St. Louis Urban Vitality and Ecology Initiative (UVE), which was coordinating the community-driven design of green infrastructure installations in neighborhoods afflicted with high levels or property abandonment. Like many Rust Belt "legacy" cities, St. Louis suffers from a bloated inventory of vacant and derelict properties that drain municipal resources and elicit the wrath of neighbors due to the perceived and real effects on crime, real estate values, and quality of life. The crisis of property vacancy in St. Louis has given rise to several planning initiatives aimed at shrinking and consolidating the built environment through strategic demolition and green space installation. Through the UMSL Department of History's partnership with the UVE and membership in its successor organization, the Green City Coalition, public history was formally embedded within the array of workshops, forums, and public events that ultimately produced design proposals. UVE leadership saw the Place Stories exercise as a way to gauge levels of popular attachment to green spaces and the historic built environment prior to the start of formal community engagement events. Under UVE's direction, the digital Place Stories collected in the earliest stages of neighborhood activity were used to spark conversation at a series of neighborhood meetings along with historical landscape data.

In the Wells Goodfellow neighborhood, collective interrogation of these resources helped galvanize community support for a green corridor that would simultaneously manage stormwater runoff and provide a neighborhood amenity through the creation of orchards, gardens, walkways, and an amphitheater. The area's history of severe flooding and the prospect of increasingly violent storms convinced

Figure 5.5 Local residents and Green City Coalition volunteers gather for the unveiling of a historic marker at the edge of the Wells Goodfellow green space corridor in November 2019. (Photo by author)

citizens of the need for more effective rainwater absorption. In addition, the extraction of local historical knowledge influenced certain elements of the green space design. Several Place Stories in this neighborhood showcased a corner liquor store that, despite its unassuming appearance, earned the esteem of local residents for the civic beneficence of its proprietor and its status as one of the neighborhood's oldest African American–owned businesses. These Place Stories sparked discussion and deliberation about how to configure design features to strengthen this community asset. In the final design, the liquor store became a focal point of active-use portions of the green space such as an urban orchard and a walking path. A consensus also emerged around the desirability of signage to commemorate the area's history, thereby preserving ties to the past within a radically transformed landscape. (See Figure 5.5.)

Reflections on University-Community Partnerships in Urban Neighborhoods

Five years of collaborative engagement with a variety of civic organizations, advocacy groups, and government agencies gave us ample opportunity to reflect on some of the rewards and challenges associated with university-sponsored, activist-oriented, public history in urban settings. As representatives of a major research university, UMSL faculty and students navigated an uneven terrain of community expectations and assumptions about mixing academic enterprise with neighborhood affairs. The task of securing community buy-in was further complicated by our predetermined thematic focus on climate change, a low-priority issue for neighborhood-scale organizations. By emphasizing highly localized aspects of environmental and climatological change and tying these dynamics to matters of more immediate concern, such as property vacancy and green space creation, we managed to attain a measure of relevance. Through trial and error, this approach ultimately nudged community organizations toward greater consideration of climate change impacts in the activities and projects already falling within their purview. If these results fell short of the full-scale mobilization that drastic climatic changes may require, they nonetheless gave communities an opportunity to assess environmental threats in the context of equally urgent problems. To the extent that our work introduced novel frameworks for understanding and assessing urban development, our project exemplified the transformative power of public history.

Forging partnerships based on trust and active cooperation proved more delicate and sometimes required a level of community involvement that went beyond the scope of prescribed research and outreach activities. The barriers to congenial university-community relations were particularly daunting in low-income neighborhoods of color that had experienced less-than-satisfactory outcomes in previous interactions with academic researchers. The presence of three major research universities in the St. Louis area, each with a growing interest in community outreach to underserved low-income populations, produced a sense of academic fatigue among residents of frequently targeted neighborhoods. In the most severe cases, community leaders felt betrayed by transient academics who depended on the generosity of local residents without producing reciprocal benefits. This perspective was expressed forcefully in conversations with a political representative of the Wells Goodfellow neighborhood who demanded, prior to endorsing the project, that the Place Stories exercise produce something beyond useful knowledge that residents could employ directly to spark revitalization. To satisfy this request, we pledged to compile selected Place Stories in a neighborhood history booklet that could be distributed to potential investors.

As our work in Wells Goodfellow unfolded, we realized how important it was, from an ethical as well as a project efficacy standpoint, to create goodwill by immersing ourselves comprehensively in community affairs and leveraging additional university resources for the benefit of our community partners. Attending social gatherings, delivering updates at ward meetings, providing local nonprofit organizations with student interns, and offering garden clubs the expertise of horticulturalists from the university's extension program demonstrated a deep and extended commitment. When the director of an organization that assisted substance abusers requested a university presence at its weekly rehabilitation intake sessions, we did our best to supply students and faculty, even though the activity had little to do with climate change or urban history. Although university participation did not contribute directly to project goals, the weekly event gave us an opportunity to connect with a segment of the residential population we might not have otherwise encountered. For the nonprofit organization, the university presence was valuable for provoking educational aspirations among its constituents. Expanding community interactions beyond the scope of our authorized grant obligations required certain sacrifices on the part of university personnel. The work was uncompensated in terms of both monetary and academic remuneration. Students performed these extracurricular services on a purely voluntary basis and faculty members contributed their time without any expectation that these activities would appear in annual accomplishment reports. While we never received any pushback from university administrators and our work was often appreciated, the absence of formal recognition mechanisms meant that recruitment of university personnel primarily invoked people's feelings of social responsibility.

For students who devoted time to the project, primarily as paid graduate research assistants, the assignments took them out of the archives and away from their computer screens into the sometimes uncomfortable realm of face-to-face interpersonal exchange. Graduate students in our Museums, Heritage, and Public History program as well as our MA History program worked intensively on the project for durations ranging from one to four semesters as paid research assistants. Reliance on a relatively small number of students afforded us the luxury of careful vetting to ensure that staffing advanced project goals as well as student recruitment and retention goals. African Americans, who constitute almost half the population of the city of St. Louis and 18 percent of the wider metropolitan area, are underrepresented in the UMSL History program. Work performed in African American neighborhoods proved appealing to African American students to whom we gave preference in hiring decisions. Although white research assistants outnumbered Black research assistants, two to one, the project indicated that public history, for all the benefits it bring to communities, can also contribute to the diversification of academic programs.

NOTES

1. "This August, One of the City's Wettest in 109 Years, More Rain Coming," *St. Louis Post Dispatch*, August 14, 1946, 1; "Torrential Rain Maroons 50 Here," *St. Louis Post Dispatch*, August 15, 1946, 1; "Heavy Damage in Record 8.98 Inch Rain; 2 Missing; 400 Marooned on East Side," *St. Louis Post Dispatch*, August 16, 1948, 1; Horner and Shifrin Engineers, St. Louis Sewer and Drainage Study, 1950, folder 109, box 8, St. Louis Metropolitan League of Women Voters Collection, State Historical Society of Missouri, St. Louis, Missouri.

2. U.S. Bureau of the Census, *Census of Population and Housing*, accessed July 6, 2015, available at https://www.census.gov/prod/www/decennial.html.

3. For an example of recent interest in climate change issues among public historians, see Cathy Stanton, ed., *Public History in a Changing Climate*, Public History Commons of the National Council on Public History, March 2014, accessed July 8, 2015, available at http://ncph.org/phc/social/public-history-in-a-changing-climate-march-2014.0.

4. Yale School of Forestry and Environmental Studies, Project on Climate Change Communication, "Yale Climate Opinion Maps,", accessed July 6, 2015, available at https://climatecommunication.yale.edu/visualizations-data/ycom-us//. In a recent survey of community residents in one inner-city St. Louis district, the category of "air, water, energy, sanitation, and environment," ranked last among nine choices in a list of planning priorities. RISE Community De-

velopment, "Kick-Off Event Takeaways, Gravois-Jefferson Historic Neighborhoods Plan," November 10, 2016, in author's possession.

5. Richard Longstreth, "Architectural History and the Practice of Historic Preservation in the United States," *Journal of the Society of Architectural Historians* 58 (September 1999): 326–333; David Hamer, *History in Urban Places: The Historic Districts of the United States* (Columbus: Ohio State Press, 1998), 25–53; Robin Elisabeth Datel, "Preservation and a Sense of Orientation for American Cities," *Geographical Review* 75 (April 1985): 125–141.

6. National Science Foundation, Experimental Program to Stimulate Competitive Research, "The Missouri Transect: Climate, Plants, and Community," Award Number IIA-1355406. Under the auspices of this award, the following students were supervised by Andrew Hurley: Lauren Cooley, Paige Fensterman Ballard, Shuron Jones, Mark Loehrer, and Eliza Murray,. Supplemental funding was provided by a Creating Whole Communities, University of Missouri–St. Louis, research grant. Under the auspices of this grant, Rebecca Rea and Brenda Thacker were supervised by Maris Gillette and Andrew Hurley.

7. Maris Gillette and Andrew Hurley, "Vision, Voice, and the Community Landscape: The Missouri Place Stories Pilot Project," *Landscape and Planning* 173 (May 2018): 1–8.

8. See the Missouri Place Stories project, accessed June 1, 2019, available at https://placestories.missouriepscor.org/.

9. The literature on cultural landscapes and cultural landscape history is vast and the following references include only a small sample of relevant works: Maggie Roe and Ken Taylor, eds., *New Cultural Landscapes* (London: Routledge, 2014); Richard Longstreth, ed., *Cultural Landscapes: Balancing Nature and Heritage in Preservation Practice* (Minneapolis: University of Minnesota Press, 2006); Arnold R. Alanen and Robert Z. Melnick, eds., *Preserving Cultural Landscapes in America* (Baltimore, MD: Johns Hopkins University Press, 2000).

10. In adopting this localized perspective, we followed those scholars in the field that have advocated microscale interventions as best suited to the skills that public historians bring to projects. See, for example, Leah Glaser, "Let's Sustain This: A Review," *Public Historian* 36 (August 2014): 130–144; David Glassberg, "Place, Memory, and Climate Change," *Public Historian* 36 (August 2014): 17–30; Georgina H. Endfield, "Exploring Particularity: Vulnerability, Resilience, and Memory in Climate Change Discourses," *Environmental History* 19 (April 2014): 303–310.

11. Jerry M. Melillo, Terese (T. C.) Richmond, and Gary W. Yohe, eds., *Climate Change Impacts in the United States: The Third National Climate Assessment*, U.S. Global Change Research Program, 2014, accessed July 15, 2015, doi:10.7930 /J0Z31WJ2.

12. Adriana X. Sanchez, Jeroen van der Heijden, and Paul Osmond, "The City Politics of an Urban Age: Urban Resilience, Conceptualisations, and Policies," *Palgrave Communications* 4, no. 1 (March 2018), doi:10.1057/s41599-018-0074-z;

Judith Rodin, *The Resilience Dividend: Being Strong in a World Where Things Go Wrong* (New York: Public Affairs, 2014).

13. On this phenomenon, more generally, see Scott Gabriel Knowles, *The Disaster Experts: Mastering Risk in Modern America* (Philadelphia: University of Pennsylvania, 2011).

14. Eric Klinenberg, *Heat Wave: A Social Autopsy of Disaster* (Chicago: University of Chicago Press, 2002); C. A. Bridger, "Mortality in St. Louis, Missouri, during Heat Waves in 1936, 1953, 1954, 1955, and 1966: Coroner's Cases," *Environmental Research* 12 (August 1976): 38–48; T. Stephen Jones et. al., "Morbidity and Mortality Associated with the July 1980 Heat Wave in St. Louis and Kansas City, Mo.," *Journal of the American Medical Association* 247 (June 25, 1982): 3327–3331. It should be noted that air-conditioning generates its own distinct hazards. The increase in outbreaks of Legionnaire's disease in the United States has been attributed largely to the malfunction of air-conditioning systems in large buildings. Winnie Hu and Noah Remnick, "Belated Look at Top Suspect in an Outbreak," *New York Times*, August 5, 2015, A1.

15. John McQuaid and Mark Schleifstein, *Path of Destruction: The Devastation of New Orleans and the Coming Age of Superstorms* (New York: Little, Brown, 2006).

16. American Society for Civil Engineers, "Report Card for America's Infrastructure," Infrastructure Report Card (website), 2017, accessed February 8, 2018, available at https://www.infrastructurereportcard.org/.

17. *St. Louis Post Dispatch*, 1993–2015, Lexis-Nexis Academic search, July 17, 2015.

18. Deborah Peterson, "Many Pools Won't Open in Time for Swimmers to Take Holiday Plunge," *St. Louis Post Dispatch*, May 23, 1998, 9; Eric Stern, "County Parks Will Shorten Pool Season, End Horseback Patrols in Budget Cuts," *St. Louis Post Dispatch*, C1; Phillip O'Connor, "Pool Pivotal in Race Relations City's Decision in '49 to Integrate Swimming Pools Sparked Violence That Triggered Change," *St. Louis Post Dispatch*, June 21, 2009, A1.

19. Tim O'Neil, "A Look Back: Searing Heat Wave Killed 153 in St. Louis in 1980," *St. Louis Post Dispatch*, July 10, 2011.

20. Anne Whiston Spirn, *The Granite Garden: Urban Nature and Human Design* (New York: Basic Books, 1984), 52–55.

21. Kathleen C. Sitter, "Taking a Closer Look at Photovoice as a Participatory Action Research Method," *Journal of Progressive Human Services* 28 (January 2017): 36–48.

22. More information is available at http://placestories.missouriepscor.org/.

23. D'Vion Harris, "Fire Hydrant," 2016, Missouri Place Stories, accessed June 1, 2019, available at http://placestories.missouriepscor.org/.

24. Emily Rasinski, "St. Louis Kids Keep Cool in Spray from Hydrant," *St. Louis Post Dispatch*, July 22, 2011, available at http://www.stltoday.com/news/local/metro/photos-st-louis-kids-keep-cool-in-spray-from-hydrant/article_ae

998f92-b468-11e0-a881-001a4bcf6878.html; Carolyn Tuft, "Child's Play Could Lead to Fine, Jail," *St. Louis Post Dispatch*, July 9, 1994, 1.

25. Paul Brown, "Empty Lot," 2016, Missouri Place Stories, accessed June 1, 2019, available at http://placestories.missouriepscor.org/.

26. Edna Sanford, "Ashland Flooding," 2016, Missouri Place Stories, accessed June 1, 2019, available at http://placestories.missouriepscor.org/.

27. John W., "Plover Avenue Trees," 2017, Missouri Place Stories, accessed June 1, 2019, available at http://placestories.missouriepscor.org/.

28. Jacque Foster, "Church Lot," 2015, Missouri Place Stories, available at http://placestories.missouriepscor.org/.

29. Antwan Pope, "Alleys," 2016, Missouri Place Stories, accessed June 1, 2019, available at http://placestories.missouriepscor.org/.

6

Critical Tourism and Embodied Geographies

*Touring Southern California with
the Bureau of Goods Transport*

CATHERINE GUDIS

L ately, I have been performing my public history. Several times this spring, for instance, I have donned the costume of a business suit and blouse, artificially straightened my hair, and adopted the cheerful demeanor of a corporate publicist. I introduce myself as a principal and CEO of the Empire Logistics Group (ELG)—a faux trade association that a faculty colleague and I invented. I explain that I am there to promote yet another fabricated entity, the Bureau of Goods Transport, *the* chamber of commerce and clearinghouse for all-things logistics. I tout the bureau's proudest achievement: the one and only heritage guide to industry sites in Southern California related to global goods movement and the modern marvels of containerization, intermodality, and information networks that enable the logistics revolution.[1] With a smile and a set of slides, I tour my audience along the path of a container, transported from ships at the Ports of Long Beach and Los Angeles (*behold the Pacific!*) onto a succession of freight trucks and trains through Southeast Los Angeles (*the Diesel Death Zone!*) to the Amazon (*warehouses!*).[2] *Now, who wouldn't be fascinated by a guided tour following a shipping container?*

I boast the magnificent assets of a travel corridor rife with environmental toxicity and economic precarity, whose scenic wonders range

Figure 6.1 View of container ships at the Port of Los Angeles—the busiest port in the nation. (Copyright Port of Los Angeles)

from diesel-belching cargo ships in the Los Angeles Harbor, where multicolored stacks of containers carry 40 percent of all goods coming into the United States (see Figure 6.1), to the subterranean trench of the Alameda Corridor's triple tracks of cargo-carrying rail, to the over a billion square feet of warehouses comprising Southern California's magisterial inland ports, where air is thick with a toxic stew that has won awards for San Bernardino and Riverside as *the* most particulate- and ozone-polluted counties in America.[3] (*Way to go Inland Empire!*)

I delight in proclaiming how much I *just love* history ("*don't you?*" I ask), before offering the quiz show version of a lesson. *Did you know* (pointing to an aerial view of California's Inland Empire carpeted in warehouses; see Figure 6.2) that this same acreage once hosted orange groves as far as the eye could see—the stuff of postcards, for Midwesterners to write home about—and garnered Riverside status as the wealthiest city in the nation per capita in 1895?[4] Sixty miles east and inland of Los Angeles, it was the epicenter of the "Orange Empire," where "citrus gold" had brought prosperity and prestige, its rows of emerald green trees bejeweling the landscape and the imagination.[5] Not so today, my alter ego sadly admits, acknowledging that ware-

Figure 6.2 Warehouses dominate Southern California's Inland Empire and encroach on homes and open space, 2014. (Courtesy of Jesse Kaplan, Los Angeles)

houses now stretch as far as the eye can see, built on land declared "cheaper than dirt." But luckily (tone switching to boastful overconfidence), I assure armchair tourists, the ELG is here to *pave the path back to the middle class*.[6] Dismissing naysayers, I wave my hand to brush off claims that warehouse work is a race to the bottom—temporary, by demand, low waged, lacking in benefits, and conducted under poor conditions largely by immigrants and people of color. *The* poster child for logistics in the Inland Empire, after all, Mira Loma, is centrally located where you can still chase a piece of the American Dream: your own single-family house with a patch of green grass lawn, on a cul-de-sac, in a walled community. Granted, the walls are legislated—the only separation from the millions of square feet of distribution centers that moved in next door, when, soon after, the Technicolor of the post–World War II suburban vision became clouded with smog and filtered through the haze of diesel exhaust from the thousands of trucks driving by daily or idling as they wait in front of the kids' school for a turn at the loading dock.[7] Still, *if* the walls were not so high, and *if* jobs remained after automation or were not just occasional, residents of this 90 percent Latinx neighborhood might, in a minute, hop right over to get to work.

Now, who wouldn't be proud of such a booster mission and legacy?

My performance follows a script drawn straight from primary sources, including quotes by the most frequently referenced pundits for warehouse development in the region. Delivered with the sincerity of booster belief in commercial capitalism, it utilizes sites and stories represented in the Bureau of Goods Transport heritage guidebook, a tactical media project that my friend, colleague, and media studies scholar Kenneth Rogers and I began in 2012, originally at the University of California, Riverside (UCR), with students and political scientist and gender studies professor Juliann Emmons Allison, who is long active in documenting the impacts of global goods distribution on labor and the environment.[8] Both my performative tour and the guidebook highlight historical and contemporary facts on the ground, narrating them through what you can see if you visit and what you surely cannot discern without a guide to get you there. Deploying the tropes of cultural heritage tourism—a celebratory tone, focus on patrimony and lineage, and emphasis on the scenic, among them—the *official* guide to goods movement and industry sites locates the toxicity, precarity, and unequal power relations of capitalist enterprise. It does so not through earnest polemics but through a tongue-in-cheek *performance of truth* that I have taken to calling the *parafactual*.[9]

As part of that performance, the guide vexes the expectations for what we understand heritage to mean or look like and where we commonly find it. It does so by showcasing what is typically hidden by being too big to notice, too mundane to call attention to, or too seemingly inevitable to think about challenging, despite the huge impact it has on every aspect of all of our lives, especially the frontline communities experiencing its deepest effects. Moreover, it locates sites and stories where we can address the structural forces producing environmental injustices.

This is not to say that affected community members have not challenged and contested the impact of logistics on their lives—they have, dramatically, and with global reverberations—but rather that more of us ought to, and a historical context can help. Out of hundreds of students in just one teaching quarter, I have met plenty who work in warehouses and some who live next door to them. Many more have not considered the connections between their next-day delivery orders from Amazon Prime and the overwhelming expanse of fulfillment centers built—often at the expense of housing—along existing and promised transportation corridors, leading to the corresponding increases in trucking, traffic, and toxicity. When I have played out pieces of the guide or taken students to "heritage" sites—whether to witness the colossal baby blue post-Panamax cranes unloading containers at the Port of Los Angeles's Pier 400 (the largest single proprietary terminal in the world), choke up at kids' soccer games alongside the BNSF Intermodal Yard in San Bernardino, or take a leisurely "scenic drive" from Amazon to Amazon (with views en route of colossal, nearly identically constructed distribution centers for Kohl's, Target, Costco, Pepsico, Mattel, Home Depot, and Stater Bros.)—they do, however, get the point. It also becomes evident to them that this is not the typical tour and that the bureau's use of contrasts or juxtapositions between what we typically celebrate and what we actually find at ground (and underground) level—or in the ether—are aimed to provoke a closer look at logistical landscapes and the related flow of goods, capital, people, and pollution.

Our strategy is also to interrogate notions of heritage that implicitly fortify hierarchies of (white) power and capital development. That is the reframing of our brand of tourism as "critical," part of a robust practice that has emerged in the past decade or so among artists and scholars, who deploy the discursive framework of the tour and guidebook to vex the "financial and attention economies of tourism" that traditionally prioritize commercial profit and superficial investigation.[10] For many of us, the goal is to recontextualize the built and natural environment to highlight its ideological workings. Among the many projects in Southern California alone that are engaged in critical tourism are Laura Barraclough, Wendy Cheng, and Laura Pulido's *A People's Guide to Los Angeles*, which foregrounds sites of racial, class, gender, and environmental struggle; the Los Angeles Urban Rangers (for which I serve as a senior ranger), which offers guided hikes and interpretive tools for traversing the wild undergrowth of infrastructure, regulation, and forgetting that defines the terrain of the megalopolis; and the Center for Land Use and Interpretation's infrastructural tours, exhibitions, and Land Use Database of sites illustrating "humankind's interactions with the Earth's Surface." Radical field guides also fit the genre and informed our quest for alternative tour strategies, including the newsprint series by Llano del Rio (my favorite being the group's *Guide to Assholes of L.A.*, which maps power, from politicians to polluters and war contractors), the interventions into Chicanx history by Sandra de la Loza's *The Pocho Research Society Field Guide to L.A. Monuments and Murals of Erased and Invisible Histories*, and the multisensory audio guide *Invisible 5*, in which community voices, ambient sounds, and expert testimony narrate the sites of environmental justice along the route of the I-5 freeway from Los Angeles to San Francisco. A growing number of "alt-institutions" push the genre further, including Superfun!, whose website for the United States Environment + People Agency (or, EPA), mirrors the design and bureaucratic legalese of the real EPA.[11]

My own quest to engage alternative interpretive strategies comes out of dual frustration with the earnestness of many public projects around environmentalism and the musty-fusty elements of "ye olde" that often permeate local historical societies, where erasure of complexity and contestation, especially around race, racial capitalism, and state violence, is the apparent norm.[12] By refiguring familiar tropes of cultural heritage, the bureau's goods-movement guide and related projects aim to open space for critique, through the gap between tradition and its unraveling, of fact and its *feeling* of fictionality.

Multiple Approaches to Place-Based Collaborative Practices

At UCR, many faculty, students, and research centers are involved in identifying the regional and global impacts of goods movement, often in partnership with community-based organizations that are representative of our area's majority Latinx population and that address the disproportionate burden placed on working classes, people of color, and vulnerable populations (children, the elderly, the disenfranchised, and those whose health is compromised, either due to preexisting conditions or their work in the industry or residence nearby). Our students—on a campus where over 85 percent are of color and nearly 60 percent are first in their families to attend college—also represent affected community members; they too live next to the rail yards and freeways, hold some of the warehouse jobs about which we study, and sometimes enter careers where they agitate for change and social justice. My colleagues do the scientific and social scientific work that such grassroots environmental justice and labor organizations can actually use, some of it quantitative and all of it lending cognitive authority that can validate for politicians and policy makers what community groups might also say and know to be true.[13]

But where does this leave those in the public humanities and arts? For me, as a cultural historian of the built and natural environment, and for many of the public historians I work with, our skill sets do not contribute to the quantitative assessment of public health impacts or the composition of policy briefs. So how might the public humanities contribute? One way to figure this out is to *play*, literally and conceptually, with interpretive practices that we regularly participate in creating, consuming, and offering a critique of: the tour and the guidebook. My deployment of these tools is much like what artists do in engaging critical spatial politics, though aimed to play with how we "do" history, as a means of activating a political agenda of social and environmental justice. Can historians expose in situ forces of logistical capitalism that are abstract and difficult to comprehend and, therefore, typically omitted from public discourses of civic memory and cultural heritage?

While I began this essay with the faux bureau and heritage guide, I also wish to highlight here the ways in which our public practice may vary, both in the types of collaborations we forge, with and beyond the university as the fulcrum, and how playful (or not) our desired outcomes might be. For instance, since 2018, UCR faculty, students, community-based organizations, and I have taken a more documentary approach than that of the Empire Logistics Group and its tongue-in-cheek Bureau of Goods Transport. We have done so through our participation in the Humanities Action Lab (HAL) traveling exhibition and digital platform, *Climates of Inequality: Stories of Environmental Justice*. Currently a coalition of twenty-three universities working with issues-based organizations and public venues (museums, libraries, parks, etc.), HAL produces participatory public memory projects on socially pressing and contested topics; prior projects are the *Guantánamo Public Memory Project* and *States of Incarceration: A National Dialogue of Local Histories*.[14] For *Climates of Inequality*, each university-community team produced a local chapter that contributed to a global narrative and will take a turn at presenting the exhibition in

Figure 6.3 Installation view of the opening of HAL's traveling exhibition, *Climates of Inequality: Stories of Environmental Justice* at Rutgers University, Newark, New Jersey, October 2019. (Photo by Shelley Kusnetz. Courtesy of Humanities Action Lab)

their area, adding local content to the presentation, digital platform, and programs along the way. (See Figure 6.3.)

HAL's praxis and pedagogy go to lengths to avoid Western traditions of "extractive" research, by which universities treat the communities they study as laboratories for their own research without sharing their findings or deploying their results for community benefit. The group also avoids what indigenous scholar Eve Tuck calls "damage-centered" research, in which neighborhoods and tribes are presented as depleted or broken. Rather, recognition is paid to the survivance (a term Anishinaabe scholar Gerald Vizenor uses to extend the meanings of survival to include "active repudiation of dominance, tragedy, and victimry") and self-determination of neighborhoods and tribes as well as the context of centuries-long histories of dispossession, disinvestment, and other forms of systemic oppression.[15] With each successive project, the coalition has devoted more intellectual energy and funds to formalize community-centered, coalition- and change-oriented project values of respect and reciprocity.[16] For *Climates of Inequality*, the local teams "activate the histories of 'frontline' communities: those who have contributed the least to the climate crisis but bear its heaviest burdens."[17]

By sheer number of students, faculty, community participants, and venues, HAL projects have the capacity to amass both a sizable audience (over five hundred thousand people visited the Guantánamo Public Memory Project) and an archive reflecting multigenerational experiences and strategies for resistance, resilience, and repair. With much more representation of people of color, working classes, and industrial and postindustrial neighborhoods than one might find in dominant archival institutions and museums, HAL makes inroads into recording what Yusef Omowale, director of the Southern California Library, describes, in the context of community archives, as "lives lived in spaces of impossibility" and "suffering slow deaths of incarceration, poverty, and environmental toxicity."[18] By uplifting and preserving the voices of people living in "spaces of impossibility" we also highlight survivance, and reimagine a different future, beyond current fact or category (of poverty, carcerality, toxicity, etc.).

The Los Angeles and Inland Empire chapter of *Climates of Inequality* produced by UCR is locational, its multimedia portraits and stories hinged to seven sites from ocean to inland ports, with overlap of sites also represented in the bureau's heritage guide, though with a different tenor to the presentation. In what follows, I intertwine HAL and the bureau as a means of doing two things. One is to focus on the history, impact, and activism around goods movement and the often invisible forces shaping infrastructural landscapes in Southern California—the content embedded in our work for HAL. The other is to address form: multiple ways to render such structures of power and multiscalar histories visible and palpable and thus subject to the critique that is necessary to instantiate a different model—to mobilize change.

My colleague Liz Sevcenko, founder/director of HAL, asserts that, in our "post-truth" era of mass political mediation, we need multifaceted and participatory practices to uncover the deep roots of social issues, to resist the powerful undercurrents of historical denial that make social problems seem intractable, without precedent, and inevitable, and to create the means by which to publicly reckon with state violence and injustice to shape solutions. It is ever more pressing, she adds, to carve out space for the humanities to regain significance as an agent of dialogue and discovery and to bridge the gaps that academia often has created between "past and present, heritage and human rights, scholarship and social movements."[19]

I also wonder how and whether we can create "multifaceted and participatory practices" that operate at different affective registers to encompass the pedagogical and polemical as well as irony and play through performative, *parafactual* practices. I would like to add to the mix, in other words, public humanities frameworks that perform their own tongue-in-cheek versions of truth by highlighting the strangeness—absurdity, even—of what we often find at ground level. By framing the ways we look at and affectively experience infrastructural landscapes through familiar institutional forms (agencies, departments, chambers of commerce, tour guides, etc.), perhaps we can also reveal how authoritative structures and claims of objectivity influence belief, enabling new modes of inquiry and resistance.[20]

Historical Backdrop: De/Material Flows and the Slow Violence of the Supply Chain

Rather than merely a management science of distribution, logistics today is a global set of circulatory systems that encompasses all phases of production (including resource extraction, design, and manufacture), distribution, and consumption. While this description focuses on material flow—goods to be made, assembled, and circulated along concrete and steel corridors and conveyances (ships, trains, trucks traveling along rails and freeways, etc.), logistics is also fully about the quest for dematerialization, which undermines labor and the conditions of work through the elimination of human time (in favor of speed), bodily presence (in favor of automation for workers and algorithms for managers), and human subjectivities.[21] The wishful thinking of logistics is about the removal of workers' bodies, for sure, with the container "the very coffin of remote-labor power."[22] It is also about rendering invisible the obdurate materiality and impact of the information systems enabling it, as if data has no attendant physical matter just because we do not usually see or visit with the network servers, microchips, wires, cables, and so on. Yet, data and its digital transmission are what enabled the information and communications technologies that revolutionized logistics and "just-in-time" production, put the final nail in the coffin of America's domestic mass industrial production, and reconfigured the capitalist social relations of production. Data and its management is how Walmart helped change a world that Amazon would colonize. This is the empire of logistics—a violent terrain.

After all, the circulatory systems of logistics and their data supply and management are rooted in the arts of war—think Genghis Khan mobilizing his troops across the Gobi, the military origins of the internet (with Vietnam-era Arpanet, the precursor of the web), and contemporary surveillance uses.[23] They stretch across time and space in an "attritional lethality" of what Rob Nixon identifies as "slow violence," and Deborah Cowen specifies as "the deadly life of logistics."[24] Stefano Harney and Fred Moten locate the violence in the founding moments of commercial logistics, with the "first great movement of commodities, the ones that could speak," the Atlantic slave trade. In the ship's hold, the status of the slave was "not just property but commodity," also marking the elimination of the subject, substituted by human capital. This prioritization of objects and their movement was the "dream of logistics."[25] What was true for the ship's hold held true as well for the boxcar and the prison, which contained then distributed the commodity labor required for modern infrastructures of capitalist accumulation: indentured servants on Pacific trade routes, migrants supplying mass industrialization in the Americas, and prisoners sent to settle colonies.[26] This defines the roots of logistical capitalism as racial capitalism and maps the slow violence of the supply chain temporally and spatially.

The social and spatial implications of both the material constitution of globalization and the efforts to dematerialize human labor become evident at ground level by tracing goods-movement corridors through Southern California with those who experience it firsthand— the people who live, work, and go to school there. For me and my students, *Witnessing the Slow Violence of the Supply Chain* became both the name for our contributions to the HAL exhibition *Climates of Inequality* and shorthand for the long historical trajectory of racialized state violence. As we journeyed spatially through the region we realized temporal implications, from mission-era displacement of Native people and native uses of the land (and its water) to settlements during Spanish Colonial, Mexican, and then American rule, with a straight line from citrus and other agriculture and the kinds of migrant and immigrant labor that required, to logistics and the same forms of extraction from the land and people. We saw the long histories of logistical and racial capitalism intertwine as a slow violence that we could witness in our current day and that the community-based organizations we have partnered with, East Yard Communities for Environmental Justice, Center for Community Action and Environmental Justice, People's Collective for Environmental Justice, and Warehouse Worker Resource Center, narrated (literally and metaphorically) with every action.

In the Inland Empire, scholars and community organizations have worked together, at various junctures also with artists, grappling with how to bring local environmental justice battles related to the logistics industry—including the poor labor practices involved, the impact on the air we breathe and the spaces we traverse, the encroachment of distribution centers on residential neighborhoods, and potential solutions to the problems—into wider view. In 2009–2010, a network of media scholars (including my bureau colleague Ken Rogers) and artists in Southern California began to look for ways to render visible the forces shaping largely hidden infrastructures and the capital flows behind it. They focused on the then unincorporated Mira Loma area of the Inland Empire, which at that time had the largest concentration of distribution centers in the nation, using it as a case study for assessing the "'externalized costs'—human, economic, social, and environmental—of the international flow of things" (the global supply chain).[27] They also were mapping financialization and logistics. The timing was significant: shortly after the economic crash and foreclosure and subprime mortgage crisis that hit the inland region hard and would ultimately ripen conditions for an even more expansive takeover of the landscape by mile after mile of distribution warehouses. Logistics became promoted regionally during the hard times of the Great Recession (which lasted longer in the Inland Empire of Southern California than elsewhere) by, among others, the Inland Empire Economic Partnership, a private nonprofit composed of prologistics industry leaders and public agencies, which claimed that warehouses were the best possible use for such rapidly devalued land. In the name of economic recovery, and in the name of job opportunities (which would later fail to materialize), city and county agencies approved industrial warehouse developments based on "overriding considerations": that economic benefits outweigh the significant impacts on the environment, including poorer air quality and greenhouse gas emissions, conversion of open land and farmland into low-return industrial use, and aesthetic degradation. Even after the Great Recession's 15 percent unemployment rate in the Inland Empire reduced to some 4.5 percent, this same language of crisis—jobs at any cost, though without much attention to how many, for how long, and with what benefits—continues to be used, as profits flow outward to global corporate stockholders rather than back in to the local community.[28]

Mira Loma was an instrumental place to agitate around this. In 2009, warehouse workers and community organizers blocked the intersection of a heavily trafficked truck route leading to and from warehouses, choking the supply chain, and setting a stage for ongoing campaigns that would focus on the cluster of a dozen Walmart-serving third-party logistics warehouses in the area, in partnership with other labor groups representing workers in contiguous parts of the Walmart supply chain.[29] The warehouse workers were publicized as the "hidden face of Walmart," and, just as they also wielded protest signs "Invisible No More!" in prior actions, they sought to "undo an act of erasure that wiped them from the map of global capital flows."[30]

These labor campaigns acknowledge the fact that the various impacts of goods movement are difficult to bring into view. This is as surely the case for labor as it is for environmental impacts on public health. Scholars Vivien Hamilton and Brinda Sarathy describe in *Inevitably Toxic: Historical Perspectives on Contamination, Exposure, and Expertise* that "toxic environments are often invisible or appear innocuous, though such spaces are more prevalent in our day-to-day lives than we either know or care to admit."[31] The challenges in this case are even more formidable, since logistics is both that which we cannot see and that which operates at an unfathomable scale: global circulation of mass data and zillions of products; millions of containers, trucks, railcars, and miles of tracks and intersecting freeways and highways; and a billion square feet of warehouses, in Riverside and San Bernardino's inland ports alone. In Sarathy's research on another "invisible" toxic site nearby, Stringfellow Acid Pits, which was declared California's first Superfund site in 1983 based on the dumping of military-industrial waste there from 1955 through 1971, she found that boosters in the Inland Empire in the 1950s held arms wide open to industrial waste, inviting growth at any cost—a pattern repeated in the decades following, particularly in the face of deindustrialization (1980s) and military base realignment (1990s). Marketing the region as free from the kinds of regulations and environmental restrictions that were beginning to be imposed on other cities, the in situ waste of industrial dumping became mobile and airborne, carried by diesel trucks, trains, and airplanes with the growth of logistics.[32]

In turning her sights to Mira Loma, as Sarathy explains in her interview for a HAL exhibition video, she began to realize the roots of logistics not just in the political moment of 1970s disinvestment but earlier. In fact, she found that the Inland Empire was ground zero for logistics by the 1940s, when the U.S. Army Quartermaster Supply Depot located a command center first in San Bernardino for the distribution of war materials and then expanded with millions of square feet of distribution centers in Riverside County. The rapid growth of the supply depot at Mira Loma had an additional purpose: to distribute goods and supplies, including perishable foodstuff, to the Manzanar concentration camp being simultaneously constructed and populated by people of Japanese descent in the Owens Valley, over two hundred miles due north, and to other western wartime relocation centers. The Army quartermaster regularly supplied forty thousand and a peak of sixty thousand incarcerated Japanese.[33] Mira Loma also supplied the Desert Training Center in the Mojave Desert, where some one hundred twenty thousand soldiers were readied for combat in Northern Africa and Europe. As Sarathy explains, the warehouses were both a physical and a discursive site for the construction of a racialized geography of labor as well as containment. In promotional films and the records of the quartermaster general's historian (hired to record the events as they were unfolding), industrious (white) civilians work "at all hours to make sure that provisions reached interned Japanese." Incarcerated Japanese American citizens, on the other hand, were invariably described in pejorative racial terms and as unworthy of the advanced techniques of supply chain management that enabled them to get fresh milk at camp, especially when "deserving" *real* Americans could not always get it themselves.[34] Perishable items and the Japanese goods the Army picked up for cut-rate prices from Los Angeles warehouses (well stocked with what Japanese shops had been forced to quickly divest) also tested existing infrastructure and know-how. Though the Army warehouses were located adjacent to the crisscrossing railroad lines that had enabled the citrus empire to develop over the prior half century, advances in trucking, new additions to U.S. 395, and proximity to Route 66 paved the way for the region's postwar development as the empire of logistics.[35] In the decades after World War II, Mira Loma remained part of the military's supply side, storing and distributing provisions for troops in Korea in the 1950s. Tract housing grew around it, even after the Air Force took over the depot for the storage and dismantling of Titan I intercontinental ballistic missiles.[36]

Today, the now decommissioned Military Depot is part of the Mira Loma Space Center commercial warehouse complex. The remaining 101 homes in Mira Loma Village are walled in by massive distribution facilities and traffic from thousands of trucks that load and unload daily.[37] This isolation has led to a decline in community services (there are no grocery stores or other shops in the area) as well as poor health. The mostly Latinx residents breathe some of the worst smog and diesel particulate pollution in the United States, with long-term reverberating health impacts. The rapid rate of residential displacement and its impacts prompt protests today. "Kid's Health before Wealth," neighbors chanted during 2018 demonstrations, "Our Lungs Are Not for Sale."[38] (See Figure 6.4.)

Yet, despite robust community opposition, massive new distribution centers continue to be developed not just in the Mira Loma area and the adjacent unincorporated area of Bloomington to its north but also in the postindustrial towns of Colton and Fontana, and on and around former military lands at San Bernardino's Norton Air Force Base and Moreno Valley's March Air Reserve Base, where air cargo hubs are also planned.[39] These stories of coalition building and legal actions to oppose further air cargo development and resist encroachment on wildlife preserves in Moreno Valley (where the 40 million-square-foot World Logistics Center is being contested) as well as the deep and recent historical backdrops, including strikes by warehouse workers, the role of military logistics at Manzanar, and changing land and labor regimes from citrus to logistics, form the centerpiece of our contributions to the HAL exhibition and website. They derive from

Figure 6.4 Community members protest new warehouse development in Bloomington, an area of San Bernardino County heavily burdened by the impacts of logistics, 2018. (Courtesy of Anthony Victoria-Midence)

firsthand experiences of local community members and organizers and with interviews, oral histories, and site-based research that was realized through both a series of classes and involvement in the activist campaigns.

Tactical Media

The minidocumentary format we used for the HAL project is just one mode of public presentation, didactic in form, and with a process that ultimately weaves contemporary voices together with historical discovery. With HAL, though, process matters, and the ways in which the project brings people together—in the three years of annual conferences to plan the projects, the multiple classes run by each university, the convenings and programs at each exhibition launch, and the other forms of translocal learning opportunities we forge together—gives presence or embodiment to issues and bridges gaps between university and community, people and bodies of knowledge. The Bureau of

Goods Transport aims to get at many of the same issues, but with a different form of tactical intervention and critique of touristic modes of spectatorship that take place in the public history forums that are the bailiwick of many of us who participate in HAL.

Using "tactical" to describe the bureau's guide to goods-movement industry sites is apt, given the military origins of both the term and the terrain of logistics in Southern California. In the 1980s and 1990s, the artistic/activist practice of tactical media hit its stride, as a way to challenge global capitalism through, as scholar Rita Raley puts it, "a micropolitics of disruption, intervention, and education." Its DIY practices were made possible by the easy availability of inexpensive electronics (camcorders, printers, etc.) and continually expanding means of distribution (from public access cable to internet, social media, vimeo, YouTube, etc.), which tacticians used to take back space (electronic and geographic) and power from institutional forces to refashion a public sphere that was, in the face of privatization and neoliberalism, not seeming very public at all.[40]

The Bureau of Goods Transport is tactical insofar as it is calculated to get at the everyday, commonplace elements of commodity capitalism—how you get your stuff, and get it fast—and to both render visible what is hidden in plain sight and make "strange" what is utterly familiar yet rarely recognizable as meaningful until you hold it up for scrutiny or frame it in ways that enable attention. The tactics in our case appropriate the language of the trade to reveal the forces of power at work in trade, create a "fissure" in "what is considered objective reality" or assumed to be inevitable in order to invite discourse, and subvert the intended meanings or claims by various actors who speak both for and against the geopolitical and local forces enabling and facilitating the global supply chain.[41]

In making our alternative agencies, first, Ken Rogers and I declared ourselves the CEOs of ELG and worked with a designer on a corporate logo that mimics those you can see anywhere you go globally, emblazoned on containers carried by ship, rail, and truck (think of Maersk, Hapag-Lloyd, Translogics).[42] These logos are the clip art of capital mobility, what you produce when there is nothing else you produce. Distribution—moving, not making—is a core metaphor that logistics industry logos incarnate in their literal depictions. In contrast to ELG, the Bureau of Goods Transport pictures its role as a quasi-

Figure 6.5 The logo for the Bureau of Goods Transport mimics county and city seals, in this case to mark the history and industry of logistics. At its center is the upraised fist and cargo hook used by ILWU longshoremen during 1971 strikes, when labor sought to address the impacts of containerization and mechanization. (Courtesy of the Bureau of Goods Transport)

public agency, with its own insignia borrowed from the seal of the County of Los Angeles but with a longshoreman's cargo hook (lifted from 1971 International Longshoremen's and Warehousemen's Union [ILWU] strike imagery) at its center in place of the original seal's scales of justice and as among the representable icons of distribution culture. (See Figure 6.5.)

From the start, the *real* model for our heritage guide has been New York State's *Path through History*, a brochure, web portal, and plaques with QR codes installed all over the state, from subways to rest stops, which is part of the I Love New York™ official tourism campaign.[43] We take its tone, adjectives, types of images, and more. And while we make strange the spaces of the already unbelievable areas through which we journey, our work is parafactual—*way beyond* truth, when truth is stranger than fiction. *You can't make this stuff up!*

We riff on the idea of heritage and how cultural patrimony is conferred on certain sites and simulate tourist attractions where they otherwise do not exist. We do so by staging photos of happy tourists interacting with living history reenactors (us, our students, and other partners, with the help of Hollywood studio prop shop rentals). We play curious visitors for shots that serve as proof that our sites are historically authentic—whether a park (built on a contaminated brownfield site), an asphalt parking lot (with stories to tell), or a vacant corner (where the Wobblies staged actions)—as if to create our own version of a postindustrial Sturbridge Village.

I enlisted my spouse to play a stevedore at a historic warehouse and then to change costume to reenact Upton Sinclair at the 1923 Liberty Hill rally in support of striking Industrial Workers of the World maritime and dockworkers. The guide suggests audiences do the same:

> Rally here to celebrate the right to free speech and assembly. Channel the spirit of Upton Sinclair and raise your cargo hook high in solidarity with the thousands of interethnic Industrial Workers of the World and their supporters in May 1923, when the local Marine Workers Union went on strike to protest low wages, poor working conditions, and the Criminal Syndicalism Act (prohibiting organizing activities). Read the U.S. Constitution aloud, just like Sinclair, parade past the stone memorial with interpretive plaque, and sigh in relief that your reenactment doesn't include jeering Klansmen, American Legionnaires, violent vigilantes—and jail time! Keep celebrating—most of the six hundred arrested on that day were released in the face of media attention, and the event galvanized the labor movement and formation of the Southern California ACLU and ILWU. *California Historic Landmark; plaque legible 24 hours daily.*[44]

For another site, then-Ph.D. student Todd Luce played Malcom McLean, the former North Carolina trucker and "founding father" of the intermodal shipping container in the 1950s, whose simple invention revolutionized global trade. Also referred to as "the box" or the "sea can," the standardized corrugated steel container could move among ship, rail, and train or be stacked and stored on a wharf or rail yard without having to "break bulk"—unpack or repack the goods being transported.[45] It sent shivers down the spine of the ILWU for its impact on labor. It did far more when mobilized for the Korean and, especially, Vietnam Wars, when the transpacific route *to* Cam Ranh Bay with troop-bound supplies was made profitable (and, therefore, possible) because the ship would continue from there to Japan, where the empty containers would be loaded up with U.S.-bound consumer goods. Military logistics was essentially handed over to commercial carriers like McLean's SeaLand and South Korea's Hanjin. The container might have "made the world smaller and the world economy bigger," as author Marc Levinson writes in *The Box*, but it also fused the empire of (Cold War) liberty with the empire of logistics.[46]

Playing McLean, Luce surveys the vast shipping empire of TraPac Container Terminal at the Port of Los Angeles, where colorful containers stack high with nary a human in sight, thanks to automation, and, of course, the efficiencies of "the box." From his vantage, atop the grassy berm of Wilmington Waterfront Park, one of the grandest industrial buffer zones to come out of an environmental mitigation lawsuit, he can catch a glimpse of the petroleum flare stacks in the distance as they belch buoyant fire plumes at dusk, courtesy of Conoco Philips Oil Refinery to the west. The guide includes a color-coded Advisory Note to the site: "Prior to aerobic activity without a HEPA respirator, consult EIR mitigation plan on increased levels of NO_x, O_3, CO, SO_2 in the region."[47]

Public historian Hannah Brown and I posed, as well, as stand-ins for the missing Japanese, Italian, and Croatian cannery women, in front of the ruins of industry on Terminal Island, where thousands of families once lived, ads jingled ("Ask any mermaid you happen to see. . . . What's the best tuna? Chicken of the Sea"), and ghosts from the Lost Village (the Japanese enclave of some three thousand people) still roam.[48] (See Figure 6.6.) All but a few storefronts of the village were razed, in 1942, after the FBI's widespread arrests of Issei fisherman just after the bombing of Pearl Harbor and forced removal of remaining inhabitants of Japanese heritage—most to Manzanar. The area redeveloped as Roosevelt Base, named for the president who issued the call for Japanese American incarceration, Executive Order 9066. Terminal Island still gives a nod to the carceral, as the only people still living there are at the federal prison down the way (pictures NOT allowed).

Many other sites also offer the opportunity to consider sovereignty and empire, including indigenous perspectives. For instance, the tour enables the exploration of the city of Carson's Watson Industrial Center, a 6.67-million-square-foot master-planned community of goods assembly, logistics, and distribution owned by the Dominguez-Watson family, whose ancestors held the first Spanish land grant in the state. Their grant included the land eventually used for the harbor, which was given to Los Angeles in exchange for railroad operating rights. Operated by the port as a foreign-trade zone—a place deemed outside

Figure 6.6 Reenactment photo, with Hannah Brown and Catherine Gudis posed next to a former cannery on Terminal Island that employed immigrant women from Japan, Italy, Croatia, and Mexico, among others. Today, most of Terminal Island is operated by the Port of Los Angeles and the Port of Long Beach, with the tip occupied by the Federal Correctional Institution. (Courtesy of the Bureau of Goods Transport)

U.S. territory and jurisdiction so free from U.S. Customs duties and taxes—the Watson Industrial Center does a number of things.[49] It charts a global trail of tears, as the ground beneath visitors' feet contains human remains and prehistoric artifacts of the village of Suangna. The bronze plaque for Los Angeles Historic Marker No. 13 (what some critics call the feeble "sorry plaque"[50]), attached to a boulder on a strip of manicured lawn beside a desolate stretch of sidewalk, surely never used by humans, is all there is to call attention to the profundity of the site, where Tongva villages, burial grounds, and north-south routes to the ocean were concentrated.

The Bureau of Goods Transport trains a keen eye on these ironies and contradictions embedded *in place*, where mobility of goods and capital has historically been prioritized without heed to its environmental impact or human costs, and where indigenous dispossession and the flow and restriction of migrant and immigrant labor have also marked tidal shifts in land use and continuities in labor regimes throughout the region over multiple generations and centuries.

The project aims at injecting a hearty dose of irony into tropes of cultural heritage tourism, from the authority of the tour guide, to the authenticity of living history, to the promotional practices aimed at monetizing heritage. Humor, play, and the performative are the essence of the guide and tour, with mimicry its central practice and deadpan its cry of disbelief. Yet, the project is fundamentally about investigating modes of public presentation to create the context for public dialogue and an embodied means of knowledge production that eschews pure polemics.

In other words, like the HAL exhibition, this critical tourism project is fundamentally about bringing different voices together, aimed toward improving our engagement with what seems too big to reckon with and offering grounds for having the dialogues that might also make the issues resonant outside of the academy or the locality. It is an underhanded way to bring to light the agents and actors of slow violence, alongside the impacts of racialized state violence, with history as our foil.

Irony is easily critiqued as a game of insider knowledge, or privileged standing. In this case, though, if the guide is making fun of anything it is the people who generally produce such guides: me. In other words, I am playing in a performative field that I know well and where I do have privileged standing. I occupy a subject position that allies with my own; as a practitioner of public history, I have worked on dozens of tours and with cultural organizations, docents, and state and other park agencies. I have written about advertising and the movement of goods and distribution culture and have mined a too-vast arena of related trade journals. These inform my ELG character, too, who stands in the professional middle class that I also occupy, though our political leanings and values might be different—or they might not be. Some of the great culture jams that riff on commercial advertising have been by designers working in advertising who had the know-how to effectively mock their own industry. That said, I am not using mockery or sarcasm. I am just looking for another way to highlight the ghostly presence of those who populate the urban archive, including colonizers and those subjected to their violence, prologistics industrial leaders as well as those who live with its heaviest impacts and who seek to challenge and reform it.

All of these related interventions commonly employ *play* as an operative element and mode of knowing, connecting, and transforming: the idea that we toy with ideas and language, game the system, perform a role as an act of productive re-creation or transformation. Play, in other words, and, even in the face of frivolity, can be potent, not only as a mode of critique or active public engagement but as a tool for seeing and feeling past your own subject position. All of which, of course, is why I am interested in it as a public engagement strategy—for my own tactical use and to illuminate how our given tools of pedagogy, tourism, or public presentation might be redeployed for more than spectatorial touristic consumption. Embodiment and affect are part of that shift from mere visual apprehension to a multisensorial connection and more egalitarian form of knowledge transmission or way of knowing that also promises more in terms of how we understand and participate in the production of space, our actions potentially part of a choreography of change. Critical tourism and embodied geographies can shift the nature of the space we traverse by virtue of our participation in a different set of expectations around it, instantiating a public realm or sphere in the face of overwhelming privatization, or create a form of knowledge on which action is more possible. If nothing else, perhaps it breeds curiosity.

Can tourism be critical? Can it have an activist agenda? Or is it always only speculative in nature, bound by our colonizing gaze? Might the performative generate an affective experience of otherwise difficult to comprehend social and geopolitical terrain? Can it enable empathy as well as comedy, sensitize us to different subject positions, or acknowledge political discordance in productive ways? We all ought to consider these questions when forging community-based and co-produced research and representational strategies and find ways to add the politics of play to our portfolio of public practices and to the ways we experience not only logistical landscapes but power and place more generally. In the meantime, and on behalf of the Bureau of Goods Transport, *thank you for touring*!

NOTES

1. On the "logistics revolution," see Edna Bonacich and Jake B. Wilson, *Getting the Goods: Ports, Labor, and the Logistics Revolution* (Ithaca, NY: Cornell University Press, 2008); Deborah Cowen, *The Deadly Life of Logistics: Mapping Violence in Global Trade* (Minneapolis: University of Minnesota Press, 2014); Juan D. De Lara, *Inland Shift: Race, Space, and Capital in Southern California* (Oakland: University of California Press, 2018); Keller Easterling, *Extrastatecraft: The Power of Infrastructure* (London: Verso, 2014); Jesse LeCavalier, *The Rule of Logistics: Walmart and the Architecture of Fulfillment* (Minneapolis: University of Minnesota, 2016).

2. De Lara, *Inland Shift*, 55–58.

3. Inland ports describe the use of exurban spaces or "metropolitan hinterlands" to absorb ocean port container traffic, usually due to the challenges of finding the cheap land, labor, and reduced environmental restrictions needed for massive distribution warehouses. De Lara, *Inland Shift*, 43–47, 55–58; Ellen Reese and Jason Struna, "'Work Hard, Make History': Oppression and Resistance in Inland Southern California's Warehouse and Distribution Industry," in *Choke Points: Logistics Workers Disrupting the Global Supply Chain*, ed. Jake Alimahomed-Wilson and Immanuel Ness (London: Pluto, 2018), 81–95; Juliann Emmons Allison, "What Happens when Amazon Comes to Town? Environmental Impacts, Local Economies, and Resistance in Inland Southern California," in *The Cost of Free Shipping: Amazon in the Global Economy*, ed. Ellen Reese and Jake Alimahomed-Wilson (London: Pluto Press, 2020), 176–193; Anthony Victoria, "Inland Empire Once Again Ranks as Worst in Nation for Air Quality," KCET, April 22, 2022, available at https://www.kcet.org/shows/earth-focus/inland-empire-once-again-ranks-as-worst-in-nation-for-air-quality; Susan A. Phillips, "Op-Ed: We Mapped the Warehouse Takeover of the Inland Empire. The Results Are Overwhelming," *Los Angeles Times*, May 1, 2022; Gilbert Estrada, "An 'Evil System'? Planning for Environmental Health in America's Mobile and Most Polluted Metropolis, 1959 to the Present" (Ph.D. diss., Department of History, University of Southern California, 2011).

4. Vincent Moses, "Machines in the Garden: A Citrus Monopoly in Riverside, 1900–1936," *California History* 61 (Spring 1982): 17.

5. Other writings on the Inland Empire include Genevieve Carpio, *Collisions at the Crossroads: How Place and Mobility Make Race* (Oakland: University of California Press, 2019); Karen Tongson, "Empire of My Familiar," *Relocations:*

Queer Suburban Imaginaries (New York: New York University Press, 2011), 112–158; Thomas C. Patterson, *From Acorns to Warehouses: Historical Political Economy of Southern California's Inland Empire* (New York: Routledge, 2016).

6. Bonacich and J. Wilson, *Getting the Goods*, 134–138; Nicholas Allen, "Exploring the Inland Empire: Life, Work, and Injustice in Southern California's Retail Fortress," *New Labor Forum* 19 (June 2010): 37–43; Juliann Allison, Ellen Reese, and Jason Struna, "Under-paid and Temporary: Key Survey Findings on Warehouse Workers in the Inland Valley," working paper (Center for Sustainable Suburban Development, University of California, Riverside, June 2013), available at http://cssd.ucr.edu/Papers/PDFs/UnderpaidTempWorkers.pdf; Juan De Lara, "Warehouse Work: Path to the Middle Class or Road to Economic Insecurity," research brief (Program for Environmental and Regional Equity, University of Southern California, Los Angeles, September 2013), available at https://dornsife.usc.edu/assets/sites/242/docs/WarehouseWorkerPay_web.pdf.

7. For an analysis of the economic, demographic, and industrial transformations in Riverside County, with a focus on Mira Loma, see Alfonso Gonzales, "Race, Domestic Globalization, and Migration Control in Riverside County," *Reform Without Justice: Latino Migrant Politics and the Homeland Security State* (Oxford: Oxford University Press, 2014), 75–98. Mira Loma's concentration of warehouses—in part, related to changes in a 1987 Community Plan—came to national attention with air pollution studies, in the early 2000s, that found children had stunted lung development and increased respiratory illnesses with long-term links to "heart attacks, cancer and premature deaths." David Danelski, "Air of Concern," *The Press-Enterprise*, August 25, 2002; Michael W. Wilson, "Black Hole Base," *Journal of Aesthetics and Protest* 9 (2014), available at http://joaap.org/issue9/blackholebase.htm; Andrea Bernstein, "Land Grab: What Happens When Warehouses Move Next Door?" KPCC, October 16, 2017.

8. Work on the Empire Logistics Group was supported by a grant from the University of California Humanities Research Institute in 2013–2014; later iterations of the project since 2018 have been supported by Teresa and Byron Pollitt Endowed Term Chair for Interdisciplinary Learning and Research and the Relevancy and History Project partnership between UCR and California State Parks.

9. The idea of the parafactual relates to the space of ambiguity or uncertainty between fact and fiction, where belief is challenged and the structures of knowledge production ("truth") necessitate closer examination. Carrie Lambert-Beatty identifies its flipside in the performative artistic genre that she calls "parafiction," in which "fictions are experienced as fact. They achieve truth status for some of the people some of the time" but are deceptions nevertheless (54–55); Lambert-Beatty, "Make Believe: Parafiction and Plausibility," *October* 129 (Summer 2009): 51–84.

10. Sarah Kanouse, "Critical Day Trips: Tourism and Land-Based Practice," in *Critical Landscapes: Art, Space, Politics*, ed. Emily Eliza Scott and Kirsten Swenson (Oakland: University of California Press, 2015), 43.

11. Kanouse, "Critical Day Trips," 43–55; Emily Eliza Scott, "Field Effects: *Invisible-5s* Illumination of Peripheral Geographies," *Art Journal* (Winter 2010): 38–47; Stephanie LeMenager, "The Los Angeles Urban Rangers, Trailblazing the Commons," in *American Studies, Ecocriticism, and Citizenship: Thinking and Acting in the Local and Global Commons,* ed. Joni Adamson and Kimberly N. Ruffin (New York: Routledge, 2013), 220–236; Emily Eliza Scott, "Undisciplined Geography: Notes from the Field of Contemporary Art," *GeoHumanities: Art, History, Text at the Edge of the World,* ed. Michael Dear, Jim Ketchum, Sarah Luria, and Doug Richardson (New York: Routledge, 2011), 50–60; Alex Schmidt, "Art in the Land," *Boom: A Journal of California* 1 (Fall 2011): 62–66; on their book *A People's Guide to Los Angeles* (Berkeley: University of California Press, 2012), see Wendy Cheng, Laura Barraclough, and Laura Pulido, "Radicalising Teaching and Tourism: *A People's Guide* as Active and Activist History," *Left History* (Fall–Winter 2010–2011): 111–127. There are four more volumes in "A People's Guide Series," covering Boston, New York City, Orange County, and San Francisco. On the alt-institution of the EPA, see https://www.superfunusa.org/.

12. On the earnest and sanctimonious approaches within the mainstream environmental movement and the performative art and activism that "queers" it, see Nicole Seymour, *Bad Environmentalism: Irony and Irreverence in the Ecological Age* (Minneapolis: University of Minnesota Press, 2018), 2, 22–25.

13. See "Student Diversity Statistics," Office of Diversity, Equity, and Inclusion, University of California, Riverside, available at https://diversity.ucr.edu /student-diversity-statistics; Sandra Baltazar Martínez, "UC Riverside Enrolls Second-Highest Rate of First-Generation Freshmen in UC System," June 19, 2019, News, University of California, Riverside, available at https://news.ucr.edu/arti cles/2019/06/19/uc-riverside-enrolls-second-highest-rate-first-generation-fresh men-uc-system. Some of the collaborative work not already represented in the text and notes above has been conducted by professors Cesuna Ivey and Brinda Sarathy, the Center for Community and Environmental Justice, People's Collective for Environmental Justice, the coalition of San Bernardino Airport Communities, Sierra Club's My Generation campaign, and Warehouse Worker Resource Center, among others.

14. See the HAL website, available at humanitiesactionlab.org, and the current project website, Climates of Inequality, available at climatesofinequality .org.

15. Eve Tuck, "Suspending Damage: A Letter for Communities," *Harvard Educational Review* 79 (Fall 2009): 409–427; Gerald Vizenour, *Fugitive Poses: Native American Indian Scenes of Absence and Presence* (Lincoln: University of Nebraska Press, 1998), 15.

16. HAL "Partnership Guidelines" and "Project Values" were developed and workshopped during annual planning meetings by Aleia Brown, HAL program manager from 2017 to 2019, and as part of discussions on shared values and mutual accountability held from 2020 to 2022. Also see the United Kingdom model by Common Cause for Fair and Mutual Research Partnerships, available

at https://www.commoncauseresearch.com and the University of Kansas Community Toolkit, available at https://ctb.ku.edu/en/toolkits.

17. See Climates of Inequality "About" web page, available at http://climates ofinequality.org/about/.

18. Yusef Omowale, "We Already Are," *Medium*, September 8, 2018, available at https://medium.com/community-archives/we-already-are-52438b863e31; also reproduced in Bergis Jules, ed., *Architecting Sustainable Futures: Exploring Funding Models in Community-Based Archives* (New Orleans: Shift, Social Equity Initiatives, and Mellon Foundation, 2019), available at https://mellon.org/media /filer_public/01/58/0158e4ba-28a3-458c-ba6a-de0f8b2fd855/architectingsustain ablefutures-2019.pdf.

19. My paraphrasing and the quote by Liz Sevcenko is from her book proposal for *Public History for a Post-Truth Era: Fighting Denial through Memory Movements*, now scheduled for publication by Routledge Press in July 2022; Amy Wang, "'Post-truth' Named 2016 Word of the Year by Oxford Dictionaries," *Washington Post*, November 16, 2016, available at https://www.washingtonpost.com /news/the-fix/wp/2016/11/16/post-truth-named-2016-word-of-the-year-by-ox ford-dictionaries/.

20. Seymour, *Bad Environmentalism*, 24.

21. Stefano Harney and Fred Moten, "Fantasy in the Hold," *The Undercommons: Fugitive Planning and Black Study* (Brooklyn, NY: Automedia, 2013), 87, 92; Niccolo Cuppini and Mattia Frapporti, "The Logistics of Global Capitalism: A Dialogue with Giorgio Grappi, Brett Neilson and Ned Rossiter," *Zapruder World*, October 15, 2018, available at http://zapruderworld.org/2018/10/the-logistics-of -global-capitalism-a-dialogue-with-giorgio-grappi-brett-neilson-and-ned-ros siter/; Michael Schapira and Jesse Montgomery, "Stefano Harney (part I)," *Full Stop*, August 8, 2017, available at http://www.full-stop.net/2017/08/08/inter views/michael-schapira-and-jesse-montgomery/stefano-harney-part-1/. Also see Matthew Hockenberry, Nicole Starosielski, and Susan Zieger, eds., *Assembly Codes: The Logistics of Media* (Chapel Hill: Duke University Press, 2021).

22. Allan Sekula, *Fish Story* (Dusseldorf: Richter, 1995), 137.

23. Yasha Levine, *Surveillance Valley: The Secret Military History of the Internet* (New York: PublicAffairs, 2018); Sam Levin, "Tech Firms Make Millions from Trump's Anti-immigration Agenda, Report Finds," *The Guardian*, October 23, 2018; Hamza Shaban, "Amazon Employees Demand Company Cut Ties with ICE," *Washington Post*, June 22, 2018.

24. Rob Nixon, *Slow Violence and the Environmentalism of the Poor* (Cambridge, MA: Harvard University Press, 2013); Cowen, *Deadly Life of Logistics*.

25. Harney and Moten, "Fantasy in the Hold," 87, 93, 90; Sandro Mezzadra and Brett Neilson, *The Politics of Operations: Excavating Contemporary Capitalism* (Durham, NC: Duke University Press, 2019), 153.

26. Harney and Moten, "Fantasy in the Hold," 92.

27. In 2009–2010, Michael Wilson, Ken Rogers, and Victor Valle and their students, with Warehouse Workers United and the Center for Community Ac-

tion and Environmental Justice, began what Wilson has continued in Northern California as a mapping and data mining project that documents the global supply chain. See the Empire Logistics website, available at http://www.empirelo gistics.org; M. Wilson, "Black Hole Base"; Kenneth Rogers, "Crowdmapping the Classroom with Ushahidi," in *Learning through Digital Media: Experiments in Technology and Pedagogy*, ed. Trebor Scholz (New York: Institute for Distributed Creativity, 2011), 230–239. Other artists working more recently with regional community-based organizations include CultureStrike (see https://www.achang ingvalley.com/) and Noé Montes (see https://www.kcet.org/shows/earth-focus /photographing-air-pollution-in-the-inland-empire-noe-montes).

 28. Steven Cuevas, "Moreno Valley Continues to Debate 41-Million-Square-Foot Warehouse," KPCC, May 22, 2012; interview by Rudolph Bielitz with Sheheryar Kaoosji, Warehouse Worker Resource Center, March 14, 2019; UCR class discussions with Veronica Alvarado and Sheheryar Kaoosji, Warehouse Worker Resource Center, April 26, 2019, and with Andrea Vidaurre and Anthony Victoria, Center for Community Action and Environmental Justice, April 17, 2019. Unemployment statistics are available at https://www.pe.com/2019/10/04/man fred-keil-new-chief-economist-for-ieep-sees-more-automation-challenges-ahead -for-inland-empire/.

 29. Sheheryar Kaoosji, "Lessons Learned from Eight Years of Experimental Organizing in Southern California's Logistics Sector," in *Choke Points: Logistics Workers Disrupting the Global Supply Chain*, ed. Jake Alimahomed-Wilson (London: Pluto, 2018), 220–222, 226; Kaoosji, interview, March 14, 2019.

 30. De Lara, *Inland Shift*, 78; E. Cho, A. Christman, M. Emsellem, C. Ruckelshaus, and R. Smith, *Chain of Greed: How Walmart's Domestic Outsourcing Produces Everyday Low Wages and Poor Working Conditions for Warehouse Workers* (New York: National Employment Law Project, 2012).

 31. Vivien Hamilton and Brinda Sarathy, "Introduction: Toxicity, Uncertainty, and Expertise," in *Inevitably Toxic: Historical Perspectives on Contamination, Exposure, and Expertise*, ed. Brinda Sarathy, Vivien Hamilton, and Janet Farrell Brodie (Pittsburgh: University of Pittsburgh Press, 2019), 3.

 32. Interview by Catherine Gudis with Brinda Sarathy, Pitzer College, Claremont, California, May 21, 2019; Alvarado and Kaoosji, class discussions, April 26, 2019; interview by Rudolph Bielitz, Catherine Gudis, and Margaret Hansen with Veronica Alvarado and Daisy Lopez, Warehouse Worker Resource Center, and Yassie Kavezade, Sierra Club, at UCR, May 30, 2019; De Lara, *Inland Shift*, 12–13; Patterson, *From Acorns to Warehouses*, 205; Brinda Sarathy, "Legacies of Environmental Justice in Inland Southern California," *Race, Gender, and Class* 20, nos. 3–4 (2013): 262.

 33. James Bennett, "Supplying 40,000 Japanese Aliens," typescript dated May 23, 1943, 4, in "History of Mira Loma Quartermaster Depot by James W. Bennett, Depot Historian," National Archives and Records Administration (NARA) RG 94, Folder 1, Box No. 7, File 314.7.

34. Brinda Sarathy, "Before Amazon: Land, Labor, and Logistics in the Inland Empire of WWII," *Boom California*, September 22, 2021, available at https://boomcalifornia.org/2021/09/22/before-amazon-land-labor-and-logistics-in-the-inland-empire-of-wwii/; Sarathy, interview, May 21, 2019; Bennett, "Supplying 40,000 Japanese Aliens," 6–9; Bennett, "Early Days at San Bernardino and the Japanese Supply Problem," 42, in "History of Mira Loma Quartermaster Depot by James W. Bennett, Depot Historian," NARA RG 94, Folder 1, Box No. 7, File 314.7; "Army Engineer Depot Supplies Nation's Forces throughout Wide District," *San Bernardino Daily Sun*, September 12, 1943, 8; "Japs at Manzanar Found Well Fed," *San Pedro News Pilot*, May 31, 1943; "More Workers Needed at Mira Loma," *Chino News*, February 5, 1943. See exhibition video *Manzanar to Mira Loma*, available at http://climatesofinequality.org/story/witnessing-the-slow-violence-of-the-supply-chain/.

35. Bennett, "Early Days," 38–42.

36. Sarathy, "Before Amazon"; "Tour of Base on Mira Loma Depot Fund Drive Schedule," *San Bernardino County Sun*, November 7, 1952; "Army to Retain Storage Depots," *San Bernardino County Sun*, December 23, 1945, 11; "Giant Tract Foretells New Era for Mira Loma," *San Bernardino County Sun*, September 30, 1955, 16; "Grand Opening, Mira Loma," housing advertisements, *San Bernardino County Sun*, March 18, 1956, 22, 27.

37. Sarathy, "Legacies of Environmental Justice," 262.

38. Brian Whitehead, "Environmental Group Sues San Bernardino County, Developer over Warehouse Project in Bloomington," *San Bernardino Sun*, October 31, 2018; "Bloomington Residents Protest San Bernardino County Supervisors about Proposed Warehouse Plans," *Daily Bulletin*, February 13, 2018, available at https://www.dailybulletin.com/2018/02/13/bloomington-residents-protest-san-bernardino-county-supervisors-about-warehouse-plans/; "Concern and Confusion over West Valley Logistics Center Should Raise Red Flags," *Herald News*, January 10, 2019, available at http://ccaej.org/concern-and-confusion-over-west-valley-logistics-center-should-raise-red-flags/.

39. See HAL exhibition videos *Enough Is Enough!* and *World Logistics Center*, available at http://climatesofinequality.org/story/witnessing-the-slow-violence-of-the-supply-chain/.

40. Rita Raley, *Tactical Media* (Minneapolis: University of Minnesota Press, 2009), 1; David Garcia and Geert Lovink, *The ABC of Tactical Media* (1997), available at https://www.nettime.org/Lists-Archives/nettime-l-9705/msg00096.html; Alessandra Renzi, "Tactical Media," Public Sphere Project, available at http://www.publicsphereproject.org/content/tactical-media.

41. Renzi, "Tactical Media."

42. Tim Hwang and Craig Cannon, *The Container Guide* (New York: Infrastructure Observatory, 2015).

43. More on New York State's *Path through History* is available at https://paththroughhistory.iloveny.com.

44. Bureau of Goods Transport, *The Goods Movement Industry Tour: Path Through History, Los Angeles*, vol. 1 (Los Angeles: Empire Logistics Group, 2015), 12–13.

45. Bonacich and J. Wilson, *Getting the Goods*, 51–53.

46. Nelson Lichtenstein, *Retail Revolution: How Wal-Mart Created a Brave New World of Business* (New York: Metropolitan Books, 2009), 150; Patrick Chung, "From Korea to Vietnam: Local Labor, Multinational Capital, and the Evolution of U.S. Military Logistics, 1950–97," *Radical History Review* 133 (January 2019): 31–55; Marc Levinson, *The Box: How the Shipping Container Made the World Smaller and the World Economy Bigger* (Princeton, NJ: Princeton University Press, 2008).

47. Bureau of Goods Transport, *The Goods Movement Tour*, 8.

48. Ibid., 9.

49. On foreign-trade zones, see Dara Orenstein, *Out of Stock: The Warehouse in the History of Capitalism* (Chicago: University of Chicago Press, 2019).

50. Kanouse, "Critical Day Trips," 49.

Epilogue

Robin F. Bachin and
Amy L. Howard

The projects highlighted in this volume aim to change institutional culture in higher education and make the academy more responsive to pressing community needs at the local, national, and global levels. Initiatives to promote civic and community engagement in higher education have the potential to be transformational, for they aim at nothing less than the overturning of a century-long tendency in higher education to promote specialized knowledge over interdisciplinarity, independent research over collaborative scholarship, and pedagogy defined solely by the classroom experience rather than learning that is participatory, cooperative, and community based. Engaging with the community in multilayered and respectful ways, through a variety of academic fields, allows scholars, students, and community groups the chance to break down barriers between disciplines and among each other.

In the wake of COVID-19, the future of these campus-community partnerships is uncertain. Both cities and universities have undergone dramatic transformations as a result of the pandemic. The ascendancy of cities as magnets for creativity, innovation, diversity, and growth is no longer assured. The seemingly unassailable trend of cities being the "best" places to live, work, and play for the "creative classes," millennials, and retirees with means is no longer assured as urban amenities shutter and major companies such as Facebook and Twitter divest themselves of urban real estate and promote remotely working from home, which can be from anywhere. As *New York Times* architecture critic Michael Kimmelman notes, "Cities are epicenters of capital and creativity, designed to be occupied collectively. Pandemics are anti-urban, preying on our human desire for connection."[1] How will cities look in the future when the very factors that have shaped them historically—the need to cluster workplaces and residents in close proximity, the creation of transit systems that moved large numbers of people quickly and efficiently, and the restaurants, bars, museums, galleries, sports stadiums, and concert halls specifically designed to gather people together side by side in shared experiences—became perilous for public health?

Moreover, the changes unfolding in cities across the nation as a result of COVID-19 have exposed and exacerbated the lack of equity that has long simmered below the surface of institutions, policies, and practices in the United States. Evictions, homelessness, disparities in K-12 public education, gaps in access to higher education, and higher rates of COVID-19 illness and death among people of color have laid bare the deep and persistent racial inequalities in this country.[2] We have long known that the zip code matters as much if not more than the genetic code in determining one's long-term health outcomes.[3] Yet, the pandemic has exposed the extent to which health disparities across racial lines are exacerbated by the social determinants of health, including access to preventive care, safe and secure housing, stable jobs, and high-quality education. The killings of George Floyd, Breonna Taylor, and other Black people at the hands of white police officers in 2020 sparked a massive movement for racial justice that stretched across cities and towns in the United States and around the world. The Black Lives Matter movement has joined together demands for an end to police brutality against Black people with more sweeping calls for equity and racial justice in all arenas. That the empty streets and deserted plazas, squares, and parks of American cities became the staging grounds for these protests shows both the continued importance of cities as civic spaces and the need to reconsider the planning practices of the future to promote safe gathering as well as equitable access to participation in democratic public life.

The twin pandemics of COVID-19 and racial inequality have also upended higher education, pushing online and hybrid teaching, fueling student activism, and prompting some institutions to announce new and/or strengthened initiatives to improve diversity, equity, inclusion, and belonging on college campuses and to more fully center anti-racism.[4] To achieve these increasingly more robust anti-racism and equity goals for higher education institutions, we contend that colleges and universities need to simultaneously attend to the full participation, belonging, and equity of both campus stakeholders and local community members. By recognizing and valuing the relationship between campuses and their host cities, the interconnectedness of students, faculty, staff, and community members, and the importance of equity for all, higher education is poised to more effectively strengthen its public purpose. Meeting the urgency of the moment will require the acceleration of shifts that were slowly underway in higher education before COVID-19. Recognizing and valuing community-engaged scholarship and teaching in the tenure and promotion process across colleges and universities rather than at a select few will expand opportunities for public scholarship. Attending to an understanding and awareness of the history of each institution and its relationship in place with a clear-eyed understanding of the role higher education has played in perpetuating inequalities in their locales and nationally will fuel the process of repair needed to partner with communities in collaborative problem-solving. Reckoning with the racial disparities in access to higher education, rethinking the relationship between institutional founding myths and the realities of land appropriation and population displacement, and recasting institutional priorities through an equity lens are all processes that should be and are driving policy and planning for the postpandemic university. Just as they did in the 1960s, students in 2020 forced administrations to reconsider the courses and programs offered and the faculty who teach them. Faculty who have long focused their research and teaching on the history of anti-Black racism, social inequality, and intergroup dialogue are seeing their enrollments soar.

Yet, it is not at all clear that the longer-term institutional responses among some leaders of colleges and universities will favor this push for inclusion. As numerous articles and books have shown, higher education in America had been facing significant challenges well before

COVID-19 shuttered campuses and sent students home. Demographic shifts mean that there are fewer Americans in the target age group for college, and these trends will continue in the coming decade.[5] Many universities were experiencing fiscal troubles long before the pandemic. The need to raise funds to promote campus expansion and greater selectivity through merit aid meant that many colleges sought out not only philanthropic gifts but also students with the ability to pay. As the authors of *The Merit Myth* explain, "higher education has become a passive participant in a system that reproduces economic and cultural elites" as a result of an admissions system that privileges the privileged.[6] The competition among elite universities to provide more amenities to students, from luxury dorm living to high-tech food delivery, pushed many universities into a spiral of spending that not only is unsustainable but has exacerbated class divisions among students. Rutgers historian Carla Yanni, in her book on the history of American college dormitories, quotes a 1920s brochure from the University of Wisconsin on the benefits of dorm living. The brochure explained that, in college dorms, "the man from the well-to-do home and the man who tends furnaces to buy his text books will learn respect for each other across a common table," and "the son of banker and farmer will find mutual understanding."[7] Nonetheless, college campuses in the twenty-first century have created campus spaces that expose class differences rather than seeking to eradicate them. Examining higher education through a racial justice and equity lens highlights how universities often are complicit in reproducing hierarchies of power even as they have made concerted attempts to do otherwise.

The chapters in this book provide a range of examples through different modes and at different scales to attend with care to power differentials, historical contexts, and community knowledge and expertise in forming campus-community partnerships to advance student learning and community development and thriving. As demonstrated, the work is messy, the outcomes unpredictable, and mistakes inevitable. Yet, in the struggle to be better and do better *with* our communities, higher education institutions have the opportunity to partner in forging a more equitable future in a post-COVID-19 world. Higher education should cultivate skills that will prepare students for ongoing civic participation and democratic deliberation. This preparation in turn can support the pursuit of political equality and full participation in a democratic society.

We aim to train students to think critically, to transcend local loyalties and become citizens of the world, and to show empathy toward others who are different from themselves. University leaders must examine how universities engage with their multiple publics and reimagine the role knowledge cocreation and public scholarship can play in rethinking cities and the role of universities within them. We can amplify campus-community partnerships as vehicles for promoting racial justice and social equity in cities across the nation. To do so, universities will need to infuse the curriculum with intentional opportunities for experiential learning so that students can apply the knowledge they learn in the classroom to our most pressing social problems at the local, national, and global levels. Equipping students with humility, respect for the knowledge and expertise in communities, and an ethos of collaboration is essential for combating the town-and-gown mistakes of the past. Giving students opportunities for service and learning outside of the classroom will showcase how to engage with local knowledge and respect the expertise that emerges from lived experience, not just academic training. To meet their collective and individual missions, higher education institutions will also need to reckon with the traditional systems of rewards and recognition for faculty members that too often relegate community-engaged research, scholarship, and teaching to "service" rather than assessing the rigor, impact, and importance of public-facing work. The post-COVID-19 college can be most influential by being relevant and joining faculty, staff, and students together in reciprocal collaboration with local community members in the challenging work of repairing their campuses and communities. As Ira Harkavy has explained, it is "essential that the democratic, civic university actively engaged with the life and problems of its community and society becomes *the* model of higher education in the post-COVID-19 world."[8] If universities take seriously their role in working to address societal challenges and shape the public good, *with* rather than *for* communities, then colleges and their communities will be more inclusive, equitable, and sustainable in the long term. These commitments will help restore higher education's public purpose and the "education for citizenship" that educator John Dewey called for a century ago and that is at the core of higher education's historic mission and its future.

NOTES

1. Michael Kimmelman, "Can City Life Survive Coronavirus?" *New York Times*, March 17, 2020, accessed March 25, 2020, available at https://www.nytimes.com/2020/03/17/world/europe/coronavirus-city-life.html.

2. Elisabeth Gawthrop, "The Color of Coronavirus: COVID-19 Deaths by Race and Ethnicity in the U.S.," APM Research Lab, May 10, 2022, accessed May 20, 2022, available at https://www.apmresearchlab.org/covid/deaths-by-race; Xiao Wu, Rachel C. Nethery, M. Benjamin Sabath, Danielle Braun, and Francesca Dominici, "Air Pollution and COVID-19 Mortality in the United States: Strengths and Limitations of an Ecological Regression Analysis," *Science Advances* 6, no. 45 (November 4, 2020), accessed November 10, 2020, available at https://www.science.org/doi/10.1126/sciadv.abd4049.

3. See, for example, "Mapping Life Expectancy," Center on Society and Health, Virginia Commonwealth University, Richmond, Virginia, September 26, 2016, updated March 31, 2022, available at https://societyhealth.vcu.edu/work/the-projects/mapping-life-expectancy.html.

4. See, for example, the University of Miami, Middlebury College, Tufts University, and Amherst College.

5. Nathan D. Grawe, *Demographics and the Demand for Higher Education* (Baltimore, MD: Johns Hopkins University Press, 2018).

6. Anthony P. Carnivale, Peter Schmidt, and Jeff Strohl, *The Merit Myth: How Our Colleges Favor the Rich and Divide America* (New York: New Press, 2020), 196. See also *The Post-COVID College* (Washington, D.C.: Chronicle of Higher Education, 2020), 8–9; Davarian L. Baldwin, *In the Shadow of the Ivory Tower: How Universities Are Plundering Our Cities* (New York: Bold Type Books, 2021).

7. Quoted in Carla Yanni, *Living on Campus: An Architectural History of the American Dormitory* (Minneapolis: University of Minnesota Press, 2019), 132.

8. Ira Harkavy, Sjur Bergan, Tony Gallagher, and Hillgje van't Land, "Universities Must Help Shape the Post-COVID-19 World," *University World News*, April 18, 2020. See also *Post-COVID College*.

Contributors

Robin F. Bachin is the assistant provost for Civic and Community Engagement and Charlton W. Tebeau associate professor of History at the University of Miami. Her research and teaching interests include universities and community engagement, the history of urban planning and design, and the intersections of urban and environmental history. She is author of *Building the South Side: Urban Space and Civic Culture in Chicago, 1890–1919* (Chicago: University of Chicago Press, 2004) and *"Big Bosses": A Working Girl's Memoir of Jazz Age America* (Chicago: University of Chicago Press, 2016). Bachin is project director for the Miami Housing Solutions Lab, member of the Aspen Institute Working Group on Inclusive Innovation in America's Cities, past president of the Society for American City and Regional Planning History and serves on the National Advisory Board for Imagining America.

Alexandra Byrum is the director of communications and community relations for Equity + Community at the University of Richmond. Alongside Equity + Community colleagues, she works to catalyze civic engagement; advance diversity, equity, inclusion, and belonging on campus; deepen community partnerships; support community-based learning classes; mentor students; and collaborate with students, faculty, and community partners on public exhibitions. Previously, she held positions at the Chrysler Museum of Art and Smithsonian Institution and taught the history of photography at Old Dominion University and Tidewater Community College's Visual Arts Center.

Catherine Gudis is associate professor of History and director of Public History at University of California, Riverside, where she holds a Pollitt Endowed Term Chair for Interdisciplinary Research and Learning. She also serves as scholar-in-residence at the Skid Row History Museum and Archive. Author of *Buyways: Billboards, Automobiles, and the American Landscape* (Routledge, 2004), among other works, her public humanities projects include *Play the L.A. River*, the Bureau of Goods Transport, and *A People's History of the Inland Empire*. All explore how public space is privatized, landscapes are racialized, and inequalities of access are contested, with a focus on Southern California.

Ira Harkavy is founding director of Penn's Netter Center for Community Partnerships. His research and teaching focus on the history and practice of urban university-community-school partnerships and the democratic and civic missions of higher education. His publications include the following coauthored or coedited books: *Dewey's Dream: Universities and Democracies in an Age of Education Reform* (Philadelphia: Temple University Press, 2007), *Knowledge for Social Change: Bacon, Dewey, and the Revolutionary Transformation of Research Universities in the Twenty-First Century* (Philadelphia: Temple University Press, 2017), *The Local Mission of Higher Education: Principles and Practice* (Dublin: Glasnevin Publishing, 2019), *and Higher Education's Response to the COVID-19 Pandemic: Building a More Sustainable and Democratic Future* (Strasbourg: Council of Europe Publishing, 2021).

Rita A. Hodges is an associate director of the Netter Center for Community Partnerships at the University of Pennsylvania. She is coauthor of two books: *The Road Half Traveled: University Engagement at a Crossroads* (East Lansing: Michigan State University Press, 2012) and *Knowledge for Social Change: Bacon, Dewey, and the Revolutionary Transformation of Research Universities in the Twenty-First Century* (Philadelphia: Temple University Press, 2017). Hodges is a doctor of education (Ed.D.) candidate in higher education at Penn's Graduate School of Education. Her doctoral research focuses on the democratic engagement of colleges and universities with their local communities as anchor institutions.

Amy L. Howard is the senior administrative officer for Equity + Community and associated faculty in American Studies at the University of Richmond. She is author of *More Than Shelter: Activism and Community in San Francisco Public Housing* (Minneapolis: University of Minnesota Press, 2014) and multiple coauthored chapters on civic and community engagement, urban history, and diversity, equity, and inclusion in higher education. She is currently collaborating on a manuscript examining race, politics, and policy in Richmond, Virginia, from 1984 to 2016. Howard serves on the National Advisory Board for Imagining America.

Andrew Hurley is professor of History at the University of Missouri–St. Louis. He is the author of *Beyond Preservation: Using Public History to Revitalize Inner-Cities* (Philadelphia: Temple University Press, 2010). His current research examines the impact of extreme weather events on U.S. cities during the twentieth century.

John L. Puckett is professor emeritus of Education at the University of Pennsylvania. His areas of expertise are American education history, urban studies, and progressive education reform. His books include, among others, the following coauthored works: *Leonard Covello and the Making of Benjamin Franklin High School: Education as if Citizenship Mattered* (Philadelphia: Temple University Press, 2007), *Dewey's Dream: Universities and Democracies in an Age of Education Reform* (Philadelphia: Temple University Press, 2007), *Becoming Penn: The Pragmatic American University, 1950–2000* (Philadelphia: University of Pennsylvania Press, 2015), and *Knowledge for Social Change: Bacon, Dewey, and the Revolutionary Transformation of Research Universities in the Twenty-First Century* (Philadelphia: Temple University Press, 2017). He is founder and director of a virtual museum, West Philadelphia Collaborative History (available at https:// collaborativehistory.gse.upenn.edu/).

J. Mark Souther is professor of History and director of the Center for Public History + Digital Humanities at Cleveland State University. He is author of *Believing in Cleveland: Managing Decline in "The Best Location in the Nation"* (Philadelphia: Temple University Press, 2017) and *New Orleans on Parade: Tourism and the Transformation of the Crescent City* (Baton Rouge: Louisiana State University Press, 2006). Souther has led three National Endowment for the Humanities digital humanities advancement grants and directs the *Cleveland Historical* and *Green Book Cleveland* digital projects.

Joann Weeks was associate director of the University of Pennsylvania's Netter Center for Community Partnerships from 1993 to 2020, focusing on its regional, national, and international programs. She also served as editor of the Netter Center's *Universities and Community Schools* journal. Weeks is coauthor of *Knowledge for Social Change: Bacon, Dewey, and the Revolutionary Transformation of Research Universities in the Twenty-First Century* (Philadelphia: Temple University Press, 2017).

Index

Please note that page numbers with f indicate figures.

www.ingramcontent.com/pod-product-compliance
Lightning Source LLC
Chambersburg PA
CBHW040140270326
41928CB00022B/3278